Teaching the Prekindergarten Child:

Instructional Design and Curriculum

Teaching the Prekindergarten Child:
Instructional Design and Curriculum

BARBARA VANCE

Brigham Young University

BROOKS/COLE PUBLISHING COMPANY
MONTEREY, CALIFORNIA

A Division of Wadsworth Publishing Company, Inc.

ISBN: 0—8185—0060—3
L. C. Catalog Card No. 72—86160
Printed in the United States of America
1 2 3 4 5 6 7 8 9 10—77 76 75 74 73

*This book was edited by Anne Phillips and designed by Linda Marcetti,
with illustrations by Bonnie Oswald and cover photograph by Wallace Barrus. It
was typeset by Holmes Typography, Inc., San Jose, California, and printed and
bound by Kingsport Press, Kingsport, Tennessee.*

Dedicated to the late Erma Clark–
my friend
and
teacher of young children

Foreword

There is an old saying that relates the inclination of trees to the bending of twigs. Perhaps the teachers of preschool children see more symbolism in that saying than anyone else. They encounter twigs in great number and endless variety, already with several pronounced bends each; they also see the relative ease of straightening a few of those bends and replacing them with some advantageous ones of their own devising. Later, of course, the twigs will have thickened, and bends will be correspondingly harder to manage.

This book concerns the twiggy science of bending and unbending the behaviors of young children. In the last ten years this science has put forward some tentative principles of behavior and tested them—first with laboratory animals, then with very troubled humans, and most recently with the virtually normal children and adults of our everyday society. The tests showed that the principles were descriptive of a wide range of behavior and the conditions of its development; thus, the principles evolved into practice. In this book, Barbara Vance demonstrates the modifications in traditional preschool curriculum techniques that these newly evolved principles suggest—or, sometimes, require.

If we are to teach young children from a behavioral point of view, then we will always see them as possessors of a large number of quite malleable behaviors, and we will always see ourselves as people who will change those behaviors by interacting with them. For whenever a child displays a behavior in our presence, if we react, we contribute something to that behavior's change or to its maintenance; but if we do *not* react, we still contribute something to its maintenance or to its change. In other words, we can abstain from the bending of twigs only by abstaining from the presence of twigs. (And even that apparently clean-handed response is in fact actually a decision to leave the twigs with those benders who have *not* chosen to abstain, which is thus a contribution to *their* bending practices, whatever they may be.) An ignorance of the rules of behavior would allow us to go on bending our twigs willy-nilly, with no responsibility felt for the consequences, since we would not recognize them as *consequences*. That might be a comfort, but it would also be an error, and hardly to the advantage of the twigs. The lack of that comfort is the embarrassment of the behavioral approach; the avoidance of the error and the resultant *potential* benefit of the twigs is its great advantage.

To make a potential benefit into an actual one, it will be necessary to choose correctly from all the behavior changes possible in our classrooms and playgrounds. This book nominates some as particularly valuable, and it is very likely correct in those choices. But the key phrase in that evaluation is *very likely,* for those choices were generally made on the basis of experience and logic, rather than on the basis of proof. The proof that a given behavior change will actually be to a measurable advantage of the child in whom it is made is simply not available in the typical case, even if we agree on how to define *advantage*. This is not a new problem for teachers; they have always taught in its shadow. But the ability to choose behavior changes and implement them with reliability makes the problem correspondingly more intense. A rational choice of which behavior changes to make would be greatly aided by factual knowledge of their consequences. For example, do children who have learned these skills do better in a measurable way in their formal schooling, their peer interactions, their interactions with parents? If we knew that such consequences resulted, and if we knew that we valued those consequences, then we could much more reasonably program just those behavior changes in our preschool—that is, we would know exactly which way to bend the twigs.

Thus there is a simple recommendation to be made to any reader of a book that, like this one, teaches some elements of the growing technology of deliberate behavioral change: do not forget how often your choices will be based on something less than proof of their value. And there is a more complex recommendation as well: remember that you will be in one of the best positions to contribute to that proof if you learn the skills of research as well as the skills of teaching.

Donald M. Baer

Contents

Preface

If you are now a teacher of prekindergarten children or plan some day to teach prekindergarten children, this book is for you. This is a *how* and a *what* book for teaching children under five.

This book is about teaching the *prekindergarten child*—3 or 4 years old—who attends some type of educational group. These groups include private, university-related, or cooperative nursery schools, day-care centers, Head Start groups, and religious education programs.

Traditionally it has been the desire of those who work with prekindergarten children to teach the "whole child." Flexibility, resourcefulness, good judgment, perceptual discrimination, attention, variety of interest, curiosity, social maturity, desire to learn, self-control, independence, sense of self-worth, and well-developed conscience have been and still are the goals of childhood educators. This book provides specific instructional processes and content that can help you provide learning experiences leading to the demonstration of these behaviors.

Part 1 is a discussion of the basic principles of instructional design as they apply to the teaching of prekindergarten children. This is the *how* of instruction. The first chapter discusses the concepts of learning and instruction related to prekindergarten children. Each of the following six chapters in Part 1 discusses a major step in the instructional design process and has response exercises, which provide opportunities for you to practice the principles and test your learning.

The subject of Part 2 is the *what* of instruction. The first chapter in Part 2 provides basic curriculum guidelines. Each of the following eight chapters discusses in detail what to teach in a specific content area. The eight prekindergarten content areas are graphic arts, health and safety, living in a world of people, mathematics, movement, music, our world, and reading. Each of the chapters is followed by a sample lesson plan in the content area it covers. After reading the book and participating in the suggested learning activities, you will be able to write appropriate lesson plans for the prekindergarten children you teach.

    This book has two other important features. First, the book progresses in logical order, but the chapters are also self-contained units and therefore can be understood if read in a different order from that presented here. Second, a background course in child development would help but is not necessary in order to understand the educational principles that are discussed.

    I am grateful for the efforts of those who have discussed ideas with me and read and critiqued part or all of the manuscript. These include Owen Cahoon, Rowen Jones, Jean Larsen, M. David Merrill, Patricia Haglund Nielsen, and Carolyn Rasmus of Brigham Young University; Bonnie Ballif of Fordham University, Gabriel Della-Piana of the University of Utah, Edith Dowley of Stanford University, Alice Harris of San Joaquin Delta College, Margaret Holmberg of the University of Kansas, Lilian Katz of the University of Illinois, Evelyn Kest of Western Washington State College, and Ethna Reid of the Exemplary Center for Reading Instruction; Brigham Young University graduate students Linda Cropper, J'Ann David, Ramona Erickson, Trevor McKee, Marcella Pace, Linda Sheffield, and Conrad Taysom. A special thanks goes to Donald Baer of the University of Kansas, a humane and masterful twig bender, who wrote the Foreword for this book. For their patience and efficiency, I would also like to thank typists Susan Mickelsen and Sandra Tew. Finally, I am deeply grateful for the constant encouragement and demonstration of effective teaching techniques by all with whom I came in contact at Brooks/Cole, particularly my editors Bonnie Fitzwater and Anne Phillips.

Barbara Vance

Part 1

Instructional Design in the Prekindergarten

Chapter 1

The Prekindergarten Child: Learning and Instructional Design

This book is about *instruction.* Instruction is a simple word, a common word. It is so simple and common that many people take it for granted and assume they know what it means. After all, we all know what instruction is. Or do we?

This book is about *learning.* If an instructor instructs, a student learns. Or does he?

This book is about instructing prekindergarten* children. In such groups instructors are instructing and children are learning. Or are they?

Undoubtedly there are various answers to these questions. But there is also agreement that instruction of the prekindergarten child can and should be improved. This book is designed to help you, the teacher, develop effective learning experiences for the children you teach: specifically, to help you learn *how* to develop instruction and to determine *what* to teach.

---

*You are probably more familiar with the term *preschool* than the term *prekindergarten.* Essentially they both mean the same thing, but *preschool* seems to connote a nonlearning or noneducative period of life. Since *kindergarten* refers to an educational group experience for 5-year-olds, *prekindergarten* seems to more accurately describe the group experiences of 3-year-old and 4-year-old children.

The ideas discussed in this book are based on the following assumptions about the human family in general and about children in particular:

1. Human behavior can be changed at any age.
2. Environment can change behavior.
3. An individual can develop the ability to change not only his own behavior but that of others.
4. The environment has its greatest effect when a behavior is in its most rapid stage of development.
5. Most human behavior is sequential in development. That is, a new behavior is based on similar behavior that preceded it in development.
6. Often it is easier to learn a new behavior than to erase old behavior and replace it with new.
7. Instruction in the prekindergarten is most effective and economical (in terms of time and effort) when learning activities are planned and implemented to bring about specific desired behavior change in the child.

Let's take a look at the way children learn. If we can understand how they learn, it seems reasonable that we can develop more efficient instructional methods. Thus we can help the prekindergarten child to learn more effectively.

LEARNING

Much of an infant's behavior during the early weeks of life is based on spontaneous and random response to physical stimuli—loud sounds, variety of light intensity or color, textural stimuli, the contractions of an empty stomach, and so forth. These responses are limited by the infant's immature bodily structure and poorly developed motor skills. For example, he can cry, randomly wave his arms, and kick his feet when he feels hungry, but he does not yet possess the bodily structure or skill to move toward the source of satisfaction of his need. As a matter of fact, in the beginning he is not even aware of the source of that satisfaction. His need just *is*, and his response is *spontaneous*, a result of maturation only—that is, a result of the developing physical structure and physiological functions. Learning is not apparent in such early random and spontaneous behavior.

But very soon a change is noted in the infant under similar circumstances. When he is hungry, he begins to cry and thrash about. The intensity of his cry and movement increases. Suddenly the crying and random body movement cease. There is a brief tense moment of absolute quiet. Mother's footsteps and soft voice are heard as she enters the room. Then the body movement begins in earnest again, but the frantic cry has changed to gurgles and bubbles. If the bottle or breast is immediately offered, the infant relaxes into contented but enthusiastic sucking; if not, the crying and thrashing begin again, this time with greater intensity. Observation of the infant over a period of days reveals a similar behavior pattern under similar circumstances. In other words, the infant has *learned* a new and fairly stable behavior pattern.

Learning is a process of more or less permanent sequential behavior change resulting from an individual's own performance, special training, and/or observation (Munn, 1965). It is inferred from the observable behavior of an individual. The sequential nature of the behavior change indicates that one behavior is built on the foundation of another that precedes it. For example, the young child learns to sit on his tricycle and propel himself by pushing both feet against the ground at the same time. Later he learns to put his feet on the pedals and slowly push alternately with one foot and then the other. After practicing this skill for a while, the child eventually rides the tricycle rapidly, negotiating turns around corners and play equipment with greater and greater ease. The skill was developed in a step-by-step sequence. The child needed the bodily structure and muscular strength (maturation) to develop such skill. But the skill was learned only as a result of appropriate environmental conditions: availability of a tricycle of adequate size, other children riding tricycles to serve as models of trike-riding skill *(observation),* and perhaps a child or an adult giving necessary verbal instructions, such as what comes first, and what comes next *(special training).* But the child still would not have developed his trike-riding skill without applying what he had been taught *(performance).* Changing *behavior* reveals whether or not he is *learning.*

Almost all human behavior, especially after the first few weeks of infancy, is a result of the process called learning. That is, behavior is a result of special training, observation, and/or the individual's own performance—verbal, motor, or both. Bodily maturation is necessary before learning can occur, but it is not sufficient to account for most human behavior. Almost all human behavior is learned behavior resulting from changes in the environment.

WHAT IS LEARNED?

The child learns only what his physical and social environment teaches him. The child—indeed, every human being—is learning all the time. The individual learns regardless of whether or not the learning environment has been planned (because the environment is always changing). In other words, much of what we learn is accidental and incidental, largely the result of chance. Even in "planned" learning situations we often do not learn what we are expected to learn.

Although much of our chance or random learning is beneficial, some of it can be detrimental to further development. For example, some people who learn to play the piano "by ear" have greater difficulty than other people learning musical notation and keyboard technique. It is difficult to drop old ways of doing things and to substitute new behavior for old. It is better for the child to learn the appropriate and acceptable behavior from the beginning rather than unlearn the old behavior at a later date and replace it with a new behavior.* For example, the young child who learns to get what he wants with temper tantrums may find a hostile, unpleasant world awaiting him in kindergarten or first grade.

Regardless of his circumstances, each child is learning every moment. Will much of this learning need to be undone later? Will it interfere with later learning? The answers to these questions depend on the child's learning experiences during the years before age 5.

*It is often necessary to eliminate some behavior before teaching new behavior. Behavior-elimination techniques are evaluated in Chapter 6 in a discussion on extinction.

HOW A CHILD LEARNS

The behavior of young children is less complicated than that of older children or adults for at least two reasons. First, young children have lived fewer years than older children and adults and therefore have had fewer experiences to complicate their behavior patterns. Second, young children tend to "wear their personalities on their sleeves"—that is, they seldom hide their feelings and attitudes and ideas. What they learn often stands out in bold relief. Therefore it is probably easier in many important ways to discover the process by which all people learn by observing how young children learn. This process begins with perception, moves on to forming a mental picture, then to actual performance, and finally to feeling. We'll call these steps (1) perceive, (2) think, (3) do, and (4) feel.

Perceive

All learning begins with a sensory experience—that is, with perception. Therefore, the learner has contact by one or more of his senses with objects, people, places, or events.

The average infant is bombarded with a wide variety of sights, sounds, smells, textures, and body pressures. (The variety of taste stimuli is probably small to begin with.) The infant has little ability to screen out stimulation except through the medium of sleep. As the child grows older, he develops greater ability to screen out certain stimuli while attending to others. When too many sensory stimuli bombard the child at one time, the child may suffer from "perceptual indigestion," a confusing situation in which behavior becomes erratic and uncontrolled.

Learning is more effective and appropriate when sensory stimuli are available a few at a time. Kagan (1968) refers to this as *distinctive* stimuli. He reports a comparison study of the amount of talking to infants by middle-class and lower-class mothers. The *amount* of vocalization in both groups of mothers was essentially the same, while the *distinctiveness* of the vocalizations of the middle-class mothers was greater than that of lower-class mothers. That is, the vocalizations of lower-class mothers apparently could not be distinguished by the infant from the almost constant blare of the television and the sounds of other members of the family. In middle-class homes an infant is usually apart from the center of household activities when the mother vocalizes to him. Therefore, what the mother says to the infant is more likely to be distinct from other sounds in the environment. This distinctiveness of vocalization, rather than amount, may account for greater facility with language in middle-class children as compared with their lower-class counterparts.

Young children are natural explorers of their physical environment. They are receiving information constantly in a variety of sights, smells, sounds, tastes, pressures, and textures. In a sense young children are building their sensory "data banks." The quantity and quality of these sensory experiences determine the quantity and quality of the child's thinking, the next stage in the learning process. If sensory experiences are a result of *direct contact* with *actual* objects, people, places, or events, there will be less chance for error in the next stage of the learning process.

When one or more of the child's sensory organs are damaged or become nonfunctional, the learning messages received through the senses are limited in scope and complexity. Early identification of sensory handicaps and correction when possible will assure greater learning capacity for the child.

Learning, then, begins when the child perceives something.

Think

Objects, people, places, or events, once perceived, become a part of the total realm of perceptual experience by which one thinks and performs. The child formulates some sort of mental picture of his sensory experience. This mental picture is made up of past sensory experiences, feelings, and actions related to the present sensory experience.

No two children form the same mental picture of the same sensory experience. For example, two 3-year-old children are looking at a kitten, which the teacher is holding. One child has never seen a real kitten before but has a soft, fluffy, toy kitten, which she always takes to bed with her. She associates the soft, furry, real kitten in the teacher's lap with her own toy kitten and moves closer for a better look and perhaps an opportunity to hold the kitten. The other child was recently scratched by a mother cat while trying to pick up one of her kittens. This child physically retreats from the presence of the teacher who is holding the kitten. Past sensory experiences, feelings, and actions related to kittens have been quite different for these two children. Therefore their mental pictures of kittens are very different.

The mental pictures formed by these two children are inferred from their actions. Forming a mental picture is an internal process that cannot be directly observed. This is why we depend so completely on the next step in the learning process, the action (do) step, to tell us what the child is thinking.

Do

What a person thinks and is reinforced for doing determines to a great extent how he will act. Of course, not all action is the result of conscious thought, nor does all thought produce action. But sensory experiences lead inevitably to mental pictures that, in turn, lead to observable behavior or action under given circumstances. For example, one child in the previous illustration enthusiastically approached the teacher and real kitten while another child drew away. We can *infer from the behavior* of these two children that each had a very different mental picture of kittens and what kittens do. We can be sure that the sensory experiences of the two children related to cats and kittens were very different. If we know something about the past sensory experiences of each child, we can be more accurate in our inference. Basically, the consequences of a child's past experiences determine his actions in the future.

The do step in the learning process gives basic data on each child. It is the child's observable behavior, or "doing," that tells you what and how he is learning. Let's look at some behavior patterns—psychomotor, cognitive, and affective—that can be expected in most prekindergarten children.

Psychomotor behavior.   Virtually all behavior is muscle response if it is observable. *Psychomotor* behavior is a term used to identify behavior that is principally based on the movement of muscles, joints, and the skeleton of the body. Psychomotor behavior includes skills of locomotion, manipulation, and body balance. During infancy and toddlerhood psychomotor behavior is paramount. The skills we take for granted as adults are just being developed during the years before age 3, which Piaget describes as the sensorimotor stage.

By age 3 "the round toddler becomes a linear runner" (Cratty, 1970). The long bones of the arms and legs have lengthened, making it easier for the child to control his locomotor movements. The basic locomotion skills of walking and running are developed in virtually all prekindergarten children without motor handicaps. However, there are wide differences among children in the more complex motor skills such as throwing, drawing, and game-playing skills. All body movement is more integrated. That is, movements are done more quickly and with greater ease and economy of body movement. For example, the 3-year-old no longer needs to monitor his moving feet as does the toddler. Arms move closer to the body, in a synchronized fashion with the feet. Age 3 usually marks the beginning of experimentation with the variety of ways one can perform each skill, such as running backward and sideways.

The locomotor skills change during the prekindergarten years. True running does not occur until age 2½ or 3. The speed of running increases during ages 4 and 5. Start and stop control increases.

Jumping is a skill that only about half of 3-year-olds can accomplish. It is not unusual to see a child at 4½ who has not yet learned to jump. Jumping often looks more like a gallop.

Hopping can be done by most 3-year-olds but for only one to three steps on one foot in any single sequence. Most 4-year-olds can hop four to six steps on one foot. Most prekindergarten children alternate feet after a few steps.

Skipping is a complex variation of forward hopping and is not usually demonstrated by prekindergarten children. A child may call what he is doing skipping when in reality it looks more like galloping.

Manipulative skills are those requiring the use of the small muscles in the hands and fingers. Tasks used to measure manipulative skills include touching each finger to the thumb, winding thread on a spool, dropping marbles into small holes, threading beads, and placing matchsticks in a box.

Prekindergarten children take far more time performing such tasks than older children. However, it is not necessarily true that prekindergarten children are more able to use large muscles than they are to use small muscles. This could be simply a matter of the child's training. The child probably has more large-muscle play equipment than small-muscle play equipment in his physical environment. He also probably gets reinforced more often for his large-muscle activity than his small-muscle activity.

Balance, which increases as the head becomes proportionately smaller in relationship to the rest of the body, can be demonstrated in one position or while moving. Prekindergarten children can stand on one foot for a few seconds using their arms for balance. If they fold their arms while balancing on one foot, they are unable to maintain the position very long. Three-year-olds can walk a 1-inch wide straight line. Four-year-olds can walk a circular line.

Throwing and catching are skills that are more complex than those usually engaged in by most prekindergarten children. Throwing can be done in a variety of ways, including underhand, overhand, and sidearm. There is little control in the speed and direction of a ball, regardless of size, when thrown by the average prekindergarten child. Catching is usually done in one of two ways. The least effective way is with the arms straight and the elbows locked to form a cradle for the ball. A more effective way, but still immature, is with the elbows fixed and the hands cupped to receive the ball. The most effective way, seldom demonstrated by prekindergarten children, is arms and elbows held at the side with flexibility to "give" as the ball arrives. The child's success at catching will depend on the size of the ball, the distance from the other person, and the speed of the ball.

Stair climbing is usually accomplished in a "marked time" fashion by 3-year-olds (that is, both feet on the stair before ascending to the next step). Many 4-year-olds can alternate feet when climbing stairs. The height and width of the stairs influence the way a child climbs them.

Hand and foot preferences are marked during the prekindergarten years. Children even turn their bodies in a preferred direction.

The overall growth rate of the body is about twice as much between ages 1 and 3 as between 3 and 5. This slowed growth probably gives the body of the prekindergarten child the time necessary to consolidate and integrate the psychomotor skills learned in infancy and toddlerhood.

Cognitive behavior.   The prekindergarten years see a marked change in behavior emphasis from psychomotor to cognitive. *Cognitive* behavior is that which is dependent on the symbolic processes, especially language. It is man's cognitive ability that distinguishes him from the lower animals by allowing him so much freedom to adapt to his environment. This cognitive ability is probably due to the nature of the cerebral cortex in the brain, which makes it possible for man to store not only object symbols but language symbols for use in any new experience. The number of possible symbolic combinations in man is endless. But these symbolic or cognitive processes take a relatively long period to develop. We see these processes in bold relief during the prekindergarten years.

The prekindergarten child is learning to pay attention to the distinctive features of the objects, people, places, and events in his world. Thus he is able to discriminate more and more clearly between things. Language labels help make stimuli distinctive. But the child does not notice everything around him. For example, when he looks at a picture he may notice just a few things he is familiar with, such as a boy, a dog, and a tree. The figures that are distinctive in a particular stimulus, such as color or action, will be noticed. The background often goes unnoticed unless the child's attention is drawn to it.

Prekindergarten children need more cues before they can recognize and label something. For example, if a child looks at a dotted outline drawing of a man, he may not recognize the figure as a man until the dots are connected. Similarly, he may have to hear the entire song, or at least a favorite chorus, before he recognizes it.

During the prekindergarten years the child is adding about 50 new words per month to his vocabulary. (This is a higher rate than that found in children before the age of television.) These words are related basically to the child's concrete or firsthand experiences. As the vocabulary grows, so do the child's flexibility and efficiency in the use of the language. Sentences are not long, averaging four or five words, and are primarily simple subject-verb sentences. Occasionally the child will use compound and complex sentences if he is in an environment where he hears such sentences. Articulation changes, especially during the latter half of age 3, so that interpretation by other children is usually unnecessary during age 4. By age 3 the basic rules of grammar are mastered even though the form of the word may be confused. For example, one child was heard protesting, "I'm are, too, a big girl!" The verb was in the correct place, but an incorrect form was used. Occasionally the child will learn the grammar rules of his subculture well but find he is out of place in the larger subculture, which uses different rules of grammar. The child is thus limited in the number of people with whom he can communicate and in what he can learn from his experiences. This limits the experiences he could have in a broader environment.

When the child develops a basic understanding of the language of his culture, his learning experiences become more and more dependent on language. For example, even though many motor skills can be learned without verbal instruction, it becomes easier for the child to learn motor skills when he can receive instruction verbally. In addition, the child who understands the basic elements of his language can learn to give himself instructions, thus moving him closer to self-control.

It is difficult for the prekindergarten child to adapt his speech to the interests and needs of his audience. He seldom explains things clearly, often relating a series of his own concrete experiences as they happen to come together in his head. There appears to be little logic in much of what he says. One reason the language of the prekindergarten child is often so delightful to adults is because it isn't restricted by adult logic.

The cognitive processes include memory, imagination, concept formation, and problem solving. The simplest and probably the easiest form of cognitive behavior is *memory*. This is simply the retaining and recalling of past experience. A child remembers names of people, places, objects, and events. He remembers the chronological order of things. He remembers poems or nursery rhymes or favorite stories. He even has "kinesthetic" memory. The list of things children retain in their memories is endless.

Imagination does not necessarily represent something that can be perceived by one or more of our senses. For example, close your eyes and imagine a cat sitting on your lap. Now picture one-half of that cat as something else, such as a bird or a fish or some other animal. Have you ever seen anything like it in "reality"? (This doesn't count a drawing or sculpture or some such representation of an imaginative idea.) This is an example of imagination. Young children are often accused of having wild imaginations. If this is true, it may be a result of relatively fewer sensory experiences compared with adults and the fact that their experiences have not given them the same number of restrictions on what something is "not." Imagination is the result of mentally combining actual past experiences into possible and impossible new combinations. It can be a type of "playfulness" in thinking. When we look at a young child's painting (or some modern paintings) we put our imagination to work to make something out of what we see.

Concept formation is a process whereby we learn to classify experiences into common categories because of similar attributes or common properties. Complex cognitive behavior requires a good deal of perceptual experience in order to develop effectively. For example, many young children will classify any animal with four legs, two ears, and fur as a "doggy" or a "kitty" or a "horsey" (depending on which term they hear first and most often), regardless of whether that animal is a cow, a toy tiger, or a teddy bear. Eventually most children learn the difference between a horse and a cow and a dog and a cat and so on. In other words, regardless of what dog he sees, a child can eventually name that particular animal a "dog" because there are some common "doggy" attributes among dogs that make them different from cats and horses and other animals. If a child sees only a few animals in his life and/or hears only one animal name, he is likely to call all four-footed furry creatures by that one name and not grow beyond this early stage of concept formation.

It has been said that man's highest achievement is his *problem-solving* ability. This is man's ability to relate one idea logically to another or one experience to another in order to arrive at a solution. Some adults develop the ability to solve problems in terms that are highly hypothetical, abstract, and unobservable. Children under 5 have the ability to reason but on a more limited basis. They can put two or three events together in a related series if the events are based on concrete experience (that is, actual sensory experience).

A child's ability to engage in cognitive behavior is aided by the verbal symbols that accompany his sensory experiences. It is quite possible that the ability to use language unclutters the mind of other forms of symbolic representation that may be unwieldy. It may allow more complex forms of thought. For instance, it is more economical to think "Two plus two equals four" than to picture two blocks plus two more blocks farther apart, then to picture the act of putting those two sets of two blocks together to form a set of four blocks. In addition, the principle "two plus two equals four" can be generalized. But direct, firsthand experience is prerequisite to appropriate use of such language symbols.

Affective behavior.   Affective behavior is a term that refers to the emotions as well as to interests, attitudes, and values. It is most closely related to the next step (feel) in the learning process.

Feel

Certain consequences in the environment tend to accompany or follow each of our acts. Our responses to these consequences are basically physiological and involuntary. When we become conscious of such involuntary responses, we call them feelings and label them "fear," "anger," "joy," "happiness," "frustration," "shyness," and so on. Interests, values, and attitudes are a result of feelings. They tend to determine whether or not we will engage again in the "do" step that preceded them. If the feeling was pleasant, we probably will engage in the "do" step again under similar circumstances. If the feeling was unpleasant, we probably will not repeat it. Psychologists call this "approach-avoidance" behavior. We tend to do things we enjoy and not to do things we don't enjoy. Adults learn to act despite their feelings. The behavior of young children, however, tends to be governed by feelings that develop involuntarily as a result of the consequences accompanying or following their behavior.

We infer feelings from the observable behavior of an individual (that is, from the "do" step). The enthusiastic approach of one child to the kitten on the teacher's lap indicated that pleasant feelings had accompanied her previous behavior related to cats. The second child, on the other hand, avoided any contact with the kitten as a result of unpleasant feelings that had accompanied previous behavior with cats.

WHAT A CHILD CAN LEARN
IN THE PREKINDERGARTEN YEARS

It has been suggested that we might make better use of our educational resources and have a better educational system if we took the present system and stood it on its head (Sava, 1968). This means we would use the $2500 average now spent each year to educate each college sophomore and spend it, instead, on the 3-year-old and 4-year-old. The suggestion is based on the assumption that Bruner's (1960) hypothesis, "any subject can be taught effectively in some intellectually honest form to any child at any stage of development" (p.33), is fundamentally a fact, not an educated guess. Though evidence seems to support this hypothesis, Bruner hastens to add that "the task of teaching a subject to a child at any particular age is one of representing the structure of that subject *in terms of the child's way of viewing things*" (p. 33, italics added). It is this second statement by Bruner that is frequently overlooked in planning the curriculum for the prekindergarten child. Our experiences determine the way we think and act. It seems obvious, then, that prekindergarten children think and act in ways that are different from older children and adults because they have had fewer experiences and less opportunity to integrate these experiences. It seems reasonable to assume that many ideas are simply too difficult for the prekindergarten child to understand, no matter how well they are presented.

Ausubel (1962), however, states some reasons for believing that young children, under certain circumstances, can learn more efficiently than older and more intellectually mature persons. First, older individuals must often "unlearn" what they've learned before they are ready for new learning. Such an unlearning process is time-consuming and frequently unsuccessful, thus blocking the effectiveness of new learning. Second, many older persons develop mental or emotional blocks in certain subject-matter areas. Though they have the capacity, such people will not allow themselves to learn in the areas they block out. Third, and possibly most important, there is a distinct decline in enthusiasm for learning as the individual gets older, particularly in intellectual areas.

Some ideas, when stated in highly academic terms, are very difficult if not impossible for the young child to understand. However, many academic ideas, when recast in terms of their basic elements, can be translated into a child's way of thinking. For example, one college student remembers an unpleasant experience in second grade trying to grasp the idea of subtraction. The abstract idea that "so many minus so many equals some other lower number" just didn't sink in, no matter how many examples the teacher put on the chalkboard and described to the class. The more the student struggled with the idea, the more frustrated she became. One day she happened to watch a group of boys on the playground engaged in a game of marbles. One boy showed his five beautiful, multicolored spheres to a friend and said, "Yesterday I had eight of these. But Fred won three in a game. So now I only have five left." Suddenly the abstract idea of subtraction became a concrete reality to her. So many (eight marbles to begin with) minus (take away) so many (three marbles lost to the other boy) equals ("is the same as" or "ends up as") some other lower number (the five marbles that are left). A concrete experience with real objects had recast an abstract idea, a fundamentally simple one, into terms she could understand. Thereafter, the abstract idea had meaning for her.

People learn more than ideas. When we think of a skill, we think of some specific proficiency with the hands or the body. Occasionally we engage in a skill as an end in itself, such as the simple motor acts of walking or running. Especially when first learning a new skill, we engage in it for its own sake. When a child first learns to ride a bicycle, he rides it endlessly just because he revels in being able to do something new and difficult. However, he may use a bicycle in adulthood either to take him someplace or in order to remain in good health. That is, his skill of bicycle riding can become largely a means to an end rather than an end in itself. Young children engage in a new skill simply for its own sake rather than as a means to an end. A toddler may walk just to be walking. A 3-year-old may talk just for the sake of talking or ride a tricycle just for the sake of using a new skill. But these skills can and do become means to other ends. The ideas and attitudes that can be developed by means of these skills can take on prime importance.

The problem of structuring the child's learning so that his experiences are built in the appropriate sequence is not easy. We don't want to frustrate him by making them too difficult. The problem becomes one of "the match" where his learning experiences are just enough discrepant from previous ones that he becomes motivated to keep on trying, practicing, and learning. The child's behavior will give us clues as to what the next learning experience should be. The question, then, is not really, "What *can* the prekindergarten child learn?" as much as *"How* can the prekindergarten child learn and *what* can we do about it?"* The purpose of this book is to help you answer these questions.

INSTRUCTION AND INSTRUCTIONAL DESIGN

Teaching, in a broad sense of the term, takes place when the "teacher" is not aware of it. For example, prekindergarten teachers have discovered they were responsible, through unconscious means of physical and verbal reinforcement (discussed in Chapter 6), for maintaining such behaviors as crying (Hart, Allen, Buell, Harris, & Wolf, 1964), crawling (Harris, Johnson, Kelley, & Wolf, 1964), aggression (Brown & Elliott, 1965), and isolate behavior (Allen, Hart, Buell, Harris, & Wolf, 1964).

Gage (1964) suggests that teaching is a misleading term because it covers too much. For example, reading about highway accidents in the newspaper "teaches" people to drive more cautiously. Stepping on a sharp object "teaches" a child to wear shoes. Getting a sunburn "teaches" a young person to stay in the shade. Losing money in penny stocks "teaches" someone to use more wisdom in his financial investments. Because "teaching" is something virtually everyone has done, it often is described in a poetic, ambiguous, and even mystical sense. *Instruction,* on the other hand, *is a specific effort by the instructor to modify the environment in such a way that specific learning will result in the learner.* It is based on the learning process (perceive, think, do, and feel). As used in this book, teaching refers to this more specific process of instruction.

It is important to distinguish the difference between instruction and curriculum. Instruction is a process. It is the *how* of teaching. Curriculum is the content on which the instructional process is based. It is the *what* of teaching.

Much of what a child learns is unsystematic, accidental, and incidental. It does not occur in a step-by-step, methodical fashion; it occurs unexpectedly and unintentionally; it occurs by chance. Such learning has at least two pitfalls. First, it is uneconomical. It takes more time and effort because of the trials and errors involved. Imagine how much simpler (and safer!) it is to learn how to drive a car when someone can give you specific instruction, rather than to learn through the discovery process of trial-and-error. Second, it has a tendency to lead to inappropriate or inaccurate learning. For example, those who have learned the "hunt-and-peck" system on the typewriter find it very difficult, even with expert instruction, to train their fingers to hit the appropriate keys when not looking at the keyboard and, thus, to speed up their typing and increase their accuracy.

To avoid these pitfalls of learning, you can *plan* the learning environment of the children you teach in a step-by-step process that will lead to desired learning by each child. A plan for instruction tells you where you're going, how you're going to get there, and when you'll know you've arrived. The term used for this plan for instruction is *instructional design.* Instructional design *is a process that occurs before instruction takes place—the process of specifying the particular environmental conditions that will cause the learner to respond with the desired specific behavioral change. Teacher* refers to the person who plans and implements such a design. *Teaching,* as used in this book, means the same as *instruction.*

STEPS IN THE INSTRUCTIONAL DESIGN PROCESS

The flow chart in Figure 1-1 outlines the six steps in the instructional design process. This is a good order to follow when planning instruction for prekindergarten children.

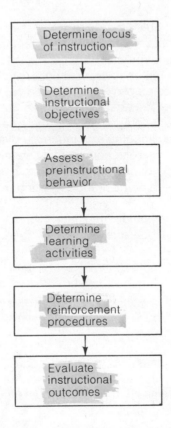

Figure 1-1. Steps in the instructional design process.

In the next six chapters, each of the steps in the instructional design process will be discussed in detail. Programmed exercises have been included in each of these chapters to provide practice in each instructional design step.

REFERENCES

Allen, K. E., Hart, B., Buell, J. S., Harris, F. R., & Wolf, M. M. Effects of social reinforcement on isolate behavior of a nursery school child. *Child Development,* 1964, **35,** 511–518.

Ausubel, D. P. Can children learn anything that adults can—and more efficiently? *Elementary School Journal*, 1962, **62,** 270–272.

Brown, P., & Elliott, R. Control of aggression in a nursery school class. *Journal of Experimental Child Psychology,* 1965, **2,** 103–107.

Bruner, J. S. *The process of education.* Cambridge: Harvard University Press, 1960.

Cratty, B. J. *Perceptual and motor development in infants and children.* New York: Macmillan, 1970.

Gage, N. L. Theories of teaching. In E. Hilgard (Ed.), *Theories of learning and instruction.* Sixty-third yearbook of NSSE, Part I. Chicago: University of Chicago Press, 1964.

Harris, F. R., Johnson, M. K., Kelley, C. S., & Wolf, M. M. Effects of positive social reinforcement on regressed crawling of a nursery school child. *Journal of Educational Psychology,* 1964, **55,** 35–41.

Hart, B. H., Allen, K., Buell, J. S., Harris, F. R., & Wolf, M. M. Effects of social reinforcement on operant crying. *Journal of Experimental Child Psychology,* 1964, **1,** 145–153.

Kagan, J. His struggle for identity. *Saturday Review,* December 7, 1968, 80–88.

Munn, N. L. *The evolution and growth of human behavior.* (2nd ed.) Boston: Houghton Mifflin, 1965.

Sava, S. G. When learning comes easy. *Saturday Review,* November 16, 1968.

Chapter 2

The Focus of Instruction

Instructional design probably sounds like something that should be taught in an art or architecture department. Or it may sound too mechanistic, not taking into account the refreshing flexibility, curiosity, activity, and humor of the young child. Maybe you are thinking it sounds too "scientific" to be applied to the "art" of teaching the prekindergarten child.

If you have ever used a camera to take a picture, you know that one of the first things you do is bring your subject into focus. In other words, you make certain you have a distinct, clear image rather than a blurred, cloudy image. That is exactly what needs to be done when you begin to design a lesson or group of lessons. You make your subject clear and distinct.

Subject can have two meanings. First, it can refer to the prekindergarten child you are teaching. Second, it can refer to the subject matter or content of the curriculum you wish to teach. This chapter is concerned with the subject matter around which you will design your instruction.

DETERMINE THE CONTENT AREA AND SUBDIVISION OF THE CURRICULUM

The human brain seems to impose some degree of order on the chaos of experiences bombarding it during every moment of life. In other words, experiences are classified or categorized. These categories might be of a high, general order, such as "pleasant experiences" and "unpleasant experiences." Or they may be of a lower, more specific order, such as "playing with a new toy" or "treating a sunburn." In the same way, we can impose some sort of order on the content of our learning. Eight basic content areas or categories seem to emerge from an examination of various preschool and elementary school programs. In alphabetical order, these content areas are graphic arts, health and safety, living in a world of people (the social sciences), mathematics, movement, music, our world (the biological and physical sciences), and reading. These are the major divisions, or content areas, of the prekindergarten curriculum. When you begin to design your lesson plan, you first decide on which one of these eight content areas of the curriculum you wish to focus.

But that is only the beginning. Your focus is not distinct enough yet. Each of these major content areas can be subdivided. For example, the content area *our world* can be divided into at least two major groups:

    I. Our world
        A. The world of living things
        B. The physical world

Each of these can be further divided. For example, A can be subdivided into these categories:

        A. The world of living things
            1. Animals
            2. Insects
            3. Birds
            4. Fish
            5. Plants
            6. Food
            7. Trees

Each of these smaller divisions can also be subdivided. For example, 1 could be broken down to these categories:

1. Animals
   a. Pets
   b. Farm animals
   c. Forest animals
   d. Zoo animals
   e. Prehistoric animals

And there are even further subdivisions. Part 2 of this book contains a list of the major content area subdivisions most useful for teaching prekindergarten children. However, you may add others; there is nothing sacred about the classification scheme used here.

    You probably need practice in subdividing major areas, so let's try a couple of additional examples before you take some trial runs on your own. *Graphic arts* is another major content area of the curriculum. It can be subdivided as follows:

I. Graphic arts
   A. Elements of art
   B. Art media

B can be divided:

B. Art media
   1. Drawing media
   2. Painting media
   3. Fingerpainting media
   4. Food-printing media
   5. Papers
   6. Collage media
   7. Pastes and glues
   8. Linear three-dimensional media
   9. Tapes
   10. Modeling or sculpture media

One can be further subdivided:

1. Drawing media
   a. Crayons
   b. Chalk
   c. Oil-base pastels
   d. Felt-tip pens and markers

Here is an example in the content area of *music:*

I. Music
   A. Music skills
   B. Elements of music

Now it's your turn. Scattered throughout the reading material will be boxes containing exercises for you to practice. Cover the answer until you have done the exercise.

---

1. Add further subdivisions to A, music skills:

   1. _____

   2. _____

   3. _____

   4. _____

   5. _____

   6. _____

You could have listed the following:

1. Listening
2. Singing

      3. Moving
      4. Playing instruments
      5. Creating
      6. Reading

Switch gears now and consider the content area *living in a world of people.*

---

2. Add subdivisions in the blanks:

   C. Holidays and other special days

      1. National holidays

      2. _____

      3. _____

You could have listed:

      2. Religious holidays
      3. Special holidays and events

---

3. Add subdivisions in the blanks:

   4. Special occasions in the family

      a. _____

      b. _____

      c. _____

      d. _____

      e. _____

      f. _____

You could have listed:

- a. Birthdays
- b. Family outings
- c. Holidays
- d. Reunions
- e. Vacations
- f. Weddings

Going back to the content area *our world*, try subdividing the topic farm animals:

---

4. Add subdivisions in the blanks:

   b. Farm animals

      1. _____
      2. _____
      3. _____
      4. _____
      5. _____

- -

You could have listed:

1. Identification of farm animals
2. Where farm animals live
3. What farm animals eat
4. How farm animals move
5. Farm animal babies

Now you know how to do it. Part 2 of the text includes a system of classification for the various content areas of the curriculum. Add or delete items as you wish. The numbering system used in Part 2 provides a quick and easy filing and cross-reference system as you prepare lesson plans for use in the prekindergarten. Table 2–1 shows each content area of the curriculum with the major subdivisions in each area.

Table 2–1. Content areas and subdivisions of the prekindergarten curriculum.

---

1. Graphic arts
   1.1. Elements of art
   1.2. Art media
2. Health and safety
   2.1. Caring for the body
   2.2. Safety at home or school
   2.3. Accidents
3. Living in a world of people
   3.1. Living in a family
   3.2. Homes people live in
   3.3. Holidays and special days
   3.4. Preparing foods
   3.5. Learning to live with others in the prekindergarten
   3.6. Money
   3.7. People and places in the community
   3.8. Subcultures within the community
   3.9. People in other countries
   3.10. People of other times
4. Mathematics
   4.1. Sets
   4.2. Counting
   4.3. Number symbols
   4.4. Addition
   4.5. Subtraction
   4.6. Time
   4.7. Miscellaneous mathematics concepts
5. Movement
   5.1. What the body does
   5.2. Where the body moves
6. Music
   6.1. Music skills
   6.2. Elements of music
7. Our world
   7.1. The world of living things
   7.2. The physical world
8. Reading
   8.1. Letters
   8.2. Words
   8.3. Sentences

SUMMARY

The first step in instructional design is to determine the focus of instruction. After selecting one of the eight major content areas of the curriculum, you then determine which specific category in that content area you wish to use as the focus of a given lesson. If you select the smallest subdivision of any topic in a content area, you can build an appropriate sequence of lessons focusing on each of the subdivisions within that topic.

After you have selected the focus of your lesson, you are ready to move on to the next step in instructional design: determining the instructional objectives of the focus of your lesson.

Chapter 3

Instructional Objectives

Someone once defined a fanatic as "a person who doubles his speed when he's lost his aim." Far too frequently teachers feverishly plan learning experiences for children without any idea why they want the children to engage in these experiences other than "to have a pleasant experience in an atmosphere of warmth and acceptance" or "to learn about spatial relationships." Any lawyer, doctor, farmer, chemist, business executive, or salesman who plans his daily experiences in terms of such nebulous goals will soon find himself without the means of earning a livelihood. It is just as important for you to plan specific objectives as anyone else. Otherwise your lesson planning can take on a fanatical flavor, and what the child learns can become simply a matter of hopeful happenstance. When you carefully plan the purposes or objectives of a lesson, you are in a position to assess what each child is learning and, thus, the success of your own teaching.

INSTRUCTIONAL OBJECTIVES
AS BEHAVIORAL OBJECTIVES

The purpose of instruction is to change behavior. In other words, you want the child to act differently in some way at the end of an instructional period from the way he acted (or behaved) at the beginning. Such desired behavior change should be stated specifically in the lesson plan. When an instructional objective states a specific activity, it is called a behavioral objective. A *behavioral objective is a statement that describes desired, specific, observable behavior expected in each child as the result of learning activities in a given lesson.* The objective "each child will correctly point to three red objects in the room" is a *behavioral* objective because it describes specific observable behavior, which the child will perform as the result of learning activities in a given lesson.

Instructional objectives that are stated in vague, abstract terms make it impossible to measure effectiveness of instruction. When an instructional objective does not state a specific, observable child activity, it is not a behavioral objective. Many instructional objectives, sometimes referred to as educational goals, are stated in nebulous terms. It is often up to you, the teacher, to state such objectives or goals in terms of specific, observable behavior. The objective "each child will know the color *red*" is not a behavioral objective. The objective does not state an observable activity or behavior on the part of the child.

Verbs such as *know* and *understand* are not specific and observable. For example, the objective "each child will know five different shapes" does not state an observable activity. On the other hand, the objective "each child will select and pick up from a mixed group of shapes a triangle, a square, a rectangle, a circle, and a diamond" specifies observable behavior.

When writing instructional objectives, it's a good idea to avoid using the following words because they do not specify observable behavior:

feel	appreciate
know	realize
nurture	comprehend
understand	

If you wish to use these verbs in instructional objectives, be sure you clarify their meaning by further stating what type of observable behavior is meant by each term. For example, the objective "the child will demonstrate that he understands the meaning of the concept *over* by jumping over three items of his choice in the room" clarifies the meaning of *understand* by further stating an observable behavior, *jumping over.*

The following words specify observable child activity or behavior. Therefore, these are examples of suitable verbs to use in writing behavioral objectives:

tell	name
select	draw
pantomime	point
sing	recite
choose	

In the objective "each child will name one red object in the room," the observable child behavior is *"name* one red object." Therefore this is a behavioral objective. In the objective "the children will grasp the meaning of the preposition *under,"* there is no observable child activity specified. Therefore it is not a behavioral objective.

Let's pause now in the discussion of instructional objectives so you can evaluate what you are learning.

---

1. Define in your own words the term *behavioral objective:*

- -

You should have written something similar to the following:

A behavioral objective is a statement that describes desired, specific, observable behavior expected in each child as the result of learning activities in a given lesson.

---

2. The following list of verbs includes some of those used in writing instructional objectives. Check those verbs that describe specific and observable behavior and therefore are useful in writing behavioral objectives:

    ___✓___(a) tell   ___✓___(e) sing
    _____(b) comprehend   ___✓___(f) point
    _____(c) appreciate   _____(g) know
    ___✓___(d) pantomime   _____(h) feel

    You should have marked (a), (d), (e), (f). The verbs in (b), (c), (g), and (h) do not describe observable behavior.

3. Check the instructional objective that is a behavioral objective:

    _____(a) Each child will realize the importance of rules in the prekindergarten.
    ___✓___(b) Each child will state two rules of the prekindergarten.

    You should have checked (b) because it has an observable activity *state*. The verb *realize* in (a) does not describe specific or observable behavior.

4. Check the instructional objective that is a behavioral objective:

    _____(a) Each child will comprehend the meaning of safety in the home.
    ___✓___(b) Each child will role play one appropriate activity he would engage in when approaching a dangerous object.

You should have checked (b) because it has an observable activity, *role play.* The verb *comprehend* in (a) is neither specific nor observable.

---

5. Check the instructional objective that is a behavioral objective:

    _____(a)   Each child will know the colors red, yellow, and blue.
    _____(b)   Each child will appreciate classical music.

- -

If you marked neither one of these objectives, you are correct. Objective (a) included the verb *know* with no clarification in terms of specific, observable child activity. The problem is the same in objective (b) where the verb *appreciate* is not clarified.

---

6. Change the following objective to a behavioral objective: Each child will understand how to care for his teeth.

- -

You could have written something like the following:

(a)   Each child will tell at least three ways to care for his teeth.
(b)   Each child will demonstrate the correct way to brush his teeth using a real toothbrush, toothpaste, and water.

7. Change the following objective to a behavioral objective: Each child will know the difference between the four seasons: autumn, winter, spring, and summer.

You could have written something like the following:

(a) Each child will correctly select from a group of pictures those that show autumn, winter, spring, and summer scenes.
(b) Each child will demonstrate one child activity that is appropriate for each of the four seasons.

Some teachers have a tendency to write objectives in terms of what the teacher is expected to do during a lesson rather than what the child is expected to do. Teacher activities, however, should always be planned *after* the behavior objectives and learning activities have been planned. Unless desired child behavior is planned for each lesson, the teacher's activities may become entertainment only. Teacher activities are based on desired child behavior.

Three Elements of a Behavioral Objective

If you are to evaluate the effectiveness of your teaching, it is not enough to state only the observable child behavior in each objective (to *name*). Mager (1962) suggests that a behavioral objective should consist of *three* elements:

1. The desired observable behavior (for example, "point to").
2. Under what circumstances or conditions the behavior is expected to be performed ("when given a group of objects").
3. The measure of successful performance of the desired behavior— that is, how well you want the child to perform ("three correct out of four").

If only the desired observable behavior is written in an objective, some questions about the desired behavior are likely to arise. For example, where and when is the behavior to be exhibited? Will it be performed in class, at home, or somewhere else? If the activity is to occur in class, by what procedure? What will be the signal for the behavior to begin? How will you know when the child has accomplished what is expected of him?

Let's examine the following objective and see whether these questions are answered:

Each child will demonstrate that he understands the concept *over* by using his body correctly to go over at least two objects in the room.

What is the desired behavior? The following words suggest the behavior: "by using his body correctly to go over." Where and when will the behavior be exhibited (that is, the circumstances or conditions under which the behavior is to be exhibited)? This is stated in the objective by the words "objects in the room." How will you know when the child has accomplished what is expected of him (that is, what is the measure of successful performance of the desired behavior)? This is answered in the objective by the words "at least *two* objects." There are many ways that a child could demonstrate his understanding of the concept *over*. The teacher must define first the observable desired behavior and then the standard of performance, or how well the child is expected to perform. Other ways might be:

Out of a group of five pictures, each child will correctly select the two pictures that illustrate people or objects going over something.
While watching the teacher move a wand over and under objects in

the room, each child will correctly tell the teacher when he moves the wand *over* an object.

Stating the observable behavior alone is not enough if teaching effectiveness is to be measured. Let's try another behavior objective:

Each child will pantomime one way he can help his mother during the week using at least one of the five props provided by the teacher.

What is the desired behavior? The words "will pantomime" specify the observable child behavior. What are the conditions or circumstances under which the behavior is to occur? The words "using at least one of the five props provided by the teacher" indicate these conditions. Is the measure of successful performance of the desired behavior indicated? Yes, by the words *"one way* he can *help his mother* during the week."

If you include the desired observable child behavior, the conditions under which the behavior is to occur, and the measure of successful performance of that objective each time you plan a lesson objective, you will have a way to measure the effectiveness of your teaching.

Here are more trial runs.

---

8. Examine the following behavioral objective and write the words that indicate (a) the desired, observable behavior, (b) the circumstances or conditions under which the behavior is expected to be performed, and (c) the measure of successful performance:

    After hearing all except the end of the story, each child will tell one way he thinks the story could have ended.

    (a) _tell_____

    (b) _after hearing all except the end of the story_

    (c) _one way he thinks the story could have ended_

You were correct if you had the following:

(a) *behavior:* "tell"
(b) *circumstances or conditions:* "After hearing all except the end of the story"
(c) *measure of successful performance: "one* way he thinks the story could have ended"

9. Examine the following behavioral objective and write the words that indicate (a) the desired observable behavior, (b) the circumstances or conditions under which the behavior is expected to be performed, and (c) the measure of successful performance:

Given a series of four pictures in scrambled order, each child will put the pictures in appropriate order according to the proper sequence of events illustrated in the pictures.

(a) *put pictures in order*
(b) *given a series of 4 pictures in scrambled order*
(c) *appropriate order ... proper sequence ..*

You were correct if you had the following:

(a) *behavior:* "put the pictures in ... order"
(b) *circumstances or conditions:* "Given a series of four pictures in scrambled order"
(c) *measure of successful performance: "appropriate* order according to the proper sequence of events illustrated in the pictures"

10. Examine the following behavioral objective and write the words that indicate (a) the desired observable behavior, (b) the circumstances or conditions under which the behavior is expected to be performed, and (c) the measure of successful performance:

Using paint colors of his choice, paint brush, and easel paper, each child will paint his own impression of what he feels when he listens to "Waltz of the Flowers."

(a) _will paint_

(b) _using paints colors ... easel paper_

(c) _his own impression ... "Waltz of the Flowers"_

You were correct if you had the following:

(a) *behavior:* "will paint"
(b) *circumstances or conditions:* "Using paint colors of his choice, paint brush, and easel paper"
(c) *measure of successful performance:* "his own impression of what he feels when he listens to 'Waltz of the Flowers' "

TYPES OF BEHAVIORAL OBJECTIVES

The task of writing behavioral objectives is simplified and clarified if you determine the *class* of behavior desired in a given learning situation. If you learn to use a behavior classification system, it won't be necessary for you to determine a unique behavior every time you write an objective. You can select the desired behavior to be learned from a limited set of classes or categories. In other words, instead of selecting hundreds of unique behavioral objectives to fit the hundreds of objectives you write for the various content areas of the curriculum, you simply select from types of behavior in a classification system consisting of twelve basic categories of behavior. This behavior classification system, adapted from one developed by Gagné (1970) and another developed by Merrill (1971b), is outlined in Table 3–1.

Table 3–1. *Categories of learned behavior.*

Levels of learned behavior	Divisions of learned behavior		
	1	2	3
PSYCHOMOTOR	single neuromuscular response	motor sequence	complex skill
COGNITIVE Memorized	naming	serial memory	component memory
Complex Cognitive	concept learning	rule learning	problem solving
AFFECTIVE	emotion	motivation interest	attitude value

Constructed from data in: Merrill, M. D. Necessary psychological conditions for defining instructional outcomes. In M. D. Merrill (Ed.), *Instructional design: Readings.* Englewood Cliffs, N. J.: Prentice-Hall, Inc., 1971b; and Gagné, R. M. *The conditions of learning.* New York: Holt, Rinehart and Winston, Inc., 1970.

You will note in Table 3-1 that learned behavior is categorized or classified into four levels and three divisions of each level. This implies that some classes of behavior must be learned before other classes or types of behavior can be learned. There is a hierarchy in learning, with simple behavior being learned before complex behavior in each level and division. This also implies that there is a logical sequence of subject matter within each area of the curriculum. Any subtopic can be taught as several different kinds of behavior.

Each level and division of learned behavior will be discussed separately. In addition, you will have the opportunity to write some behavioral objectives for each class or category of behavior.

Psychomotor Behavior

Psychomotor behavior is neuromuscular activity associated with mental processes. That is, this type of behavior is observable neuromuscular or motor activity under conscious control of the individual. Psychomotor behavior, the first level of learned behavior, is the simplest type of behavior that is a voluntary process. Psychomotor behavior occurs when the child is able to perform rapidly a specific muscular reaction in the presence of a specific stimulus. The observable behavior is a muscular response carried through to completion without hesitation. There are three basic divisions of psychomotor behavior: single neuromuscular response, motor sequence, and complex skill.

Single neuromuscular response. The most simple psychomotor behavior is the single neuromuscular response, which is a single new neuromuscular reaction such as lifting a foot, raising a finger, or taking a step in the presence of a specific stimulus. Writing behavioral objectives in this classification is probably unnecessary unless you are working with children who have perceptual-motor handicaps.

Motor sequence. A motor sequence is a linking of several muscular reactions into a coordinated series of reactions occurring in rapid succession. It is usually one portion of a complex skill. Such motor skills as running, jumping, hopping, climbing, sliding, hammering nails, throwing a ball, and galloping are motor sequences in young children. That is, each skill consists of a coordinated series of reactions occurring in rapid succession. These, therefore, are sequences of single neuromuscular responses. The observable behavior must be smooth, well integrated, and seemingly automatic. Some examples of motor-sequence objectives in the prekindergarten follow.

Each child will:

1. Cut off at least one piece of paper the width of the construction paper without tearing the paper or dropping the scissors when given a pair of blunt scissors and a piece of 9″ × 12″ construction paper.
2. Use his hands and fingers to spread the fingerpaint in horizontal, vertical, and circular strokes on the fingerpaint paper when given a piece of dampened fingerpaint paper and a helping of colored fingerpaint the size of an egg.
3. Demonstrate with a toothbrush, toothpaste, and water that he can brush his front teeth with an up-and-down motion of the brush without dropping the brush and while keeping the toothpaste in his mouth.
4. Demonstrate with an article of his own clothing that he can put each button in the correct buttonhole smoothly and without hesitation.
5. Use a spoon to dish up the desired amount of food from the serving dish to the plate without spilling any before it reaches the plate when given a serving dish of food, a serving spoon, and a plate.
6. Jump over three objects of his choice without touching the objects.

Now try writing some motor-sequence behavioral objectives yourself.

---

11. Write below a *motor-sequence* behavioral objective focusing on the manipulative skill *throwing:*

- -

You could have written an objective similar to this:

Given a bean bag each child will throw the bean bag beyond the marker 15 feet from him in four out of five tries.

---

12. Write below a *motor-sequence* behavioral objective focusing on the music skill *playing the autoharp:*

- -

You could have written an objective similar to the following:

While holding the autoharp on his lap, each child will stroke with one finger all the strings of the autoharp at least five times in rapid succession.

It is easy to assume that the children you teach have already developed the necessary motor sequences before they enter prekindergarten. But motor sequences are necessary to demonstrate learning in each of the other classes of behavior. A child who is having difficulty demonstrating problem-solving ability, for example, may be deficient in one or more motor sequences. If the child can demonstrate sufficient skill in a desired motor sequence, there is no reason to teach him something he already knows. If the child cannot demonstrate sufficient skill in a specific motor sequence, this skill can be taught. But first you need to identify the motor sequence to be learned.

Complex skill. A complex skill is a coordinated series of motor sequences occurring in the presence of a large set of cues. On the adult level, for example, the game of tennis is a complex skill. That is, specific motor sequences such as serving the tennis ball over the net into the correct court, returning a high volley within the correct boundaries of the opposite court, returning a serve with a backhand or forehand shot within the correct boundaries of the opposite court, and other motor sequences are necessary in order to play an effective game of tennis. The cue for each motor sequence depends in large part on the actions of the opponent. The effective and successful tennis player responds appropriately in smooth, integrated fashion and without hesitation to each cue provided by his opponent.

Complex skills are required in all sports, in dance, and in many occupational areas such as auto mechanics, secretarial work, engineering, commercial art, plumbing, carpentry, and so on. But young children also engage in complex skills such as riding a tricycle, painting a picture, brushing teeth, building an object of wood with nails, hammer, and saw, climbing the jungle gym, and crawling through a maze, to mention only a few. For example, riding a tricycle requires the motor sequences of pedaling with alternating feet, using the hands to guide the moving tricycle over constantly changing terrain, and decreasing and increasing speed on the tricycle. Each of these sequences is a smooth, integrated response to a specific cue performed without hesitation.

When an individual has learned to engage in a complex skill, he responds in a habitual pattern so that he doesn't have to think about each response to a cue before he makes that response. In other words, he responds voluntarily but does not have to think about the steps involved in each response. As a matter of fact, verbal prompts during the complex-skill response would interrupt the response.

Here are some complex-skill objectives in the prekindergarten.

Each child will:
1. Make a collage of his choice by correctly using a paste brush, paste, paper, fabric scraps, and construction paper.

2. Demonstrate how to wash his hands, arms, and face by appropriately using water, soap, washcloth, and towel.
3. Role play one activity performed by his parent or guardian at work.
4. Participate in the making of cookies by doing at least three of the following activities: measure correct amounts of flour, sugar, salt, milk, and vanilla in the appropriate container; add one or more ingredients to the cookie dough; mix the dough with spoon or hands; roll out the cookie dough with a rolling pin and flour; cut at least three cookies from the rolled-out dough with a cookie cutter; place at least three cookies in an appropriate spot on the cookie sheet.

Now it's your turn to try some complex-skill objectives:

_____

13. Write below a *complex-skill* behavioral objective focusing on the topic *locomotor skills*.

- -

You could have written an objective similar to this:

Each child will demonstrate three different locomotor skills of his choice (for example, walking, sliding, leaping, galloping, jumping, hopping) when moving from one end of the room to the other.

_____

---

14. Write below a *complex-skill* behavioral objective focusing on the topic *how plants grow.*

- -

You could have written an objective similar to this:

Each child will plant his own individual bean seed, correctly using a large planter can, soil, bean seed, soil scoop, water can, and water.

---

15. Write below a *complex-skill* behavioral objective focusing on the topic *care of pets*.

- -

You could have written an objective similar to this:

With a real dog and using real food, a real brush, old rags, and a box, each child will demonstrate how to feed the dog and how to prepare a box in which the dog can sleep.

When writing behavioral objectives at the psychomotor level, remember that the objective must emphasize some kind of smooth, integrated neuromuscular performance by the child in the presence of a given stimulus or several stimuli in succession. If verbal behavior is required, the class of behavior is usually at another level.

Cognitive Behavior

The term *cognitive* is an adjective describing the mental processes through which we gain knowledge. The word is associated with the mental processes of memory, imagination, concept formation, and problem solving. All of these processes involve some type of symbolic or representative activity. *Symbolic* refers to those processes that represent or stand for something else. For example, language is a symbolic process because the written, verbal, and gestural symbols used in language are not the actual objects, persons, places, or events but represent or stand for these objects, persons, places, or events. Some form of language is the observable behavior by which cognitive behavior is measured. It is cognitive behavior in man that distinguishes him from the lower animals and allows him to adapt to his environment. Psychomotor behavior is a prerequisite to the expression of cognitive behavior inasmuch as verbal, written, or gestural language is fundamentally a motor activity. That is, psychomotor behavior is the means by which cognitive behavior becomes observable.

There are two major levels of cognitive behavior: memorized and complex cognitive. Memorized behavior has three divisions of increasing complexity: naming, serial memory, and component memory. Complex-cognitive behavior, which uses memorized behavior as a foundation, also has three divisions of increasing complexity: concept learning, rule learning, and problem solving.

Memorized behavior. When memorized behavior takes place, the child either recognizes or reproduces a symbolic response in the presence of cues identical to those he has experienced before. A symbol is something that represents something else. For example, a word is not the thing itself but "represents" verbally or on the written page something else. The word *cat* is not a real cat but a symbol or, in other words, something representing the real thing. Observable behavior in a memorized response can be either verbal (talking) or psychomotor (pointing or drawing). Therefore, psychomotor skills are considered prerequisite to memorized behavior. The emphasis in memorized behavior is the reproduction or recognition of symbols identical to those experienced in the past.

   Naming. Naming is the least complex type of memorized behavior. An example of naming is the infant or toddler who learns specific labels for specific stimuli such as *baby, bed, cup, doll, mama, ball, sleep, horse,* and so on. In this case a single verbal response (symbolic response) is associated with and either recognized or reproduced in the presence of a specific stimulus. The child is able to recognize or reproduce the appropriate symbol whether the stimulus is the real thing, such as his own pet dog, or a representation of the real thing, such as a picture, a toy reproduction, or a movie of a dog. The ability to appropriately name objects, people, places, or events is prerequisite to the development of higher cognitive processes. Most children who have learning disabilities in school, particularly those from disadvantaged neighborhoods, probably have not yet learned to correctly label the stimuli in their environment. Thus, when more complex behavior is expected of them they are unable to respond appropriately because of a deficiency in naming behavior.
   The following are examples of naming behavioral objectives suitable for prekindergarten.

   Each child will:
   1. Give the correct label for each item used in the making of his collage.
   2. Correctly label verbally each shape in a group of wooden shapes provided by the teacher.
   3. Correctly label verbally the denomination of each of five coins provided by the teacher.
   4. On a picture of a community, correctly point to and state the name of at least five places where community helpers work.
   5. When asked by the teacher to identify each of the rooms in a house in a picture, point correctly to each room named by the teacher.

6. Correctly state the name of each of the percussion instruments in the music learning center.

7. While watching children demonstrate each of the locomotor skills, correctly identify verbally the locomotor skill demonstrated by each child.

---

16. Write below a *naming* behavioral objective focusing on the subject *identifying forest animals.*

- -

You could have written an objective similar to this:

Each child will correctly label verbally each picture of a forest animal when asked by the teacher.

---

17. Write below a *naming* behavioral objective focusing on the subject *varieties of weather.*

- -

You could have written an objective similar to this:

Each child will point to at least five pictures depicting the four seasons and correctly label each one according to the season it depicts.

18. Write below a *naming* behavioral objective focusing on the subject *tasting*.

You could have written an objective similar to this:

Each child will correctly label each of six substances he tastes as salty, sour, bitter, or sweet.

Serial memory. Serial memory is demonstrated when the child can place in their correct order specific single naming responses in the presence of specific stimuli. The order is always the same. The most common type of serial memory occurs when the child can quote verbatim a poem or piece of prose or when he can sing the exact words to an entire song. Incidentally, singing a song includes two examples of serial memory—memory for melody and memory for words. In serial-memory behavior, the sequence of responses is always the same and the order is demonstrated without hesitation and without prompting from someone or something else. Listing things in chronological order is also serial-memory behavior.

Examples of serial-memory behavior objectives in the prekindergarten include the following.

Each child will:
1. Place real materials in the correct sequence of use in planting a vegetable seed without prompting from the teacher or other students.
2. Place pictures of the four seasons in chronological order without prompting.
3. Tell the appropriate steps to follow in order to make Jell-O.
4. Demonstrate with his body three nonlocomotor skills in the order verbally suggested by the teacher without prompts or additional cues other than the teacher's instruction.

19. Write below a *serial-memory* behavioral objective focusing on the subject *rhythm*.

You could have written an objective similar to this:

Each child will play on the drum at least two identical rhythms demonstrated by the teacher.

20. Write below a *serial-memory* behavioral objective focusing on the subject *singing*.

You could have written an objective similar to this:

Each child will correctly sing all the words of a given song without the use of prompts such as pictures, objects, or cues from the teacher.

21. Write below a *serial-memory* behavioral objective focusing on the subject *number symbols*.

You could have written an objective similar to this:

Each child will place in correct order felt numerals from one to five.

Component memory. Component memory is the most complex kind of memorized behavior. Component memory occurs when a child can recognize or reproduce correctly each member of a given set or class in the presence of a specific stimulus he has experienced before. You probably have had numerous multiple-choice examinations during your years in school. In these exams, you selected from a number of possible choices or discrete items for each question the correct response appropriate to the cue given in the question (or initial statement). In order for this to be an example of component memory, however, you must have had previous exposure to the correct response in each item. Therefore your task in such a multiple-choice test becomes one of recognizing or reproducing (discriminating) a response with which you previously have had experience. By the same token, when a child selects out of a group of objects the one asked for by the teacher, he is demonstrating component memory, provided he has learned to label that object in previous experience (naming behavior).

Gagné (1970) suggests that this type of learning is "often concerned with distinctive features [p. 157]." That is, a child learns to differentiate between stimuli in the same set according to distinguishing characteristics such as color, shape, texture, and size. He learns to distinguish among faces, toys, eating utensils, furniture, the location of objects, and so on. For example, in the set called *balls,* he can distinguish among such characteristics as size, shape, texture, and surface decoration to identify a golf ball, a tennis ball, a volley ball, a baseball, a basketball, or a football. In the set called *dishes,* he can discriminate the difference between a plate, a bowl, a cup, a pitcher, or a platter.

Component memory is similar to naming except that in naming the child has learned in isolation the labels for specific objects, persons, or events. By contrast, component memory involves the possibility of *interference* while learning to discriminate each stimulus in a set of stimuli and thus *forgetting,* especially if the discrete elements being learned are quite similar to one another. For instance, a child can learn in an isolated instance to attach the verbal label *cow* to the real cow (naming). A little later he learns to attach the verbal label *horse* to the real horse. But there are several characteristics about cows and horses that are similar, such as approximate size, texture of the fur, number of legs, shape of the face, length and texture of the tail. Therefore, when someone points to a real cow and asks the child what it is, the child may say, "It's a horse," because of his more recent experience with a horse. Or he might say, "I forget," because a similar learning condition to that of naming the cow, but a more recent one, has "interfered" with his ability to remember the correct label. Cows and horses belong to the set called *animals,* or more specifically, *farm animals.*

Some members of a set are easily distinguished from one another such as bowls, plates, and cups in the set *dishes.* Some members of a set are difficult to distinguish from one another, such as the members *p, b,* and *d* in the set *letters.* In other words, if a child develops component memory, he learns what something is *not* as well as what something *is.* More about this idea in Chapter 5.

Some examples of component-memory behavioral objectives that might be suitable in the prekindergarten follow.

Each child will:
1. Correctly select from a random group of shapes at least four different shapes he has worked with before.
2. Correctly select from and place in separate piles all the pieces of blue fabric, pieces of red fabric, and pieces of yellow fabric used in previous demonstrations.
3. Given pictures of community helpers he has seen before, correctly select the policeman, the doctor, the postman, the nurse, and the bus driver.
4. From a group of flannel figures of family members he has seen before, correctly select one suitable for the mother, for the father, for the baby, for the brother, and for the sister.

Now it's your turn:

---

22. Write a *component-memory* behavioral objective focusing on the subject *texture*.

- -

You could have written an objective similar to this:

Each child will correctly select from a group of textured objects he has worked with before those that are smooth and those that are rough.

---

23. Write a *component-memory* behavioral objective focusing on the subject *body direction* (forward-backward, upward-downward, sideways).

- -

You could have written an objective similar to this:

Each child will correctly name at least three of four body directions he has practiced when demonstrated by another child.

24. Write a *component-memory* behavioral objective focusing on the subject *number symbols*.

You could have written an objective similar to this:

Each child will correctly select from a random pile of numerals printed on cards he has seen before the number symbols 2, 5, and 7.

Much if not most of the curriculum K through 12 is based on these three classes of memorized behavior—naming, serial memory, and component memory.

Complex-cognitive behavior.   Psychomotor and memorized behavior are prerequisite to complex-cognitive behavior. However, the divisions of complex-cognitive behavior are similar to those in psychomotor and memorized behavior, with the first division involving the learning of single elements, the second division involving the combination of two or more single elements, and the third division involving a choice among elements. Complex-cognitive behavior is the highest level of behavior. It includes concept-learning, rule-learning, and problem-solving behavior. Memorized behavior usually occurs without hesitation in the presence of given stimuli, while complex-cognitive behavior may take a period of time before it is expressed. In each class of complex-cognitive behavior, the child "makes an appropriate response to a previously unencountered instance of some class of stimulus objects, events, or situations [Merrill, 1971b]." Therefore, complex-cognitive behavior goes beyond memorized behavior.

Concept learning. Concept learning "occurs when a [child] is able to correctly identify the class membership of a previously unencountered object or event or a previously unencountered representation of some object or event [Merrill, 1971b]." Concept learning is similar to naming "except that what is distinguished is a class rather than a specific object [Gagné, 1971]."

Any word or term can be a concept. What is meant by *concept* is a category or class, not a name for something specific. If a child points to a chair and says "chair," we don't know if he is demonstrating naming or concept behavior unless we are certain the child has never seen that particular chair before. *Chair* can refer to an abstract quality shared by any number of objects in the same class. Or it can refer to one chair only. In the latter case, the child's use of the term *chair* is naming behavior. In other words, concept learning is demonstrated when the child can label or select an item he has never seen before as fitting a particular class or category. If the child has seen that particular object before and called it by name, his subsequent correct labeling of the object is naming behavior, a form of memorized behavior. So the test of whether or not a child has learned a concept is to present him with a situation or object or event he has never experienced before and see whether he can respond to that single new stimulus appropriately. If a child labels correctly a spoon he has never seen before, he is demonstrating concept learning related to the class *spoon*.

It can be said that a child who demonstrates correct concept learning is thus demonstrating ability to both generalize and discriminate. *Generalization* is the child's ability to distinguish the members within a given category. For example, the members of the category *pets* include cats, dogs, hamsters, and guinea pigs. Each of these animals is distinguished as belonging to this particular category or class because of certain abstract properties. Thus generalization within an appropriate class has occurred. *Discrimination* occurs when the child can distinguish between the members of several classes. For example, a child can discriminate if he can identify cows as farm animals, dogs as pets, deer as forest animals, tigers as wild animals, and dinosaurs as prehistoric animals. This distinction between discrimination and generalization is illustrated in Figure 3–1. Discrimination and generalization are also characteristic of component memory, previously discussed.

Figure 3–1. Concept learning as discrimination and generalization.

Concepts can be of a higher order or a lower order. *Spot* may be the name of a particular dog. There are no other members of this class, except other dogs named Spot. But Spot belongs to a higher-order class, *dogs.* That is, many kinds of dogs belong to the category *dogs.* (Incidentally, the category *dog* is also made up of many other categories such as spaniels, terriers, poodles, and so on.) *Dogs* belongs to the higher-order category *pets. Pets* in turn belongs to the higher-order category *animals.* In most cases, prekindergarten children demonstrate concept learning with lower-order classes or categories, especially if the objects in these classes are concrete objects or if their representations are in pictures, films, or models.

Here are some examples of concept-learning behavioral objectives in the prekindergarten.

Each child will:
1. Correctly select from a group of pictures he has never seen before those three that show rainy weather.
2. Correctly point to three cooked foods in a group of six foods not previously seen in the lesson.
3. Correctly sort into sets from a pile of wooden shapes he has never seen before those that are triangles and those that are squares.
4. Correctly select the triangles from a group of nonpitched percussion instruments he has never seen before.

---

25. Write a *concept-learning* behavioral objective focusing on the subject *holidays:*

You could have written an objective similar to this:

Each child, when hearing a list of holiday activities not mentioned during instruction, will identify two that are appropriate for a Thanksgiving holiday.

26. Write a *concept-learning* behavioral objective focusing on the subject *pitch* (high, low):

You could have written an objective similar to this:

Each child will correctly put his hands above his head when the teacher sings high notes and put his hands near the floor when the teacher sings low notes in a song he has never heard before.

27. Write a *concept-learning* behavioral objective focusing on the subject *hearing* (tone quality):

You could have written an objective similar to this:

> While the teacher makes sounds behind a wooden screen using objects the children have not seen or heard before, each child will identify correctly whether each sound remains constant or changes tone.

When testing whether or not the child has learned a concept, be sure that you do not use an item you have already used during instruction. If you use previous instructional material, the child's response is memorized behavior, not a demonstration of concept learning.

Rule learning. Rule learning is the second division of complex-cognitive behavior. A rule is a relationship between two or more concepts. When a child has learned a rule, he has learned to respond to a particular class of stimulus situations with a specific class of behavior (Gagné, 1970). For example, the rule (class of stimulus situations) that "you turn the doorknob to open the door" can be responded to with a turning motion of the hand grasping the doorknob (a specific class of behavior) whenever a closed door blocks the entrance of a child into another room. The child may not say the rule to himself as he approaches and opens a door, but his behavior indicates he is functioning on the basis of the rule. If someone says to the child, "Show me the rule that you turn the doorknob to open the door," and he responds appropriately, the assumption is that the child understands the rule. In order for you to evaluate whether or not a child understands a rule, he must be able to demonstrate (apply) the rule in some way; being able to verbalize a rule is not sufficient to indicate the rule has been learned. If you say to a child, "What is the way to open a door?" and he replies, "Turn the doorknob," you have tested only the child's memory for stating a rule. Stating a rule is memory, but demonstrating the rule illustrates rule learning.

Technically, any statement is a rule in that several concepts are necessary to make a statement. These individual concepts are related to one another in some way, depending on the nature of the sentence. For example, the statement, "Babies cry when they are hungry," is a statement of a relationship between a baby's crying and hunger. Rules are also known as ideas (Gagné, 1970) or principles (Merrill, 1971a).

Much of our behavior is a demonstration of one kind of rule or another. For instance, you know that when you turn on the light switch, the light will turn on. You know that if you put your pencil on the edge of the table, it will roll off. You know that when you rub soap on your hands with water, a lather will form. You know that if you walk a certain direction down the sidewalk, you will come to a friend's house. You know that plants will grow if you give them water. You know that round objects roll on an inclined plane, that it snows only when there are clouds, that ice will melt when heated, that some animals live in the forest and others live on the farm, that your car needs gas in order to take you places. You function by rules even though you don't always verbalize each rule.

A few examples of rules you might use for lessons in the prekindergarten include:

1. Paper tears (graphic arts)
2. Scissors cut (graphic arts)
3. Paste makes things stick to paper (graphic arts)
4. Pull the brush down the hair to comb it (health and safety)
5. Wipe up spilled liquid (health and safety)
6. Use a knife or other sharp object only when a parent or teacher can watch you (health and safety)
7. When you dress, begin with the underclothes first (health and safety)
8. Use your voice instead of your hands when you are angry with someone (living in a world of people)
9. Telling a child you like him can make him feel good (living in a world of people)
10. We pay money for things we need or want in a store (living in a world of people)
11. We buy medicine at the drugstore (living in a world of people)
12. We put as many on one side of the equal sign as we have on the other (mathematics)
13. Songs can be sung with a soft voice or a loud voice (music)

14. Sometimes a melody goes up, sometimes it goes down, sometimes it stays the same (music)
15. Songs can be very slow and they can be very fast (music)
16. Wool comes from sheep (our world)
17. Birds fly (our world)
18. Plants grow from seeds and bulbs (our world)
19. We wear coats outdoors when it is cold (our world)
20. Cows live in barns (our world)
21. A magnifying glass makes things look bigger than they really are (our world)
22. Wheels roll (our world)
23. Air cannot be seen (our world)

Some concepts are so abstract that they can be learned only by definition. Such concept learning is really rule learning. The concept *uncle* is an idea or definition stated as "an uncle is the brother of a parent." In such a case, the child would need to demonstrate his understanding of such concepts as brother, parent, husband, and sister before he could use them in the appropriate relationship. Thus the child would be demonstrating a concept by definition or, in other words, a rule (Gagné, 1970).

If you are planning a behavioral objective related to rule learning, you need to determine a statement of the rule before you plan the objective. Most topics used for lesson focus can be subdivided into one or more rules. For example, rules related to the topic *how plants are used* might include:

A. Some plants give us food.
  1. Carrots, potatoes, beans, lettuce are some plants that give us food.
B. Some plants are used for clothing.
  1. The cotton plant gives us cotton for many things we wear.
C. We use some plants for decoration.
  1. Flowers are used for decoration at home, in church, at school and many other places.

2. Weeds are plants that sometimes can be used for decoration.
    (a) Thistle and cattails are weed plants that can be used for decoration.

Each of these rules probably can be further subdivided if desired. It becomes apparent as you read such rules that the child can understand them only if he first can demonstrate an understanding of the concepts that comprise the rules. In the preceding example the child would demonstrate understanding of such concepts as plant, food, clothing, decoration, and weed before learning the rules or ideas that tie these concepts together.

A further example of a lesson topic divided into rules would be *hospital.*

A. A hospital is a place where sick and injured people go to get well (concept by definition).
    1. Doctors and nurses work in a hospital to help sick and injured people get well.
    2. Hospitals are also places where mothers go to have babies.
    3. A hospital has many kinds of rooms.
        (a) A hospital room is where a sick person can have his own bed.
        (b) A waiting room is where people wait before going to a hospital room.
        (c) A delivery room is where babies are born.
        (d) The operating room is where doctors operate on people who need surgery.
        (e) The dispensary room is where nurses and doctors go to get the medicine to help make people well.

Again, these ideas can be further subdivided as desired or additional rules (ideas) can be added. You can subdivide any topic in the curriculum into desired rules or ideas.

Once you have determined the rule you wish to teach, you can determine the behavioral objective or objectives related to that rule. Remember that a child demonstrates his understanding of a rule by applying the rule, not by restating it.

Some examples of rule-learning behavioral objectives that might be useful in the prekindergarten follow.

Each child will:
1. Demonstrate the rule "scissors cut" when given a piece of paper and a pair of blunt scissors, by cutting a strip at least 2 inches long.
2. Demonstrate the rule "wipe up spilled liquid" when the teacher pours a small amount of water on the table tops and hands the child a sponge. All water will be absorbed by the sponge and the water squeezed from the sponge into a bowl.
3. Demonstrate the rule "when you dress begin with the underclothes first" by putting real clothes on a large doll, underclothes first, so that the clothes are put on and buttoned or zippered or pulled on correctly.
4. Demonstrate the rule "wool comes from sheep" by looking at a piece of wool fleece and selecting from a group of objects (e.g., animals, buildings, fruits, vegetables) the appropriate object that expresses the rule.
5. Demonstrate the rule "we put as many on one side of the equal sign as we have on the other" by correctly completing various equations on the chalkboard with the appropriate number of marks on the right side of the equal sign.

---

28. Write a *rule-learning* behavioral objective for the rule "songs can be very slow and they can be very fast".

You could have written an objective similar to this:

> While singing a song of his choice, each child will be able to
> sing it slow and fast when the teacher gives him each signal.

---

29. Write a *rule-learning* behavioral objective for the rule "most
    animals walk on four legs"

You could have written an objective similar to this:

> Each child will select correctly from each group of four
> pictures the picture that shows the animal on one or two feet
> only or standing on his head when asked the question, "Is
> there a picture here that has something wrong with it?" As the
> child selects the "wrong" picture he will tell why it has
> something wrong with it by restating the rule.

---

30. Write a *rule-learning* behavioral objective for the rule "wheels
    roll".

You could have written an objective similar to this:

> Given a board placed on an inclined plane and several objects of different shapes, including three toy wheels, he will correctly select the wheels and roll them down the plane when the teacher says, "Show me wheels roll."

As in the teaching of concept behavior, if you select an example used during instruction to test the child's rule learning you are testing memory, not rule learning. Your examples used for testing the rule-learning behavior must be those the child has not been exposed to during instruction.

Problem solving. Problem solving is the most complex level of cognitive behavior. Problem-solving behavior is demonstrated when the child puts two or more previously learned rules together in an appropriate sequence to solve a previously unencountered problem situation.

Two types of behavioral objectives related to problem solving have been described by Boutwell and Tennyson (1971). One is the *terminal problem-solving* objective where the teacher knows the solution and encourages the child to reach that known solution. Some examples follow:

1. When given an illustrated conflict situation where one child has verbally threatened or physically attacked another child or taken away his property, each child will role play a solution that includes verbal identification of feelings and a verbal resolution of the conflict rather than a physical confrontation.
2. When shown a plant that is wilted and droopy, each child will tell why he thinks the plant is wilted (rule: plants need water to grow), what he can do about it (rule: a sprinkling can filled with water can be used to water a plant), and apply the solution.

Such terminal problem-solving behavioral objectives should be based on firsthand experiences rather than on rules that involve verbal, abstract reasoning alone. Compared with adults, young children are hampered in the process of solving problems because they have had relatively fewer firsthand experiences, are less skilled in remembering more than two or three rules at one time, and have less skill in the use of language. Effective problem solving, especially the terminal type, requires that the child hold two or three rules in his mind at the same time and juggle these rules into an appropriate sequence. Terminal problem-solving behavioral objectives probably should be used in instructional design but not nearly as often as other less complex types of behavioral objectives.

The second type of problem-solving behavioral objective is the *expressive objective*. This type of objective is related to the concepts of creativity and divergent thinking in that the solution is not known and the child reaches his own interpretation of a solution. Such objectives are common in the graphic arts, dance, music, and drama curricula. This type of objective is always open-ended. Eisner (1971) describes his concept of the expressive objective:

> An expressive objective does not specify the behavior the student is to acquire after having engaged in one or more learning activities. An expressive objective describes an educational encounter: It identifies a situation in which children are to work, a problem with which they are to cope, a task in which they are to engage; but it does not specify what from that encounter, situation, problem, or task they are to learn. ... An expressive objective is evocative rather than prescriptive ... [p. 99].

An expressive behavioral objective is thus related to discovery learning. However, regardless of whether the problem-solving behavioral objective is terminal (solution known) or expressive (solution unknown), the solution still depends on previous learning of rules.

Samples of expressive problem-solving behavioral objectives are:

1. Each child will create an original easel painting about things he likes to do with other children using easel paper, paints in each of the primary colors, and a brush ¾" wide.
2. Each child will create an original melody encompassing tones that go down, and tones that stay in the same place using five melody bells and a wooden mallet.

It is important to note that each expressive objective should include the conditions under which the behavior will take place (for example, "using five melody bells and a wooden mallet") particularly because of the appropriateness or inappropriateness of some "creative" acts. For example, poking holes in the screen or painting the piano with shoe polish may be creative but the conditions for the behavior are inappropriate.

---

31. Write a *problem-solving* behavioral objective (terminal) related to the subject "getting a new pet":

You could have written an objective similar to this:

Each child will be able to state at least one procedure not mentioned by someone else that is necessary before a pet can be obtained for the prekindergarten. He will then role play each of the steps involved in obtaining the pet (that is, determine what pet to buy, determine where the pet will live, determine what food the pet will need, decide where to get the pet, determine how much money, if any, is needed to buy the pet, determine what care the pet will need, determine who will take care of the pet).

32. Write a *problem-solving* behavioral objective (expressive) focusing on the topic *singing:*

You could have written an objective similar to this:

Each child will make up the words and melody of a two-line song about something he likes to do in prekindergarten.

The problem-solving behavioral objective is always demonstrated with a novel problem situation. If the child has previously solved the problem, his subsequent problem-solving behavior is merely a matter of memory. That is, he is putting rules together in a sequence he has demonstrated in a previous occasion.

Complex-cognitive behavior often requires some period of time before the child responds to a stimulus situation. This is in contrast to memorized behavior, which is characterized by rapid response after presentation of the stimulus.

Training for transfer is one of the prime purposes of instruction. That is, it is impossible to teach the child every specific behavior he will need to learn in order to live in this complex world. Therefore, training in the higher cognitive processes is essential in every instructional program. This is because the very nature of complex-cognitive behavior (concept learning, rule learning, problem solving) is a form of transfer. Merrill (1971b) explains that "in a transfer situation rather than a one-to-one correspondence between stimulus and response, as is the case in psychomotor and [memorized] behavior, there is a many-to-one relationship. That is, the response is made to one of a large set of possible stimulus situations [p. 179]." Thus a child is responding to a class of single objects or events in concept learning, to a class of relationships between or among concepts in rule learning, and to a class of novel problems in problem solving, all involving a many-to-one relationship. That is, if a child has learned to identify two or three randomly selected but previously unencountered objects as belonging to a particular category or concept, we assume that he will be able to do the same when he encounters other objects belonging to the same class. This principle is the same for rule learning and problem solving.

Affective Behavior

The term *affective* refers to the emotions, interests, motivations, attitudes, and values of an individual. When a person talks about what he likes and what he doesn't like he is really talking about the affective side of his life. We can also infer from a person's actions whether he likes or dislikes something. For example, if a child spends his free-choice time listening to records, we assume he "likes" to listen to records. If he leaves his blocks in a pile on the floor instead of in the proper place on the shelf, we assume he "dislikes" putting blocks away or "likes" to leave his blocks in piles. If he spends a great deal of time near his teacher, touching his teacher, or talking to his teacher, we assume he "likes" his teacher. If he pushes away the bowl of peas at the lunch table, we assume he "dislikes" peas. That is, we infer his emotions, interests, motivations, attitudes, and values from his observable behavior.

Affective behavior can be observed only in a free-choice situation. In a free-choice situation each person, whether child or adult, tends to do that which he "likes" best out of all the possible choices. Such free-choice behavior is largely involuntary. That is, the child automatically tends to do whatever he wishes. In a sense a habit has been formed that is no longer under conscious control.

It should be noted at this point that we, as adults, learn to act despite our feelings. This does not mean necessarily that we deny our feelings. It simply means that we are not governed by them. Thus we are brave despite fear, industrious despite fatigue or boredom, and polite or civilized despite anger. More about this idea in Chapter 6.

If you want to change a child's preference for some type of free-choice

activity such as blocks and trucks, music, domestic play, or books, you first
need to find out what the child's preferences are in a free-choice situation. Then
you can determine whether or not you need to plan an instructional objective to
change the child's preference during free-choice time.

When you plan behavioral objectives in the affective behavior class
you are really asking yourself, "What do I want each child to learn to like?"
Some examples of desired affective behavior in the prekindergarten follow.

Each child will:
1. Voluntarily wash his hands and dry them before snack or lunch
    without being reminded by the teacher or some other child.
2. Engage in a variety of activities over a given period of time rather
    than just one activity during free-choice time.
3. Voluntarily assist another child who is frustrated or angry or upset
    because he is having trouble solving a problem.
4. Voluntarily hang up his coat and put away his boots when he
    comes in from outdoors.
5. Put away learning materials he has been using when finished
    without being reminded by the teacher.
6. Resolve conflict situations with other children verbally rather than
    physically and without the aid of an adult.
7. Voluntarily join his learning group and participate
    enthusiastically in the learning activities.

---

33. Write in the space below additional *affective* responses in
    children that you feel are desirable in the prekindergarten.

FREQUENTLY ASKED QUESTIONS ABOUT
BEHAVIORAL OBJECTIVES

How specific do behavioral objectives have to be? A behavioral objective should be specific enough to be observable. However, many teachers when first learning to write behavioral objectives tend to write objectives that are so precise they are restrictive. A behavioral objective can be quite broad in scope and yet observable and specific. Compare the following two objectives:

a.   Each child will help his mother tomorrow by hanging up his clothes and then tell his group about it the following day.
b.   Each child will name one thing he will do to help his mother tomorrow and report what he did and how he felt about it to his group the following day.

Objective a is restricting the child to only one way of helping his mother on a given day. He has no apparent choice in the matter. This objective may be appropriate in a given lesson. However, it is also possible to broaden the objective by giving each child the choice of several alternatives as in objective b. Both objectives include specific, observable behavior, but objective a is restrictive in scope whereas objective b is broad in scope. The decision whether to make an objective broad or restrictive depends on the type of behavior you are teaching.

Is an objective a good one when it is stated in terms of observable behavior? The term *good* is a value term. What is "good" to one person may be totally unacceptable or inappropriate to another. The types of behavior we teach children are usually those we consider important for them to learn. If the curriculum in the prekindergarten is planned to include each of the twelve types of behavior in each of the content areas and in a step-by-step fashion, it is easier to determine whether or not an objective is related to the appropriate sequence of learning. Some objectives can be very trite in a content area while others can provide greater opportunity for growth in learning. If you plan your lessons according to the six steps in the instructional design process, you will be able to decide whether an objective is a "good" one or not.

It is easy to write objectives that require only verbal responses from the children. Verbs such as *name, tell,* and *say* describe observable behavior. But prekindergarten children can do many other things, such as *pantomime, draw, paint, role-play, sing, select,* and so on. You can draw on a wide variety of child activities to plan your objectives rather than get caught in the trap of planning verbal objectives only. Prekindergarten children are relatively limited in their ability to use language to demonstrate what they are learning. Their body movement often tells you what they are learning better than their language.

Will behavioral objectives guarantee better, more effective teaching?   Effective teaching occurs when children actually engage in specific desired activities as a result of a planned learning environment. Behavioral objectives are only one part of this process of planning the learning environment. You also must plan how you will find out what the child already knows about a lesson objective (that is, you assess preinstructional behavior), and then plan appropriate learning activities related to each objective. If assessment of preinstructional behavior is inadequate or learning activities are poorly planned, behavioral objectives will not guarantee effective teaching. When objectives are written in terms of observable behavior, it is much easier to plan the learning activities that will lead to the achievement of those objectives.

How do you deal with "teachable moments" when you have already planned everything you expect a child to do in your behavioral objectives?   When you plan behavioral objectives (as well as the remainder of the lesson plan) you are actually in a better position to respond to "teachable moments" than if you waited until the moment arrived before attempting to "teach" the child. The term *teachable moments* usually refers to those unexpected, unplanned events that often occur and make it possible for special kinds of learning to take place. Such events can include the appearance of a rainbow after a rainstorm, a bug crawling across the floor, a dead fish or frog, the shock waves resulting from an airplane breaking the sound barrier, the sound of a siren, an injured child, a sudden change in the weather, a special event such as a birthday, or an unexpected visitor such as the plumber. When such events occur it would be wise for you to pause in the planned lesson presentation to make the unexpected event an effective learning experience for the children. You then can go back to wherever you left off in your planned lesson. Your experience in planning behavioral objectives and preparing learning activities to accomplish them will enable you to be a more effective teacher when those "teachable moments" occur.

SUMMARY

A behavioral objective describes desired, specific, observable behavior that the child will perform as the result of a learning experience. Three elements are necessary in a behavior objective: (1) the desired observable behavior; (2) the circumstances or conditions under which the behavior is expected to be performed; and (3) what constitutes successful performance of the objective. Behavioral objectives are of 12 types: single neuromuscular response, motor sequence, complex skill, naming, serial memory, component memory, concept learning, rule learning, problem solving, emotion, interest and motivation, attitude and value.

REFERENCES

Boutwell, R. C., & Tennyson, R. D. Instructional objectives—different by design. Working Paper No. 13, Instructional Research and Development, Division of Communication Services, Brigham Young University, 1971.

Eisner, E. W. Instructional and expressive educational objectives. In M. D. Merrill (Ed.), *Instructional design: Readings.* Englewood Cliffs, N. J.: Prentice-Hall, 1971.

Gagné, R. M. *The conditions of learning.* (2nd ed.) New York: Holt, Rinehart and Winston, 1970.

Gagné, R. M. The learning of principles. In M. D. Merrill (Ed.),
    Instructional design: Readings. Englewood Cliffs, N. J.: Prentice-
    Hall, 1971.
Mager, R. F. *Preparing instructional objectives.* Palo Alto, Calif.:
    Fearon Publishers, 1962.
Merrill, M. D. (Ed.) *Instructional design: Readings.* Englewood Cliffs,
    N. J.: Prentice-Hall, 1971a.
Merrill, M. D. Necessary psychological conditions for defining
    instructional outcomes. In M. D. Merrill (Ed.), *Instructional design:
    Readings.* Englewood Cliffs, N. J.: Prentice-Hall, 1971b.

Chapter 4

Assessing Preinstructional Behavior

A teacher in a prekindergarten was presenting a lesson to 4-year-olds about the idea "food is something we eat." She started the lesson by showing pictures of various foods, asking the children to name each food as she propped each picture in the groove board. After she had shown several food pictures, she asked the children what all of them together were called. The children replied in unison, "They're called food," almost as though they had rehearsed it. The teacher replied, "Yes, food is something we eat. What do we call something we eat?" The children again replied, "Food." The teacher continued by showing more food pictures and asking the same questions as before. The children lost interest in the "game." They already had learned well what the teacher was trying to teach.

The teacher had planned carefully the focus of her lesson, the desired objectives, and the learning activities related to the objectives. However, she had failed to assess the preinstructional behavior of the children in the group before planning the learning activities. As a result, her lesson was boring for the children instead of being a pleasant new learning experience.

Assessment of the child's preinstructional behavior is a part of *each* step in the instructional-design process. It is an evaluation of the child's behavior—a specifically desired behavior related to a given lesson. For any given lesson and any given stage of instructional design, you must ask yourself "*what* can the child do and *how well* can he do it?" You need to determine (1) whether or not each child can already perform each objective, and (2) the most effective kinds of learning activities related to the objectives for children in your group according to their typical behavior patterns.

CAN THE CHILD ALREADY PERFORM THE OBJECTIVE?

In the prekindergarten it's a good idea to reserve a few minutes at the beginning of each lesson to assess what was learned from the preceding lesson in the same content area of the curriculum and whether or not the children can perform the desired objectives in the present lesson. Lesson objectives should be developed in a sequence, with one objective acting as a foundation for another objective. For example, in mathematics it is important that children be able to perform certain counting operations before they perform operations related to rules of equation. In music, some singing and movement skills are important before children can demonstrate such elements of music as high and low (pitch) or fast and slow (tempo). Therefore, a review of objectives from a preceding lesson could lead directly into a new and related objective. But it is also important to find out if the children already can perform the *new* objective. There is no point teaching children to do something they already can perform.

Often children can demonstrate an objective immediately following the related learning activities but have difficulty demonstrating the same objective later in the day or week. This often means that experiences during that time lapse have interfered, causing the child to "forget" something he once could perform. Remember that learning does not occur unless the new behavior is relatively permanent—if a child has performed well immediately after training but does not perform well at a later time, it is possible he has not "learned" the desired behavior. A review period at the beginning of a later lesson provides the opportunity for needed practice.

Mager and Pipe (1970) suggest two possible reasons for inadequacy of performance. One possibility is that the child simply does not know how to perform that which is desired. In other words, he has not "learned" the desired performance. You ask yourself the question, "Could he do it if his life depended on it?" If the answer is no, the inadequacy of performance can be overcome by appropriate instruction. However, the other possibility is that the child can perform as desired but does not *want* to perform. The performance may be punishing to the child or at least may not be followed consistently by pleasant consequences. In this case, the inadequacy of performance can be overcome by providing pleasant consequences following the desired behavior, thereby making the performance matter. You "water the performance you want to grow" (Mager and Pipe, 1970). Chapter 6 is a detailed discussion of ways to motivate children to want to perform desired behavior.

The review period at the beginning of each lesson is a good time to assess the child's preinstructional behavior. If the child has not learned the desired behavior, teach him to do it. If he can do it but does not want to do it, you can provide experiences that will make the desired performance important to the child.

WHAT ARE THE TYPICAL BEHAVIOR PATTERNS OF THE CHILDREN?

If you adequately assess preinstructional behavior, you will avoid the possibility of teaching behavior the child already can perform well. Similarly, when you determine the typical behavior patterns of the individual children in your group, you are in a better position to plan effective learning activities related to the desired objectives.

It is important that you study basic principles of child development in order to recognize behavior that is typical of the prekindergarten child—that is, the child of age 3 or 4. (Some of these typical behavior patterns are described in Chapter 1.) In addition, you need to study the behavior of the individual children in your group. If you can recognize typical behavior patterns of 3- and 4-year-olds and can relate these to the typical behavior patterns of the individual children in your group, you can plan more effective learning activities, capitalizing on each child's unique characteristics and past experiences. For example, an event in the life of one of the children in the class can be used as an example of a selected idea in the lesson. When an actual experience of a child is known and used in the form of a story, dramatization, or some other learning experience, it will be more effective in the learning process than an experience that is taken from the life of someone else.

There are several ways you can learn to recognize typical behavior patterns of the children you teach. Here are a few suggestions:

1. Observation
2. Conversation with an individual child or with a group of children
3. Talking to others who know the child
   (a) Parents
   (b) Siblings
   (c) Friends

Observation

Perhaps the most effective means of getting to know a child is to observe his behavior in a variety of situations. In other words, you become a "watcher" of individual children. Here are some questions you might be able to answer from your observations about each child:

Does he spend more time doing certain activities than others?
Does he have a favorite toy? If so, what does he usually do with it?
When he is with other children in a free-play situation, does he play the role of leader or follower?
What does he usually do when he wants something someone else has?
How does he respond in a new and strange situation?
What does he do when he bumps into a problem he can't solve by himself?
How does he usually respond when someone asks him to do something?
How does he respond in the presence of his parents?

Does he have any brothers and sisters? How does he usually respond in the presence of each one?

What are his typical eating habits?

Does he express his feelings verbally or physically or both?

How well does he verbally label his own feelings?

What situations, objects, or people seem to make him happy? Unhappy?

Children can be observed in the neighborhood, on the school ground, in the grocery store, at home, at church, and many other places. Opportunities for observation are limitless. As we observe children in a variety of situations over a period of time, we can make more accurate inferences about how they might respond in a given situation and what learning activities would be most effective.

Conversation with an Individual Child or with a Group of Children

Do things with the children you teach on an informal basis. This leads to casual conversation. Conversation should be an important part of the learning experience in any given lesson. It should also be a natural part of your behavior toward children whether you are in the classroom or not. Children enjoy talking about what they are doing as well as about their feelings and ideas. The questions you ask and your responses to the comments of the children can help them to increase their conversation ability. The mental notes you accumulate during these conversations can aid you in planning your instructional approach to a lesson.

Talking to Others Who Know the Child

Frequent opportunities generally are available to teachers in prekindergartens to talk with parents of the children in the group. Parents see their own children in a greater variety of situations than anyone else. A parent often shares with his child's teacher important events that have occurred and are occurring in the child's life. A parent may reveal special events the child has experienced, events that might influence his behavior at a particular moment or during a particular day or over a long period of time (for example, lack of sleep, no breakfast that morning, a nightmare the night before, a new baby in the family, a parent or sibling going to the hospital, a death in the family, a birthday, a vacation trip with the family, a severe wound). Seemingly unimportant events, such as a quarrel with another sibling or a child's response to a television program, may give you a clue when planning a particular learning activity related to a specific objective.

Spontaneous and informal chats with a child's brothers, sisters, and friends can help you know more about how a child may respond in given situations. Knowledge of a child's behavior, reflected in verbal descriptions and feelings of others, can aid you in planning learning experiences.

---

1. Assessing preinstructional behavior means:

- -

You were correct if you wrote something like this:

Evaluation of the child's behavior—that is, evaluation of how well he can perform desired behavior.

---

2. An appropriate place to assess whether or not a child can perform a desired behavior is at the _____ of a lesson.

- -

beginning

3. If a child demonstrates a desired behavior immediately following a lesson but not during a later review period, it is likely the child has not _____ the desired behavior.

---

learned

---

4. Write the two possible reasons for inadequacy of performance as suggested by Mager and Pipe (1970):

(a) _____

(b) _____

(a) the child does not know how to perform

(b) the child knows how but does not want to perform

---

5. If the child can perform as desired but does not *want* to perform, the performance:

(a) may be punishing to the child

(b) may not be followed consistently by pleasant consequences

(c) has not been learned

(d) either (a) or (b)

(d) is correct

---

6. If the child has not learned the desired behavior (i.e., he does not know how to do it) you can:

_____

---

teach him to do it
_____

---

7. When you determine the typical behavior patterns of the individual children in your group, you are in a better position to plan effective _____ _____ related to the desired objectives.
----

    learning activities
    _____

---

8. Name three ways a prekindergarten teacher can learn to recognize typical behavior patterns in the individual children he teaches:

    (a) _____

    (b) _____

    (c) _____

    (a) observation
    (b) conversation with an individual child or with a group of children
    (c) talking to others who know the child
    _____

---

9. Generally speaking, who can give you more information about an individual child's typical behavior patterns than anyone else?
----

    his parents
    _____

SUMMARY

Assessing preinstructional behavior is a continuing process throughout all stages of instructional design in the prekindergarten. However, it is especially important to evaluate what a child can do and how well he can perform after you have planned the instructional objectives of a given lesson. You thus can avoid the possibility of teaching the child something he already can do. You also can plan more effective learning activities, the subject of the next chapter.

REFERENCE

Mager, R. F., & Pipe, P. *Analyzing performance problems*. Belmont, Calif.: Fearon, 1970.

Chapter 5

Learning Activities

After you have planned the behavioral objectives for a lesson and have assessed preinstructional behavior in the children, you are ready to plan the learning activities. The purpose of learning activities is to help the individual child accomplish the desired behavior—that is, the behavioral objective. Learning activities should be planned with the goal of involving the child in as many *doing* and *saying* activities as possible. Regardless of whether the lesson is to be taught in a group situation or in a one-to-one situation between teacher and child, the emphasis always should be on doing and saying activities for *each* individual child.

You should keep in mind the way a child learns when you plan learning activities. The child first perceives, or has a sensory experience with objects, people, places, or events. Using what he has perceived, the child then forms some sort of mental picture of his sensory experience. This means he relates past experience to present experience or perception. This mental picture largely determines how a child will act in a given situation. What happens after the child acts will determine his attitudes and feelings about the act. These four stages of learning—*perceive, think, do, feel*—were discussed in Chapter 1; the learning activities related to these four stages of learning are *show,*

discuss, apply (Woodruff, 1961), and *reinforce.* The relationship
between learning and teaching is illustrated in Figure 5–1.

Figure 5–1. Relationship between learning and teaching.

	Perceive	Think	Do	Feel
Child Activities	See Hear Touch Taste Smell	Recall (memory) Imagination Concept formation Reasoning	Do the desired behavior	Feelings, attitudes, interests, values resulting from behavior Desire or lack of desire to *do* again
	Show*	Discuss*	Apply*	Reinforce
Teacher Activities	Show children what you want them to learn through: Firsthand experiences Vicarious sensory experiences	Ask questions Pose problems Consider each child's idea Ask for interpre- tations & feelings Allow practice of desired behavior (verbal and motor)	Plan activities that allow children to exhibit desired behavior objectives Make assignments Allow reports of related out-of-class behavior	Provide pleasant consequences for desirable behavior

Adapted from *Teacher Development Program: Basic Course.* Salt Lake City, Utah:
Corporation of the President of The Church of Jesus Christ of Latter-day Saints, 1971, 63.
*These terms adopted from Woodruff, A. D. *Basic concepts of teaching.* San Francisco:
Chandler Publishing Co., 1961.

It cannot be emphasized too strongly that assessment of
preinstructional behavior is important during the entire lesson-planning
process. Although assessment of preinstructional behavior was
necessary after planning the behavioral objectives, it continues to be
important as you plan learning activities. Your assessment will help you
determine which learning activities are most appropriate to the age and
behavior level of those being taught. For example, a panel discussion

would be appropriate for a group of adolescents or adults but would be inappropriate for children under 5. These young children have not developed the verbal skills and thinking and reasoning abilities to successfully participate in a panel discussion. On the other hand, if you asked a group of 4-year-olds to draw something related to a lesson idea with crayons, the activity would be appropriate and pleasurable for the children, whereas adolescents may find other activities more challenging.

SHOWING IS MORE THAN TELLING

Learning begins with perception, a sensory experience. This step, when you plan learning activities, is called the *show* step. In other words, you plan a sensory experience for the young child related to the objective being taught. *Show* means any kind of sensory experience or combination of sensory experiences related to the lesson objective. It does not necessarily refer to vision alone, although visual experiences are important show steps.

It is impossible to communicate some experiences or events in words alone. For example, try describing to someone a new taste experience you have had. That person will understand what you're saying only if he can have or has had that same taste experience. After a trip to the Far East and the Orient I found it impossible to describe to friends who had never traveled to these faraway lands my various experiences with pleasantly exotic and not-so-pleasant odors while on the trip. My friends would have had to experience the same odors I had experienced to understand what I was talking about.

The most effective type of show step with young children is a *firsthand experience.* In other words, children can have direct contact with actual objects, people, places, or events. Any object, person, place, or event on which the child's attention is to be focused is called a *referent.* Firsthand experiences are of prime importance at any age but particularly in the years before age 5. You should "show" the referent through one or more of the child's senses, not sight alone. The child's concepts can then be built on reality, not error. A 3-year-old boy visiting the zoo was heard to exclaim as he stared at the caged tiger in wide-eyed wonder, "He's so big! The cat and tiger in my picture book are big as each other!" The child who has never seen a real cat and a real tiger may never know the two animals differ a great deal in size.

Teachers often take young children on field trips or excursions because of the direct contact with objects, people, places, or events that such experiences provide. A story about a bus or a train has far more meaning to a child if he has had the opportunity to ride in a real one. Similarly, a story about the sea and the seashore is more effective if a child has actually taken a trip to the beach. A child will have a more realistic concept of the relationship between cows and milk if he has visited a dairy farm, watched a cow being milked, and tasted the milk after it has been refrigerated. A pre-excursion discussion telling the child what to expect, what to look for, and what the rules are will prepare the child for the trip and help to make it an effective learning experience.

Because firsthand experiences are so important in all learning, try to provide *direct contact* with the real thing whenever possible. If you are teaching color, be sure you have different items of the same color for children to see and manipulate. When you are teaching counting, give children real objects to count. When you are teaching spatial relationships (over, under, around, through, and so on), let children manipulate real objects in a variety of spatial relationships. When you are teaching about a musical instrument, let the children see, hear, and if at all possible play the real instrument. *It takes extra effort to plan and provide firsthand experiences for young children.* It is easier to plan *show* steps involving secondary or "secondhand" experiences, such as pictures, drawings, books, tape recordings, and records. But if secondary experiences are to be used for show steps, they should *follow* firsthand experiences, not precede them. Unless you provide firsthand experiences, children may not "see" in spite of your efforts to "show."

Sometimes it isn't possible to provide a firsthand experience as a show step. Perhaps the event has already occurred or has not yet occurred. Perhaps the object is not available and the person or place is too far away. If you cannot provide a firsthand experience, try a *simulated* or *vicarious* experience—come as close as possible to recreating the real experience. Models are good vicarious experiences. For instance, if the children don't live by the seashore, you can teach an objective about the seashore with a model made of sand and water and sea shells and perhaps even a fan to stir up "waves" in the "ocean." If it is not possible to visit a real dairy farm, create one of your own with toy animals and farm buildings, some hay, sod, branches from trees, and so forth. If a mother and her baby are unable to come to class, present your lesson about babies using a doll, doll clothes, a baby bottle, and other items related to care of a baby. If you wish to help children find better ways to solve problems between one another, have them role play appropriate ways of solving a particular problem.

The following list indicates show steps in descending order of their probable effectiveness. In other words, the first item on the list should be the most effective and the last item should be the least effective:

1. Firsthand experience (such as visiting a real dairy farm)
2. Simulated or vicarious experience (such as a model of a dairy farm)
3. Audio-visual representation, sight plus sound (such as a movie about a dairy farm)
4. Representation, sight only (such as a filmstrip or slides of a dairy farm, or pictures of a dairy farm)
5. Representation, sound only (such as a tape recording of someone telling about a tour through a dairy farm including sounds of cows mooing and eating and the milking machines in operation)
6. Words, hearing only (such as the teacher telling about his trip to a dairy farm, no pictures or other illustration)

As many of the five senses as possible should be involved in each show step. An experience involving one sense alone is usually less effective than one involving a combination of senses. One reason firsthand experiences and vicarious experiences are more effective than secondary experiences is because they usually involve more than one sensory experience and because they are more likely to lead to the correct mental picture of something. For example, when a real doctor visits the classroom, the children have a sensory experience of sight as well as sound and touch. A picture of a doctor would offer a sight experience, but the sight experience of a picture is limited because it is two-dimensional and usually does not represent the actual size or scope of the object or person or event. The information fed through the senses when a real doctor is present is more accurate than when only a picture of a doctor is available.

---

1. Define the meaning of *show* in the design of lesson plans.

- -

You were correct if you had something similar to the following:

Show means any kind of sensory experience or combination of sensory experiences related to the lesson objective.

---

2. The *show* step in planning learning activities corresponds to which one of the following stages of learning?

____(a) perceive   ____(c) do
____(b) think   ____(d) feel

- -

You were correct if you checked (a).

---

3. A *show* step should consist of:

_____(a) a visual sensory experience only
_____(b) sensory experiences that include two or more senses
            at one time

- -

You were correct if you checked (b).

4. A child who visits a piano factory to see how pianos are made is having a:

   (a) firsthand experience
   (b) vicarious experience

   If you checked (a) you were correct because the child is having direct contact with the real object.

5. Models are good (firsthand/vicarious) experiences.

   You were correct if you selected "vicarious."

6. Which one of the following probably would be the most effective *show* step for prekindergarten children?

   _____(a) showing the children a film of a fireman at work
   _____(b) showing the children a picture of a fireman at work
   _____(c) having a real fireman visit the class to describe his work
   _____(d) telling the children about the work of a fireman

   You were correct if you marked (c) because it is a firsthand experience. The other *show* steps are secondary experiences.

DISCUSSION IS MORE THAN TALKING

The show step is a sensory experience. However, sensory experience with the referent (object, person, place, or event) is not enough. Clarification is usually necessary and is aided by some form of discussion, either on a one-to-one basis between you and the child, or in a group discussion. You do not know what the child has perceived until the child responds in verbal or motor fashion to whatever is "shown." For example, assume a mother colors a few random strokes with a crayon on a piece of paper on the floor (show step) and then hands the crayon to her infant son. The child grasps the crayon, changes it from one hand to the other, then puts it in his mouth and chews on it. It is clear to the mother that her infant son has perceived the crayon as "something to chew on" rather than "something to draw with." Verbal discussion is impossible at such a young age. This same mother models the same behavior for her 3-year-old girl. She then hands the crayon to the child and asks, "What is this?" The child replies, "It's a crayon." Mother asks, "What do you do with a crayon?" The child says, "I can draw with it." If the mother hands the crayon to the child, who, in turn, draws with it on a piece of paper, the mother has clear evidence that the child knows not only the correct label for the referent but also its use. The child's knowledge is evident through her verbal and motor behavior. On the other hand, if the child had given an incorrect label and use for the crayon, the mother could have provided the appropriate label and stated its use. The child could then have been asked the same questions again. If the answers were correct this second time around, the child's verbal behavior would indicate appropriate thinking.

Clarification is just one function of discussion. Through discussion the child can relate everything he knows about the referent. For example, the 3-year-old in the previous illustration might state that the crayon is round and red and soft (not like chalk). She might even tell of an important past experience she had with a crayon. She could express whether or not she likes to use a crayon and what she feels when she is drawing with a crayon. The child thus can have the opportunity to express not only the factual information she knows but also her values and feelings about a referent. The mother (teacher) can lead the child into new realms of information and feeling and skill through carefully selected questions and statements. When a teacher merely "shows and tells," learning in the child is likely to take a detour toward something other than that of the desired behavior. The child's verbal and motor behavior indicates the level of his thinking.

Once the child perceives something, he begins to form a mental picture of what he perceives; he relates what he is perceiving to past experience. His mental picture may be realistic or unrealistic, depending a great deal on what happens while he is having a sensory experience. Consider the example of a person who picks up an item of fruit that looks like a peach in color and size and shape. However, the surface is not as fuzzy as other peaches he has seen and held before. He bites into the fruit and discovers that it tastes very much like a peach. It even has a pit the same as a peach. So he labels the fruit a "peach." In other words, this combination of sensory experiences gets related to past experiences and the person conceptualizes this new experience as "peach." Later this same individual is munching on a similar "peach" when a friend notices him and asks, "Could I have a nectarine, too?" The friends then discuss the differences between peaches and nectarines, and our friend with the "peach" leaves that conversation with a different label for the fruit he was eating. The "peach" isn't a peach at all—it's a nectarine. His conceptualization (or mental picture) of the fruit probably changes because a new label has been attached to it and he has had the opportunity to discuss the differences in his sensory experiences with peaches and with nectarines—that is, peaches have fuzz and nectarines have smooth skin.

A major purpose of the *discussion* step is to help children build an appropriate or correct mental picture of a sensory experience. Probably the most common and effective means to do this is by asking questions related to the show experience.

There are many kinds of questions a teacher or parent can ask a child that will enhance the process of conceptualization. Each of the following four kinds of questions requires a different kind of mental process to be appropriately answered:

1. Questions that require *remembering* (similar to memorized behavior, discussed in Chapter 3): such questions are used most frequently by teachers and parents. They require very little from

the child other than simple recall of information. They are necessary but in no way sufficient to discover what the child understands about an idea or concept.

Examples:
(a)   How many children are in our class?
(b)   What made David feel so sick? (After reading a story about David to the children.)
(c)   What did you eat for breakfast this morning?
(d)   Where did we go yesterday?

2.   Questions that require *reasoning* (similar to rule learning, discussed in Chapter 3): children need the opportunity to think about and discuss reasons for things and to relate something they are experiencing now to other settings.

Examples:
(a)   Why do you wear a coat and boots in the snow?
(b)   Why is it better to eat fruits and vegetables than candy?
(c)   How do you help Mommy and Daddy at home?
(d)   Tell me about your favorite television program. (This is a statement that requires a recall as well as a reasoning response from the child.)

3.   Questions that require *judgment* or known *solutions to problems* (similar to terminal problem solving, discussed in Chapter 3): these kinds of questions help children weigh choices, make decisions, and find ways to get answers to problems.

Examples:
(a)   If you found a penny on the sidewalk, what would you do? Why?
(b)   If someone else were riding a tricycle you wanted to ride, what would you do? Why?

(c) When you don't know which glass has hot water and which has cold water, how can you find out?

4. Questions that require *imagination* (similar to expressive problem solving, discussed in Chapter 3): this kind of question helps children come up with new ideas, create new solutions to problems, invent new ways of doing things. Often such questions do not have a "correct" answer.

Examples:
(a) What would you do if you were a bird?
(b) How would you feel if there were never any nighttime?
(c) How would you act if you walked on all four feet like an animal instead of on two feet?
(d) What would you do if you could do anything in the whole wide world?

You should use several different kinds of questions when you conduct a discussion with children. If you rely on questions that merely require rote memory or one-word replies, you fail to stimulate more complex thinking processes in the child. Note that questions requiring reasoning, choice, or imagination do not fit into hard and fast categories. There is a great deal of overlap among these categories.

A visitor to a prekindergarten, after observing the teachers and children for an hour or so, asked why the teachers didn't ask the children questions. Teachers often told the children what to do and what not to do, but seldom asked the children what they thought about anything. It is all too easy to "tell" children what to do. Perhaps we don't converse with children often enough because we haven't learned how to converse. By conversing with young children, we learn what they are thinking and why. We can share our thinking with them and provide a language model for conversation that they can practice with one another. We can get clues concerning misconceptions so we can clarify when necessary. If we adults ask questions of children, the children too will ask questions. We need to ask questions in order to learn. If the teacher does all the "telling," the child will do little thinking on his own.

After studying child-question teacher-response units in a nursery school, Haupt (1966) concluded:

> The tendency of the nursery school teachers ... to reinforce their position as the prime verbal source of information and their limited use of reciprocal questions of leading open-ended responses suggests that frequently their acts of teaching are not consciously designed to provoke thinking on the part of the children ... The teacher's behavior does not encourage an orderly sequence of questioning utilizing either the child's past experiences or the abilities of other children to have followed the thread of a story, for example ... If children are to learn how to learn to pose relevant questions, and gain skill in handling increasingly complex thought processes, these require teachers who ask thoughtful questions and stimulate reflection and thinking. They need teachers who are able to pace their teaching acts from simple descriptive, factual responses to responses which guide the child's search for understanding of processes, progression, causality, classification and so forth [pp. 288–289].*

Another purpose of the discuss step is to provide opportunities for each child to practice a specific desired behavior during a lesson presentation. This is particularly important to remember when you plan lessons for prekindergarten children because they are so limited in language and motor behavior, compared with adults. (However, the same principle applies to the teaching of adults.) These practice activities can be verbal or motor, depending on the nature of the lesson objective being taught. For example, a child practices singing the melody and words to a song until he is able to sing both words and melody without help and without hesitation. In other words, he cannot demonstrate a memorized behavioral objective related to singing until he has practiced the words and melody over a period of time. By the same token, a

*From D. Haupt, *Teacher-child interaction: A study of the relationships between child-initiated questions and nursery school teacher behaviors.* Unpublished doctoral dissertation, Wayne State University, 1966. Reprinted by permission.

child cannot demonstrate concept-learning behavioral objectives until he has practiced identifying the appropriate class for given objects, people, places, or events. Practice is an important part of the discuss step. Discussion involves more than the asking and answering of questions.

---

7. When you plan a lesson, the *discuss* step should (precede/ immediately follow or accompany) the *show* step.

You were correct if you selected "immediately follow or accompany."

---

8. The *discuss* step includes which of the following?

_____(a) asking and answering questions
_____(b) what one knows about the referent
_____(c) practicing the lesson objective

You were correct if you selected all of these items: (a), (b), and (c).

---

9. "Where did we go yesterday?" is an example of what kind of question?

_____(a) remembering
_____(b) reasoning
_____(c) judgment or known solutions to problems
_____(d) imagination

You were correct if you selected (a) because this question requires a memory or recall response only.

10. "How do you think you would act if you were a large fish in the ocean?" is an example of what kind of question?

_____(a) remembering
_____(b) reasoning
_____(c) judgment or known solutions to problems
_____(d) imagination

(d) is probably the best answer because the child can come up with a new idea or invent a new way of doing things.

11. Select where the *discuss* step begins in the following instructions to the teacher:

Place a notched rhythm stick in the center of the table (or on the rug if you and the children are seated on the floor) without the stick. Ask: "What do you think that is? What does it look like? What do you think you could do with it? What kind of a sound do you think it makes?"

You were correct if you selected "What do you think that is?" The instructions preceding this question involve a sensory experience only (*show* step).

12. Select where the *discuss* step begins in the following instructions to the teacher:

Select from a tray of various foods those that represent the category *meat, fish, and poultry.* Say: "These are foods we call *meat, fish, and poultry.* What are these called?" Let children respond.

The *discuss* step begins with the words, "What are these called?" The preceding instructions involve a *show* step or sensory experience only.

APPLYING IS MORE THAN BEHAVING

After the child has had a sensory experience with a referent, has talked about his interpretation and feelings about a referent, and has had the opportunity to practice a desired behavior (when practice is important), his ability to do the desired task can be evaluated. The child is ready for the *apply* step in learning activities.

A child came home from Bible School excited about a new song she had learned about dogs. Her mother, though familiar with most of the songs the children sang at the school, could not recall a song about dogs. She asked the child to sing the new song. The child immediately began to sing the words to "Up, Up in the Sky" as follows: "A pup in the sky, where the little birds fly. . . . " Such incidents are humorous to adults. But such an incident also indicates that the *apply* step occurred before appropriate *show* and *discuss* steps had taken place. The teacher in this case could have sung the song for the children while they listened (show step). She then could have asked the children what she was singing about (discuss step). As the children commented, she could have shown a picture representing each part of the song mentioned by the children (another show step). She could have sung the song again (a repeat of the first show step) and then asked the children in what order the pictures should be placed (another discuss step). She could have encouraged the children to sing the song with her (another discuss step), using the pictures in appropriate order as guides for singing. After the teacher and children had sung the song a few times, the pictures could have been removed and the children allowed to sing the song by memory (apply step). After such a learning experience, children are more likely to sing the song with understanding as well as from rote memory.

When you plan the apply step in the learning activities of a given lesson, you are providing a setting for the child to demonstrate whether or not he has learned the desired behavior. Therefore, the apply step is determined by the nature of the behavioral objective. For example, the behavioral objective "each child will correctly select from a group of textured objects those that are smooth and those that are rough" will provide you with a guideline for setting up an *apply* learning activity. This objective indicates you will need a group of textured objects, including some with smooth textures and some with rough textures. Inasmuch as this is a memorized behavioral objective (component memory) rather than a complex-cognitive behavioral objective, you can use the same objects in the apply step that you use during the show and discuss steps. In order to prevent the possibility that each of the children in the group will copy the responses of the first child during this learning activity, you probably need to provide a different set of rough and smooth objects for each child in the group while still using objects the children have seen and discussed before.

Use each behavioral objective as your guideline when planning not only the apply step, but also the show and discuss steps. There should be at least one show, one discuss, and one apply step related to each behavioral objective. However, you may wish to have two or more show and discuss steps related to a given objective.

---

13. Define the meaning of the *apply* step when planning learning activities:

You were correct if you wrote something similar to this:

The *apply* step provides a setting for the child to demonstrate whether or not he has learned the desired behavior.

14. How many *apply* steps are desirable for each behavioral objective?

You were correct if you wrote: one.

15. The *apply* step in planning learning activities corresponds to which one of the following stages of learning?

_____(a) perceive   _____(c) do
_____(b) think   _____(d) feel

You were correct if you checked (c).

16. Practicing a desired behavioral objective (is/is not) an *apply* learning activity.

You were correct if you selected "is not" because practice of a desired behavior is a *discuss* step preceding the *apply* step.

REINFORCING IS MORE THAN PLEASING

We wish to teach children to engage in desired behavior not only during a given lesson but also during other appropriate situations whether at school, at home, or in some other setting. That is, we wish to maintain or increase the frequency of many kinds of behavior in many kinds of situations.

If you wish to maintain or increase the frequency of a behavior, you must provide pleasant consequences immediately following the desired behavior. This is called reward or reinforcement. Teacher attention, especially verbal approval, is probably the most effective reinforcement for most prekindergarten children.

Reinforcement should be given frequently to children not only for demonstrating a desired behavioral objective but also for engaging in any kind of appropriate behavior leading to the desired behavioral objective. In other words, you should reinforce appropriate and desirable child responses during the discuss step as well as during the apply step. Reinforcement not only tends to increase the frequency of a given behavior but also tends to motivate the child to keep on trying (or responding) and therefore learning. The appropriate use of the principles of reinforcement is so important throughout the entire instructional process that a complete chapter has been devoted to the subject (Chapter 6).

---

17. If you wish to maintain or increase the frequency of a behavior, you must provide pleasant stimuli (immediately following/ immediately preceding) the desired behavior.

- -

"Immediately following."

---

18. Following a desired behavior with pleasant consequences is called:

_____(a) reward
_____(b) reinforcement

- -

Both (a) and (b) are correct.

19. Reinforcement should follow desired behavior:

_____(a) during the *show* step only
_____(b) during the *discuss* step only
_____(c) during the *apply* step only
_____(d) during both the *discuss* and *apply* steps

Answer (d) is correct.

LEARNING ACTIVITIES
AND TYPES OF BEHAVIOR

Learning activities are the procedures and materials used during the instructional process. The procedures and materials used during the instructional process are determined largely by the nature of the behavioral objective. The nature of the behavioral objective includes the class or category of a given objective as well as the specific content of the curriculum to which it is related. Twelve classes or categories of behavior were defined and described in Chapter 3 (see Figure 3–1, p. 60). The necessary instructional materials and procedures differ from one category of behavior to another. That is, you would use different materials and procedures to teach a motor sequence than you would to teach a problem-solving objective.

This section provides guidelines for you in planning learning activities related to behavioral objectives in each of the 12 categories. Once you have determined the class or category of a given behavior, you can plan the learning activities (*show, discuss, apply,* and *reinforce* steps) most suitable for that particular category of behavior. The classes of behavior, from simple to complex, include psychomotor behavior (single neuromuscular responses, motor sequences, complex skills), memorized behavior (naming, serial memory, component memory), complex-cognitive behavior (concept learning, rule learning, and problem solving), and affective behavior (emotion, motivation and interest, attitude and value).

Psychomotor Behavior

A desired psychomotor response is always a neuromuscular response of greater or lesser complexity performed smoothly and without hesitation. Typical psychomotor behavior in prekindergarten children includes painting a picture, cutting with scissors, molding clay, using a spoon, pouring juice, riding a tricycle, climbing the jungle gym, digging in the dirt or sandpile, sawing wood, hammering nails, and tying shoes.

If you plan to teach a psychomotor behavior, you first need to determine the components of that behavior. This will help you to determine the nature of a child's problem if he cannot perform a desired behavior. For example, the psychomotor behavior of cutting with scissors is made up of the following components (single neuromuscular responses): holding the scissors with the thumb and fingers in appropriate position; spreading the index finger and thumb while in the scissor holes to separate the scissor blades; closing the index finger and thumb while in the scissor holes to adequately close the scissor blades; using the forefinger to maintain balance and force while cutting.

Your learning activities should begin with a verbal description and instructions and/or a demonstration of the desired skill (show step).

For young children it is usually good procedure to provide a demonstration while you are verbally describing the steps involved. The demonstration can be given by you, by another child, or by a mechanical process such as a movie. Second, as you watch each individual child practice the behavior (discuss step), you provide feedback regarding how well he is doing (reinforce step). This feedback should be specific. That is, you would say, "You did a good job of holding the scissors; your fingers are in just the right place" rather than "You did a good job."

When the child begins to have trouble with one of the components of the psychomotor behavior, you can provide verbal and demonstration prompts (another show step). For instance, you could say to the child having trouble opening the scissor blades as you demonstrate the correct neuromuscular response, "You spread your finger and thumb like this to open the scissors."

Finally, as the child moves closer and closer to mastery of the behavior, you can fade out verbal prompts and reinforcements. The child's own success in the performance of the act provides the "internal" feedback or proprioceptive stimuli that tell him he has "got it." These proprioceptive stimuli are sensory experiences produced internally by movements of the body and can eventually become the only feedback necessary to maintain the psychomotor act.

Most psychomotor behavior is not learned in a single instructional session. This is saying that practice is important. However, practice must be accompanied consistently by feedback or knowledge of results if practice is to lead to mastery of a given psychomotor behavior. Practice without feedback may lead only to increased physical development, rather than to *motor sequence* or *complex skill* mastery. Mastery of the psychomotor behavior (apply step) occurs when the child can perform with smooth and coordinated neuromuscular responses without hesitation in the presence of a given cue. This cue can be verbal such as "Cut a piece of paper" or can be situational such as paper and a pair of scissors on the table.

When you are teaching a psychomotor behavior, pace your teaching to the learning rate of the individual child. Some children are fast learners while others learn slowly. Regardless of the child's rate of learning, the same sequence of procedures just described is necessary for learning to take place.

If a child can verbalize the components of a psychomotor act when asked, he is demonstrating memorized behavior, not psychomotor behavior. The child must be able to perform the desired psychomotor act to accomplish a psychomotor objective.

---

20. List the appropriate sequence of learning activities related to any *psychomotor* behavioral objective after the components of the behavior have been determined:

    (a) _____

    (b) _____

    (c) _____

The appropriate sequence follows:

(a) provide a demonstration of the desired behavior together with appropriate verbal description and instruction
(b) provide practice of the desired behavior accompanied by verbal feedback (i.e., knowledge of results or specific reinforcement)
(c) fade out prompts and verbal feedback as the child comes closer and closer to mastery of the behavior

---

21. Write a *show, discuss,* and *apply* step to teach the following *psychomotor* behavioral objective (motor-sequence chain):

Each child will demonstrate with a toothbrush, toothpaste, and water that he can brush his front teeth with an up-and-down motion of the brush without dropping the brush and while keeping the toothpaste in his mouth.

(Use a separate sheet of paper.)

You could have written something similar to this:

Show. (1) Have one of the older brothers or sisters of one of the children in the prekindergarten group demonstrate brushing his front teeth with appropriate up-and-down motions using his own toothbrush, toothpaste, an empty bowl, and a cup or glass of water. As the brother or sister demonstrates, describe what the child is doing, step by step. (2) Put some toothpaste on each child's toothbrush and hand each child his toothbrush, an empty bowl, and a cup or glass of water. Say, "It's your turn to practice brushing your front teeth. Remember to dip the brush in the water and brush up and down on your front teeth the way [name of child who demonstrated] did."

Discuss. As the children practice up-and-down strokes on their front teeth, tell each child what part or parts of the performance he is doing well. If a child has trouble with any component, such as pressing the bristle part of the brush against his teeth, holding the toothbrush, or manipulating the toothbrush up and down, have the child who demonstrated the complete chain demonstrate the troublesome component for the child. Then have the child try it again, reinforcing him for what he does well and encouraging him as he gets better and better (for example, "That's much better. You're brushing up and down very well." "You are holding onto the toothbrush just right." "Doesn't that feel good now?")

Apply. Have children brush their teeth following snack or lunch the same day and on several days following the lesson. Continue to give occasional verbal praise to those children who master the objective (remember this is just one part of the complex skill of brushing teeth). Give verbal prompts and encouragement to children who still have trouble.

Cognitive Behavior

Cognitive behavior consists of some type of symbolic or representational response from the learner. Verbal, written, or gestural language together with other psychomotor responses tell you whether or not the child is able to perform a desired cognitive behavioral objective. Cognitive behavior consists of two levels—memorized and complex cognitive. Memorized behavior includes naming, serial memory, and component memory. Complex-cognitive behavior includes concept learning, rule learning, and problem solving.

Memorized behavior. When a child engages in memorized behavior, he is recognizing or reproducing a symbolic response in the presence of cues identical to those he has experienced before. For example, when you point to a window and say, "What is that?" and the child responds, "Window," the child is responding symbolically (with verbal language) to a verbal and objective cue that he has experienced before. There are three divisions of memorized behavior, each requiring slightly different kinds of learning activities.

Naming. Naming is the least complex memorized behavior. The child who attaches a specific verbal label to a specific object, person, place, or event is engaging in naming behavior. The "window" example shows naming behavior.

In general, you should begin the sequence of learning activities associated with a naming-behavior objective by verbally naming each desired object, person, place, or event while showing the real thing (firsthand experience-show step) or something as close as possible to the real thing (vicarious experience-show step). Second, you immediately ask for a response from the group and individual children (discuss step) such as, "What is this?" or "Who is this?" You continue this one-two sequence of activity until you are satisfied that each child can correctly label each object, person, place, or event. Finally, you evaluate each child's ability to recognize or reproduce a label for a specific cue by asking each child to name each stimulus as you provide the same stimuli used in the first two steps (apply step). When doing this, avoid asking each child to name the same thing, one child after another, before going on to the next item; ask each child in the group to label a different object each time until each child has labeled each object.

Children should be given the opportunity to practice naming objectives in subsequent lessons. This helps to overcome the effects of interference and, therefore, forgetting.

Let's follow this sequence with the naming behavioral objective "each child will correctly label verbally the denomination of each of the five coins provided by the teacher."

> *Show, discuss.* (1) Hold up a half-dollar (50-cent piece) and say, "This is a half-dollar." Then ask the whole group, "What is this?" Next, ask individual children, "What is this?" If the child gives the correct label say, "That's correct" or "You are

correct." If a child gives no label or the incorrect label, quickly turn to a child who *does* know the answer and say, "What is this?," reinforcing the child for the correct answer. Then immediately go back to the child who gave the incorrect answer and ask the same question, providing verbal approval for the correct answer. (2) Follow this same procedure, using a quarter, a dime, a nickel, and a penny.

Apply. Hold up a coin and say to a child, "What is this?" If he answers correctly, pick up another coin and ask another child, "What is this?" Follow this procedure until every child has correctly labeled each of the five coins. If any child gives an incorrect label, use the same procedure described in the *discuss* step for handling incorrect responses. The following day repeat this *apply* procedure. Repeat in about a week.

---

22. Write the appropriate sequence of learning activities related to any *naming* behavioral objective:

    (a) _____

    (b) _____

    (c) _____

You should have written something similar to the following:
(a) verbally name each desired object, person, place, or event
(b) immediately ask for a response from the group and individual children
(c) ask each child to name each stimulus

23. Write a *show, discuss,* and *apply* step to teach the following *naming* behavioral objective:

    Each child will correctly label verbally each of five different shapes in a group of wooden shapes provided by the teacher.
    (Use a separate sheet of paper.)

You could have written something similar to this:

Show, discuss. (1) Put on the table at least three different sizes in wood of each of the following shapes: square, circle, triangle, rectangle, oval. Hold up the square and say, "This is a square." Ask the whole group, "What is this?" Then ask individual children, "What is this?" If the child gives the correct label say, "That's correct" or "You're correct." If a child gives no label or an incorrect label, quickly turn to a child who *does* know the answer and say, "What is this?," reinforcing the child for the correct answer. Then immediately go back to the child who gave the incorrect answer and ask the same question, providing verbal approval for the correct answer. (2) Follow this same procedure using a circle, a triangle, a rectangle, and an oval.

Apply: Hold up one of the wooden shapes and say to a child, "What is this?" Follow this procedure until every child has correctly labeled each of the shapes, regardless of its size. If any child gives an incorrect label, use the same procedure described in the *discuss* step for handling incorrect responses. The following day repeat the same *apply* procedure. Do this same thing in about a week.

Serial memory. Serial memory occurs when the child can place in their correct order specific single naming responses in the presence of specific stimuli. The order is always the same. The most common type of serial memory occurs when the child can quote verbatim a poem or piece of prose or when he can sing correctly the words and music of a song. Placing things in chronological order is also serial memory.

There are four basic steps when teaching a serial-memory objective. First, you demonstrate whatever behavior you are teaching (show step). If you are teaching the children to memorize a poem, you say the poem. If you are teaching a song, you sing the entire song (or play it on a tape or a record player). If you are teaching the chronological order of some events, such as seasons, you show pictures or other objects of each event in correct order, explaining the nature of each event. If you are teaching children to count from one to ten, you count from one to ten, possibly clapping your hands each time you count. Instructional materials or devices such as objects, pictures, or body movements act as memory prompts for the children as you demonstrate a given serial-memory objective.

Next, you allow the children to practice the desired behavior, providing as many prompts as necessary (show and discuss steps). If the children are learning a poem or a song, they probably will need to hear you say it or sing it several times before they are ready to try. You will need to continue saying it or singing it with the children until they have learned the poem or song. Prompts such as pictures or objects or body movements are helpful to give meaning to the poem or song and to help the children determine what comes next. It is not a good idea to teach poems or songs in parts, such as the first two lines and then the next two lines. Say or sing the entire first verse of the poem or song until it is memorized. Then move on to the next verse.

Third, you decrease prompts gradually as children move closer to mastery of the serial-memory objective (another show and discuss step). For example, you take away one picture after another used to illustrate parts of a song until the children can sing the song without looking at the pictures. Finally you can stop singing and let the children sing the song by themselves.

The final step is to let the children demonstrate that they have mastered the objective (apply step). This is a smooth transition from step three.

The children now can sing the song or say the poem or list things or events in chronological order without hesitation when asked to do so. It is important, too, that you provide opportunities on subsequent days for children to demonstrate each serial-memory objective. This helps to overcome the effects of interference and thus forgetting.

Let's look at show, discuss, and apply steps for the behavioral objective "each child will place pictures of the four seasons (spring, summer, autumn, and winter) in chronological order without prompting and correctly label each picture by its season":

Show, discuss.   Place four pictures, one for each season, in chronological order on the table, beginning with the picture for spring. Point to the picture depicting a spring scene and say, "This is a picture about spring because [describe the unique spring features such as budding flowers, birds in the nest with eggs, rain, etc.]." Then ask the whole group, "What season is this picture about [pointing to the spring picture]?" Then ask them why they know it's spring. Then point to the picture depicting a summer scene and say, "This is a picture about summer because [describe its unique summer characteristics such as sunshine, green lawns, children in bare feet, etc.]. Summer always comes after spring." Then ask, "What season always comes after spring? What season is this [pointing to the summer picture]? How can you tell that it is summer in this picture?" Now point to the picture depicting an autumn scene and say, "This is a picture about autumn because [describe its unique autumn characteristics such as yellow and red leaves on the trees, piles of leaves, fields of dried corn stalks, and orange pumpkins, etc.]. Autumn always comes after summer." Then ask, "What season always comes after summer? What season is this [pointing to the autumn picture]? How can you tell that it is autumn in this picture?" Now point to the picture depicting a winter scene and follow the same procedure. Then point to each picture in turn, beginning with the picture of spring, and say, "This is a picture of spring. After spring comes summer [point to summer picture]. After summer comes autumn [point to autumn picture]. After autumn comes winter [point to winter picture]." Then ask questions of individual children such as, "What comes after spring? Using a different season for each child, ask him to show you the picture of the season he named. Then ask each child to point to each picture in order, beginning with spring, and tell the name of the season and what season comes next.

Apply. Shuffle the pictures for each child and ask him to put the four pictures in the right order as he names the picture. If a child puts the pictures in the wrong order, put them in the correct order as you name each one, shuffle the pictures again, and give the child another try. Repeat the *apply* step the following day and one week later.

---

24. Write the appropriate sequence of learning activities related to any *serial-memory* behavioral objective:

  (a) _____

  (b) _____

  (c) _____

  (d) _____

You should have written something similar to the following:

  (a) demonstrate the desired behavior
  (b) allow children to practice the desired behavior, providing as many prompts as necessary
  (c) fade out prompts gradually as children gain mastery of the objective
  (d) allow children to demonstrate mastery of the objective

25. Write a *show, discuss,* and *apply* step to teach the following *serial-memory* behavioral objective:

     Each child will correctly sing all the words of a given song without the use of prompts such as pictures, objects, or cues from the teacher.

     (Use a separate sheet of paper.)

     You could have written something similar to this:

     Show. Tell the children to listen carefully to a new song you are going to sing because you want them to be able to sing it, too. Sing the song.
     Discuss. Ask the children to tell you what you were singing about.
     Show. Hold up a picture to represent a key word or idea in each line of the song. Put the pictures in scrambled order where all the children can see each one. Tell the children to listen to the song again so they can tell you in which order the pictures should be placed. Sing the song.
     Show, discuss. Ask the children in what order the pictures should be placed. Place them in the order they suggest. Then have the children listen to the song again to decide whether or not the pictures are in the correct order. Then make the changes in the order of the pictures, if necessary. Have the children sing the song with you, watching the pictures to help them sing the correct words. Repeat the song, gradually taking away one picture and then another.
     Apply. After all the pictures have been removed, have the children sing the song alone. You can get them started on the correct pitch. Watch the individual children as they sing. If some children stumble on some words, provide a prompt or two until they can sing the

words. Repeat this *apply* step the next day. Do the same thing on an occasional day throughout the year as the children build their repertoire of songs.

Component memory. Component memory occurs when a child can recognize or reproduce correctly each member of a given set or class in the presence of a specific stimulus he has experienced before. For example, he responds appropriately to the specific members of the set or class called *dishes* by putting food on a *plate,* drinking from a *cup,* and serving himself from a *serving dish.* There is no definite order of use or presentation that must be "memorized." The child simply responds appropriately to a specific member of a class or set when a given stimulus is provided.

Some members of sets are quite difficult to discriminate from one another, such as the letters d and b in the set *letters.* When members of a set are similar to one another, the learner has a tendency to overgeneralize and respond to or label one member as though it were another member, such as selecting a b when the child was asked to find a d.

The goal in a component-memory objective is to teach the child to select the correct member or members of a set when presented with several choices he has previously experienced. If you are teaching the child to discriminate *blue* in the set *colors,* he must have previously seen and named the objects used to test his memory for *blue.* If you are teaching him to discriminate 5 in the set *number symbols,* he must have previously seen and named the objects used to test his memory for 5.

Since you are teaching the child to identify and label members of sets, you first must present during instruction many different kinds of objects, events, people, or places that represent different members of that set (show step). If you are teaching the shape *square,* you should present several different kinds of objects that have the characteristic shape (square) such as a block, a square piece of paper, a box, a wooden piece cut in the shape of a square, a square jar, and others. As you present each item, you label the characteristic to be learned, such

as "This box is square, this block is square, this jar is square ... "
Second, have the whole group of children repeat with you the correct
shape label of each item (discuss step), occasionally asking an
individual child, "What shape is this?"

Third, you combine the objects, events, people, or places
having a similar characteristic with those that do *not* have the same
characteristic and label the unrelated members such as, "This is *not*
square" (another show step). For example, you would combine the
square items with other items that are not square, such as a ball, a
pencil, a round jar, a rectangular block. Fourth, as you label each item
you pick up, allow the children to feel it and say the label. For example,
you say, "This is *not* square. Say it with me. This is *not* square" (another
discuss step).

During the fifth step, you could have the individual children
select (from a group of items some of which do and some of which do
not have the desired characteristic) something that has the desired
characteristic or something that does not have the desired characteristic
(another discuss step). Using the square and not square items you could
say, "Hold up something that is square" or "Hold up something that is *not*
square," providing verbal praise when a child is correct (reinforce step). If a
child responds incorrectly, you could say, "No, this is _____. Say it with me.
This is _____," after which you could say to the child again, "Hold up
something that is _____." For instance, if you said to a child, "Hold up
something that is square" and he responded incorrectly, you could say, "No,
this is *not* square. Say it with me. This is *not* square." Then you could follow this
by repeating the original instruction ("Hold up something that is square") and
by providing verbal approval when the child responds correctly. If the child
continues to respond incorrectly, go on to another child and come back to this
child later.

The sixth step comes when the child can identify each member of a
given set without hesitation. You can test this immediately following practice of
the desired behavior (apply step). For example, you could hand each child a
box containing some square items and some items that are not square and say
to him, "Take out each thing that is square" or "Take out each thing that is *not*
square." It is important that these be the same items that were used in a

previous part of the lesson. If the items used to test the desired behavior are different from those used during instruction, you are testing for concept learning, not component memory.

To test for the possibility of interference, and thus forgetting, it is important to provide a review session on the objective a day later and again a few days later.

There are higher-order sets and lower-order sets. The set *square,* for example, is a lower-order set that can be conceptualized as a member of a larger set called *shapes.* Other lower-order sets or members of the set *shapes* would be *circle, triangle,* and *rectangle.* The instructional process is the same for higher-order sets. However, it is important to teach children to identify members of higher-order sets. This applies not only to the teaching of component-memory objectives but also to the teaching of concept-learning objectives discussed next.

---

26. Write the appropriate sequence of learning activities related to any *component-memory objective:*

   (a) _____

   _____

   (b) _____

   _____

   (c) _____

   _____

   (d) _____

   _____

   (e) _____

   _____

   (f) _____

You should have written something similar to the following:

(a)   present and label many different kinds of objects, people, places, or events that represent different members of a given set

(b)   have the children repeat the correct characteristic label with you

(c)   combine and label the objects, events, people, or places having a similar characteristic and those *not* having the same characteristic

(d)   have the children repeat the label for the unrelated members, "This is *not* _____"

(e)   have individual children select from a group of items that do and do not have the desired characteristic something that either has the desired characteristic or does not have the desired characteristic

(f)   have each child identify from items used during instruction each member of the set that has the desired characteristic

27.   Write appropriate *show, discuss,* and *apply* steps to teach the following *component-memory* behavioral objective:

Each child will correctly select from a group of textured objects he has worked with before those that are smooth and those that are not smooth.

(Use a separate sheet of paper.)

You could have written something similar to the following:

Show, discuss.   Put four or five objects on the table that have a smooth texture, such as a plastic ruler, a piece of silk fabric, a piece of paper, a drinking glass with smooth sides, and a fur-lined mitten. As you pick up each item say, "This is smooth. Say it with me. This is smooth." In addition to whole-group response, call individual children by name to "Say it with me." Give occasional verbal approval and encouragement as needed.

Show, discuss.   (1) To the first group, add four or five items that are not smooth, such as a piece of nubby fabric, a sheet of sandpaper, a rough stone, a small wicker basket, and a piece of unsanded wood. As you pick up each item say, "This is *not* smooth. Say it with me. This is *not* smooth." In addition to whole-group response, call individual children by name to "Say it with me." Give occasional verbal approval and encouragement as needed. (2) Then say to each individual child either "Hold up something that is *not* smooth" or "Hold up something that is smooth." Give verbal approval if the child responds correctly. If the child does not respond correctly, tell him, "No, that is/is not smooth. Hold up something that is/is not smooth." Be sure that each child has at least one chance to respond to each request.

Show, apply.   Hand each child a box containing items that are the same as those used during the *show, discuss* steps. Say to the children, "You have a box of things just like the ones on the table. Now take out of your box each thing that *is* smooth and put it by the box on the table." Watch individual children, encouraging them as they follow instruction. Do the *apply* step again the next day in class.

Complex cognitive behavior. Psychomotor and memorized behavior are prerequisite to complex cognitive behavior. Complex cognitive behavior is the highest form of human behavior. Prekindergarten children can learn the most elementary forms of complex cognitive behavior. Their level of complex cognitive behavior is not expected to equal that of an adult. The child's lower level of performance of complex cognitive types of behavior may be due to inadequately developed structures in the central nervous system, or it could be a result of a relative lack of experience in the preceding types of behavior. The answers to this controversy are still conjectural.

Concept learning. Concept learning is related to the classification of objects, people, and events not previously encountered. Whenever a child points to a chair he has never seen before and says "chair" or points to a man he has never seen before and says "man," he is demonstrating concept learning. That is, he is classifying newly encountered objects or people according to some abstract characteristics he has learned before. There is something "chairy" about a chair, possibly having something to do with four legs, a flat surface on which to sit, and some sort of a back support. There are "manish" characteristics about a man, possibly having something to do with the type of clothing worn, the hair style, a slight facial shadow denoting a place where a beard and mustache might grow, and possibly even the smell of "manish" cologne. Whatever the distinguishing characteristics of certain objects, people, places, or events, young children are quite capable of classifying many objects, people, places, or events on the basis of some of these abstract characteristics.

Any single word is really a category or set of many objects, people, places, or events with similar characteristics. The word *chair* to a very young child may stand only for a particular chair. In such a case, naming occurs, not concept learning. However, whenever a child can point to a chair he has not seen before and label it correctly, he is demonstrating ability to classify objects into appropriate sets. If he labeled a chair he had not seen before as *table,* he would be demonstrating *overgeneralization* because he would be including in the set *chair* something that really belonged to the category or set *table.* This probably means the child has not learned enough of the distinguishing characteristics of the concept *chair.* In other words, he has not learned to *discriminate* between members of two or more sets or categories (see Figure 3–1, p. 60).

When teaching concepts to children be sure they are concrete enough that the boundaries between neighboring concepts are clear. Some concepts are so abstract that even experts disagree on instances and noninstances of the concept, such as the concepts *love, good,* and *teaching.* Concepts that are clearly discernible by the senses, especially sight and touch, are particularly important for young children to learn. It is from appropriate discrimination and generalization of such concrete concepts as *cat, pencil, house, mother, flower,* and *glass* that the child is prepared to learn more abstract concepts.

Some guidelines may help you as you plan learning activities related to concept-learning objectives. First, it is important to select examples widely from among the possible members of a category or concept. It is impossible to learn a concept from a single example. For instance, the concept *farm animals* is not learned by teaching the children to identify a horse. Other animals also belong to this category or class, such as *cow, pig,* and *sheep.* If a child points to a horse every time you ask him to point to a farm animal, he is *under-generalizing* because he has not experienced other members of the same category with their appropriate labels.

Second, correctly label the concept associated with selected objects, people, places, or events as you show instances to the children. For example, as you hold up in succession a figure of a horse, a cow, a pig, and a sheep say, "This is a farm animal." Then immediately ask, "What is this?" to the whole group or to an individual child.

Third, provide concrete examples of what the concept is *not,* as well as what it is. A child has not learned a concept until he can discriminate between a member and a nonmember of the category as well as generalize among the members of a category. When teaching the concept *farm animals,* for example, show figures representing forest animals or zoo animals along with those of farm animals. Whenever you show a nonmember of a category, say something like, "This is *not* a _____. Say it with me. This is *not* a _____." Avoid saying what the nonmember *is* because you will then be teaching a category other than the one you wish to teach.

Fourth, after you have presented members and nonmembers of a category, ask individual children to point to or pick up something that *is* and something that *is not* the concept you are teaching. For instance, you could say during a lesson on farm animals, "Show me something that *is* a farm animal" or "Show me something that is *not* a farm animal." Continue this until each child can pick up an appropriate item.

The fifth and final step is to present items that have not been used in the previous instruction, some items of which are members and some of which are not members of the concept being learned. Then ask the individual children to "Show me something that is _____" or "Show me something that is *not* _____." This final step is often missed in the concept instruction process, even in a child's advanced schooling. It is impossible to evaluate whether or not a child has learned a concept until he responds appropriately to stimuli he has not previously encountered in the instructional process. If he responds appropriately to stimuli used during preceding stages of the instructional process, he is demonstrating memorized behavior, not concept learning.

Here are some learning activities related to the concept-learning behavioral objective "each child will correctly select from a group of miscellaneous items he has never seen before those that are red."

Show, discuss. (1) Put three objects on the table, two of which are red. These objects should be different, such as a red ball, a red sheet of paper, and a block of some color other than red. As you pick up the red objects say, "This is red. Say it with me. This is red." As you pick up the object that is not red say, "This is *not* red. Say it with me. This is *not* red." Allow the children to hold the items while they look at them for a few seconds. (2) Put three more objects on the table, two red, such as a red fire truck, a red crayon, and one not red, such as a blue crayon. As you pick up each red item say, "This is red. Say it with me. This is red." As you pick up the item that is not red say, "This is *not* red. Say it with me. This is *not* red." Allow the children to hold the objects while they look at them for a few seconds. (3) Put all six items in a low, flat cardboard box, and mix them up. Put the box in front of each child in turn and say, "Show me something that is red" or "Show me something that is *not* red." Be sure that each child in the group has the opportunity to respond to *both* requests. If a child points to or picks up an incorrect item, say, "No, that is (is *not*) red. *This* [picking up a correct item] is *not* (is) red. Now show me something that is *not*(is) red [you ask him the original question again]." Continue asking both questions until each child can respond correctly each time he is asked.

Show, apply. Put in front of each child a box containing four items, two or three of which are red. These items should *not* be items used in the previous instruction process. Ask each child to take out of his box each item that is red. If any child takes out incorrect items, go through the correction process described in the previous *show, discuss* step with that child. Repeat the *apply* step the following day and again a week later.

---

28. Write the appropriate sequence of learning activities related to any *concept-learning* behavioral objective:

    (a) _____

    (b) _____

    (c) _____

    (d) _____

    (e) _____

You should have written something similar to the following:

(a) Select examples widely from among the possible members of a category or concept.

(b) Correctly label the concept associated with selected objects, people, places, or events as you show instances to the children.

(c) Provide concrete examples of what the concept is *not,* as well as what it is.

(d) Ask children to point to or pick up something that *is* and something else that *is not* the concept you are teaching.

(e) Present items that do and items that do not represent the concept being taught; select items that have not been used in the previous instruction process. Ask the children to select instances of the concept from these newly encountered objects.

---

29. Write appropriate *show, discuss,* and *apply* steps to teach the following *concept-learning* behavioral objective:

    Each child will correctly select from a group of shapes of various sizes and colors and materials he has not seen before those that are triangles.

    (Use a separate sheet of paper.)

    You could have written something similar to the following:

    Show, discuss. (1) Put three objects on the table, two that are in the shape of a triangle and one that is not. These objects should be made of different materials, such as plastic, wood, and paper, and should differ in size and color. As you pick up each triangular item, say, "This is a triangle. Say it with me. This is a triangle." As you pick up the object that is not in the shape of a triangle, say, "This is *not* a triangle. Say it with me. This is *not* a triangle." Allow the children to hold the items as they look at them for a few seconds. (2) Put three more objects on the table, two of which are triangles. Again these objects should be made of different materials and should differ in size and color. As you pick up each item in the shape of a triangle, say, "This is a triangle. [Let the child hold the item.] Say it with me. This is a triangle." As you pick up the item that is not a triangle, say, "This is *not* a triangle. [Let the child hold the item.] Say it with me. This is *not* a triangle." (3) Put all six items in a low, flat cardboard box, mixed at random so the triangular objects are not separated from the objects that are not triangular. Put the box in front of each child in turn and say, "Show me something that *is* a triangle" or "Show me something that is *not* a triangle." Be sure that each child in the group has the opportunity to respond to *both* questions. If a child points to or picks up an incorrect item, say, "No, that is [or is *not*] a triangle. *This* [picking up a correct item] is *not* [or is] a triangle. Now show me something that is *not* [or is] a triangle [you ask him the original question again]." Continue asking both questions until each child can respond correctly each time he is asked.

Show, apply. Put in front of each child a box containing four items, two or three of which are triangles. These items should differ in size, color, and material. They should *not* be items used in the previous instruction process. Ask each child to take out of his box each item that is a triangle. If any child takes out incorrect items, go through the correction process described in the previous *show, discuss* step with that child. Repeat this *apply* step the following day and again a week later.

Rule learning. A rule is a relationship between two or more concepts. Any given sentence, for example, is a rule because it is a combination of two or more concepts in some type of logical relationship to one another. Rule learning is thus dependent on concept learning.

A child demonstrates concept learning by identifying appropriate instances or noninstances of a given concept verbally or through a motor sequence. Rule learning, on the other hand, is demonstrated when the child can *do* what the rule says, such as, "Open the door," "Drink your milk," or "Draw a straight line."

Gagné (1971) suggests several characteristics of the instructional process related to rule learning. First, the concepts of which a given rule is comprised must have been learned previously. For instance, if the concepts *open* and *doors* have previously been learned, a child can then learn the rule "Doors open."

Second, the rule must be demonstrated or discovered by the child. If the child performs the rule when asked, such as "Doors open; show me," he is engaging in "reception" learning (Gagné, 1971) in the process of learning a rule. If, on the other hand, you show a child two doors and ask him to show you the ways the doors are similar, he may discover among other things that doors open. This learning activity is called "discovery" learning (Gagné, 1971). Reception learning and discovery learning are both show and discuss steps.

Third, the learning of a specific rule must be tested by asking the child to demonstrate the rule in a particular case not previously encountered in instruction. If the child is to demonstrate that he has learned the rule 'Doors open," he must demonstrate that rule with one or more doors not previously encountered during the rule-learning lesson (the apply step). Regardless of whether "reception" learning activities or "discovery" learning activities are used in the rule-learning lesson plan, the child must always be able to *do* the rule with something not previously used in the lesson.

These three characteristics of learning activities for rule learning are basically the same whether the rule is a simple one, such as "Doors open" or a more complicated one such as "We pay money for things we need in a store." If we test a child's rule learning simply by having him restate the rule, we are testing memory, not rule learning.

Here is an example of learning activities related to the rule-learning behavioral objective "each child will demonstrate the rule *paper tears* by tearing at least a 2-inch strip in each sheet of paper he has not seen before during instruction" (it is assumed the child has previously learned the concepts *paper* and *tears*):

> *Show, discuss.* [Select either (1) or (2)] (1) Hold up a piece of pastel construction paper and ask, "What is this?" (Paper.) Hold up a piece of unprinted newsprint and ask, "What is this?" (Paper.) Then say, "That's correct. These are pieces of paper. Tell me how these pieces of paper are alike." If the children have trouble responding, ask, "What can you do with this piece of paper [hold up the piece of construction paper] that you can do with this piece of paper [hold up the piece of newsprint]?" Let the children respond. They may suggest such things as, "They are both paper," "We can draw on them," "We can cut them," "We can fold them," and "We can tear them." As a child suggests something that can be done with the paper, let him try what he suggests. This means you should have at least some crayons and blunt scissors available. If the children do not suggest that paper tears, ask, "Can we tear paper?" Let the children respond. Then hand a piece of construction paper or newsprint to each child and say, "Paper tears. Show me." If one or more children have trouble demonstrating the rule, have one of the children who knows how demonstrate the rule. Again say to the child having trouble, "Paper tears. Show me." Verbally reinforce the children. (This series of activities is *discovery* learning.) (2) Hold up the piece of construction paper and ask, "What is this?" (Paper.) Hold up the piece of newsprint and ask, "What is this?" (Paper.) Then hand a piece of newsprint or construction paper to each child and say, "Paper tears. Show me." If one or more children have trouble demonstrating the rule, have one of the children who knows how demonstrate the rule. Again say to the child having trouble, "Paper tears. Show me." Be sure to tell each child when he has correctly demonstrated the rule. (This series of activities is *reception* learning.)
> *Show, apply.* Hand each child two different pieces of paper at least 4" × 5" each. These pieces of paper should be other than construction

and newsprint paper, such as pages from old magazines, pieces of newspaper (printed), type paper, or fingerpaint paper. After each child has received two different pieces of paper say, "Paper tears. Show me." If a child or several children cannot demonstrate the rule, follow the correction step in the previous show, discuss steps. Repeat the apply step the following day using, again, different kinds of paper for each child. Do the same thing one week later.

Children can demonstrate rule learning with real objects, people, places, or events or representations of objects, people, places, or events that are as nearly like the real thing as possible. They also can demonstrate rule learning by role-playing or pantomime or use of the graphic arts media such as crayons, paints, clay, and paper products.

---

30. Write the appropriate sequence of learning activities related to any *rule-learning* behavioral objective:

    (a) _____
        _____
    (b) _____
        _____
    (c) _____
        _____

- -

You should have written something similar to the following:

   (a) the concepts of which a given rule is comprised should have been learned in previous lessons.

   (b) the rule must be demonstrated when the teacher asks (*reception* learning) or be discovered by the child (*discovery* learning).

   (c) the child must demonstrate the rule in a particular case not previously encountered in instruction.

31. Write appropriate *show, discuss,* and *apply* steps to teach the following *rule-learning* behavioral objective:

Each child will demonstrate the rule *liquids pour* by pouring at least two different liquids not previously used in instruction from one container into another.

(Use a separate sheet of paper.)

You could have written something similar to the following (the children will have learned previously the concepts *liquids* and *pour*):

Show, discuss. [Select either (1) or (2)] (1) Put a glass of milk on the table. Ask, "What is this?" The children probably will respond, "Milk." Then ask, "What else can we call this?" If the children do not give the correct answer, "A liquid," say, "This is also called a liquid." Put a small pitcher of juice on the table. Again ask, "What is this?" Some children will say, "Juice." If so, ask, "What else can we call this?" Again, if the children do not give the correct answer, say, "This is also called a liquid." Then say, "Tell me how these two liquids are alike." If the children have trouble responding, ask, "What can you do with this liquid [point to the milk] that you can do with this liquid [point to the juice]?" Let the children respond. They may say such things as, "They are both liquids," "You can drink it," "You can spill it," and, "You can pour it." As each child suggests something, let him demonstrate what he has suggested with the real liquid or by pantomime (you probably won't want the child to spill the milk or juice). This means you should have some empty containers on the table, one for the milk and one for the juice. If the children do not suggest that liquids pour, you can ask, "Do liquids pour?" Let the children respond. Follow up with, "Yes, liquids pour." Put the glass of milk and the small pitcher of juice in front of each child in turn

and say, "Liquids pour. Show me." If one or more children have trouble demonstrating the rule, have one of the children who knows how demonstrate the rule. Again say to the child having trouble, "Liquids pour. Show me." Verbally reinforce the children. (This series of activities is *discovery* learning.)
(2) Point to a glass of milk on the table and say, "What is this?" The children will probably answer, "Milk," so ask, "What else can we call it?" If the children do not respond "Liquid," say, "This is also called a liquid." Point to a glass of juice and ask the same questions. Then point to both the milk and the juice and say, "Liquids pour." Put the glass of milk and the pitcher of milk in front of each child together with an empty container for each and say, "Liquids pour. Show me." If one or more children have trouble demonstrating the rule, have one of the children who knows how demonstrate the rule. Again say to the child having trouble, "Liquids pour. Show me." Be sure to tell each child when he has correctly demonstrated the rule. (This series of activities is *reception* learning.)
Show, apply. (1) Put in front of each child a glass of water and a cup of prepared easel paint, together with an empty container for each liquid. Then say, "Liquids pour. Show me." If a child has trouble demonstrating the rule, follow the correction step in the previous show, discuss steps. (2) Repeat the apply step the following day using different liquids. Do the same thing a week later.

Problem solving. Problem solving, the most complex of all behavior, occurs when the child puts two or more previously learned rules together in an appropriate sequence to solve a previously unencountered problem.

Boutwell and Tennyson (1971) have suggested two types of problems, terminal and expressive. The terminal problem has a known solution. The expressive problem is open-ended because there is no known solution. Expressive problems are most frequently encountered in the graphic arts and in the movement and music areas of the curriculum in the prekindergarten.

However, the expressive problem by no means is exclusively the province of the fine arts. The entire spectrum of human and scientific endeavor is fraught with problems that have no known solution.

Learning activities related to problem-solving behavioral objectives should include three characteristics. First, the problem should be identified (show step). For prekindergarten children this usually means that some form of direct contact should be provided. If the children are to learn how to solve a conflict situation, a real conflict (such as one child attempting to take away the toy being used by another child) can be demonstrated through role-playing by two children in the group.

Second, the children should have the opportunity to search for and formulate hypotheses leading to the solution of the problem (discuss step). This means arriving at statements of various rules and putting these rules together in a logical order that might solve the problem. In the conflict situation just described, the children could formulate hypotheses guided by such questions as, "What happened when Tom took the toy away from Bob? How do you think Bob felt when Tom took the toy away from him? How do you think Bob felt when he took the toy away from Tom? Can you think of another way that Tom could get the toy he wants without making Bob angry? How will both children feel if Tom does what you just said? Is there a way the teacher can help?" The answers to such questions are really hypotheses or simple rules that, put together, can lead to a solution of the problem. Prekindergarten children have a difficult time thinking about more than two rules at a time. Even two are difficult unless the rules can be related to concrete reality. The Swiss biologist-psychologist Jean Piaget has suggested this important idea in his numerous descriptive studies of cognitive behavior in young children. You can lead the prekindergarten children you teach to the solution of a problem by the kinds of questions you ask, but you can't make them drink.

Third, the children should have the opportunity to verify the solution to the problem by applying what they have hypothesized and verbally stating the solution (discuss and apply steps). For example, in the conflict situation, the teacher could verbally summarize the appropriate steps suggested by the children, have the children repeat the solution with him, and then have the same two children role-play the conflict situation, using the new solution. Each of the children in the group then should demonstrate the solution to a similar conflict situation (that is, one child wanting something from another child) with another child in the group. If the individual children role-play the solution in a different but similar conflict situation, they are *transferring* the appropriate steps required for solution to a similar but different situation. In other words, they are using a "class" of rules that can be used to solve a class of problems. If the children in the group role-play the solution to the identical problem used during previous instruction, they are demonstrating memory behavior, not problem-solving behavior.

A good problem solver is *not* a wild guesser. Unfortunately, too many children are taught to guess indiscriminately rather than to examine the possible alternatives and come up with the best solution. For example, a teacher shows a group of five children two identical glasses filled half full with water. The teacher says, "Can you tell me which glass has warm water?" The children begin to guess, one trying to out-yell the other. The teacher quietly says, "No, you can't tell me yet which has the warm water. How could you find out?" The children answer variously, "By touching it," "By feeling it," "By putting your finger in it." The first question, "Can you tell me which glass has warm water," leads to guessing. The second question, "How could you find out?," focuses on the idea that a way can be found to solve the problem. The teacher responds to the replies of the children with, "That's correct, you touch the water and find out." He then gives each child a turn touching the water. Next he asks the original question, "Can you tell me which glass has the warm water?" Each child gives the correct answer. The teacher further questions, "How did you find out?," to which the children answer, "By touching it." The teacher then tests the learning of the appropriate solution by showing different combinations of hot and cold to each child (such as two sponges of different colors, one dampened with warm water and the other with cold water; two washcloths of different sizes, one dampened with warm water and the other with cold water) and asking, "How can you find out which one is warm? Show me." The children thus demonstrate and verbally describe the solution. The two rules related to the solution are, "One is warm and the other is cold. Find out which one is warm by touching both."

Another type of problem-solving situation deals with probabilities when the evidence is not immediately available. For example, "It is now lunch time. What do you think your mother is doing right now?" Although the children can't see their mothers right now, they can predict what she might be doing in terms of what they have seen her do in the past at lunch time. Or children in a room with no direct view outdoors could be asked, "What kind of weather is it outdoors? Why do you think so?" The children could base their answers again on what they've seen in the past, such as what the weather was like when they came to school and their knowledge of how quickly certain kinds of weather changes occur. The children can check out their hypotheses by telephoning their mothers in the first instance and going outdoors in the second instance.

You may wish to have many *expressive* problem-solving objectives (open-ended problems) in the graphic arts, movement, and music curricula. When a child is asked to paint his impression of an object, event, person, or place, he is engaging in expressive problem solving because the solution is not known. Whenever a child creates a basic body movement pattern or an original melody, he also is engaging in expressive problem solving. But rule learning, concept learning, and other types of learning are required before a child can effectively engage in terminal or expressive problem solving. When other types of behavior related to a problem have not been learned, the child's problem-solving behavior may become just another random activity to pass the time. A child, for example, who attempts to paint his impression of a bird may be considerably limited in his behavior unless he has learned psychomotor behavior (such as ways to put the paint brush in the paint and lift it out and how to move the paint brush around in contact with the paper), memorized behavior (such as labels for the paint brush, the colors of the paint, and the paper), and complex cognitive behavior (such as the rules "Paint drips from a brush" and "Mixing blue and yellow paints makes green paint").

32. Write the appropriate sequence of learning activities related to any *problem-solving* behavioral objective:

    (a) _____

    (b) _____

    (c) _____

You should have written something similar to the following:

   (a) Identify the problem.
   (b) Allow the children to search for and formulate hypotheses leading to the solution of the problem.
   (c) Allow the children to try out and verify the solution to the problem.

33. Write appropriate *show, discuss,* and *apply* steps to teach the following *problem-solving* behavioral objective:

    When presented a social-conflict problem not previously used in instruction, each child will role-play the part of the wronged child, including the appropriate behavior when something has been taken from him by another child.

    (Use a separate sheet of paper.)

You could have written something similar to the following [the children will have learned previously the concept *anger* and the rules "We tell people when we feel angry" and "We tell people a better way to act when they make us angry"]:
    Show. Say, "I'm going to show and tell you about some things that make children angry. I'll need your help because

these will be let's pretend stories." Have two children stand
beside you. Hand a ball to one of the children. Say, "Bobby
(child with ball), bounce the ball like you would if you were
playing outside. Now, Mary (other child), pretend you're
outside and you want to play with the ball Bobby has. You go
over and take the ball away from Bobby." Child takes ball.
"Now [turn to Bobby] let's pretend that Bobby gets very
angry because the ball was taken away. So he says to
Mary, 'Give me back my ball' and grabs the ball back.
Bobby, say that with me and take the ball [repeat, "Give
me back my ball" and pause while child takes back the
ball]." Turn to other children in the group. Say, "That is
not a good way to act when you are angry at someone.
Both children would feel angry now." Have the two
children sit down. Thank them for being good helpers.
Discuss.   Ask the children: (1) "How do you think Bobby
felt when the ball was taken away?" (2) "What did Bobby
do when he got angry? How did this make Mary feel?"
(3) "Could you think of a better way for Bobby to act
when the ball was taken away from him?" Verbally
encourage children as they respond.
Show.   Say, "Now, I want to show you the same pretend story,
but this time the child who has something taken away from him
does the right thing." Ask two other children to stand beside you.
Hand a ball to one of the children. Say, "Ann (child holding ball),
bounce the ball the way you would if you were playing outside.
Good. Now, Gary (other child), pretend you're outside and you
want to play with the ball Ann has. You go over and take the
ball away from Ann." Child takes ball. Turn to child who had ball.
"Now, let's pretend that Ann gets very angry because the ball
was taken away. So she says to Gary, 'That makes me mad when
you take my ball. Give me the ball. You can have a turn when I'm
finished.' Ann, say that with me, but look at Gary. [Repeat, "That
makes me mad, etc."] That is a *good* way to act when you are

angry at someone." Have the two children return to their seats.
Thank them for being good helpers.

Discuss.   Ask the children: (1) "How do you think Ann felt when
the ball was taken away?" (Angry, mad.) (2) "What did Ann do when
she got angry?" (Let children respond. Lead them to these two
ideas: she told the other child how she felt (mad); or she told
the other child a better way to act.) (3) "What should Ann do if
Gary won't give back the ball?" (Good possibilities: get an adult
to help or find something else to play with.) Verbally encourage
children as they respond.

Show, discuss.   Say, "Let's do some more pretending. We'll
try to remember the best ways to act when we're angry." Have
children role-play at least two more situations similar to the last
one. In the first situation one child takes a book away from another
child. In another situation one child takes a doll away from
another child. After each role-playing situation ask the children
the preceding three questions, relating each question to the item
taken away. Give constant encouragement to the children as they
practice. After the practice session, review with the children the
two actions that are appropriate when someone takes something
away: (1) tell the other child how you feel; (2) tell the other child
a better way to act.

Show, apply.   (1) Say, "Now let's see if you can remember the
best ways to act when you are angry at someone for taking
something away from you. We'll play let's pretend again." Have
two children role-play a conflict where one child takes the play
dough away from another. When the children need help saying
and doing the right thing, give them verbal prompts. Do the
same type of role-playing with blocks and with a puzzle being
taken away, providing prompts when necessary. Give verbal
praise when the children engage in the desired behavior. (2) One
to seven days later, do similar role-playing but use different
situations, such as taking away a tricycle, some cookies, and a
toy truck.

Affective Behavior

The term *affective* is descriptive of the kind of behavior we call emotion, motivation and interest, or attitude and value. We infer a person's affective behavior from the choices he makes when he has a free choice, when no one is directing him in a particular activity, or by the way he responds in a directed learning situation. Affective behavior is what we often call the expression of feeling, particularly when the feelings are strong ones such as love, anger, enthusiasm, and frustration.

Affective behavior becomes more differentiated and complex as a person grows from infancy to maturity. The infant responds spontaneously in what is often called emotional behavior soon after birth. Such behavior is generalized to begin with, such as "satisfied" and "distressed." As the infant grows older and has more experiences, his free-choice behavior becomes more complicated than the simple term *emotional* would suggest. Therefore, we begin to infer specific interests and motivation in the infant as we observe his behavior related to his exploration of his physical environment and his responses to other people. As the infant grows into toddlerhood and then early childhood, we begin to infer even more complicated types of affective behavior—attitudes and values. These attitudes and values probably are largely influenced by the child's growing ability with language in addition to his increasing motor ability.

The child demonstrates affective behavior in a directed learning experience when he quickly and cheerfully volunteers an answer, excitedly bounces up and down on his rug or chair, immediately volunteers to participate in a role-playing experience, excitedly digs his hands into a new graphic arts medium he has never experienced before, pushes his chair away from the table and refuses to respond to the teacher, pokes another child sitting next to him, or cries when he is asked a question. In free-choice activity the child demonstrates affective behavior when he consistently chooses one activity such as block-building over several others or when he refuses to do some things such as play the musical instruments in the music corner or look at books in the library corner. That is, we infer his likes and dislikes, or his interests and motivations, from the activities in which he chooses to engage.

The children you teach will not always be where you can direct their choices and activities. As you teach children in direct learning experiences and free-choice activities in the prekindergarten, you are helping them develop desirable or undesirable emotions, interests and motivations, attitudes and values. For example, in lessons about birds, you probably desire that the child you teach will voluntarily feed the birds at home during the winter and leave a bird's nest in the tree when he climbs up to inspect one he has discovered. Whether or not a child will engage in such desirable activity reflecting emotions, interests and motivations, or attitudes and values depends largely on the type of reinforcement experienced at school and in his home and neighborhood environment. The next chapter discusses the principles of reinforcement and desirable ways to use them in the prekindergarten.

PLAY AS A LEARNING ACTIVITY

Adults often view play as a leisure-time activity—an activity that is fun, entertaining, and to be enjoyed for its own sake. Many early childhood educators view play for children as an exploratory activity, an opportunity to test out the properties of things, an emotional release, a means of "controlling" the world, and the "work" of the child. These educators always include the idea that a child is learning when he plays.

The basic difference between most of the literature on play for young children and the prekindergarten learning activities discussed in this chapter is the desirable degree of adult direction and supervision suggested. Learning activities can and should be enjoyable and fun. The fact that a learning activity is carefully planned does not mean that the child cannot be up and about using his muscles as well as his language. The suggested importance of time, space, and appropriate adult guidance in "play" literature basically applies to learning activities as described in this chapter.

Children in prekindergarten spend so many more hours at home, in the neighborhood, or on the playground than they do at school. Therefore, it seems more economical as well as wise in terms of effectiveness of instruction to structure the learning activities at prekindergarten more than they might be away from school. All of the good effects of play can result from planned learning activities in the prekindergarten while most of the ill effects (such as learning inappropriate behavior or learning to withdraw because of a lack of motor or language skills) can be avoided.

SUMMARY

Learning activities are planned experiences for children to help them attain a given instructional objective. Learning activities consist of four basic steps: *show, discuss, apply,* and *reinforce.* These activities correspond to the steps in the learning process for the child: *perceive, think, do,* and *feel.* The nature of the learning activities depends on the type of objective being taught.

REFERENCES

Boutwell, R. C., & Tennyson, R. D. Instructional objectives—different by design. Working Paper No. 13, Instructional Research and Development, Division of Communication Services, Brigham Young University, 1971.

Gagné, R. M. The learning of concepts. In M. D. Merrill (Ed.), *Instructional design: Readings.* Englewood Cliffs, N. J.: Prentice-Hall, 1971.

Haupt, D. Teacher-child interaction: A study of the relationships between child-initiated questions and nursery school teacher behaviors. Unpublished doctoral dissertation, Wayne State University, 1966.

Woodruff, A. D. *Basic concepts of teaching.* San Francisco: Chandler, 1961.

Chapter 6

Principles of Reinforcement: Behavior and Its Consequences

Three-year-old Carla has been in nursery school for three days but cries constantly for her mother and begs to go home. The more Carla cries the more her teacher tries to comfort her and get her involved in activities with other children. When Carla is alone the crying diminishes or stops completely.

Brad, a handsome 4-year-old with seemingly endless energy, is known by the teachers as the nursery school "stirring spoon"—he seems to be stirring up trouble more often than not. He takes tricycles away from other children, pushes children out of the swings, climbs up the face of the slide preventing children from sliding down, knocks over block structures built by the other children, uses his clay as missiles in the classroom, paints the furniture as well as the paper on the easel, and stirs up a constant commotion during story or music time. The teachers feel they spend an inordinate amount of time scolding Brad or keeping him away from the other children.

Jennifer is a petite 4-year-old who never seems to run out of things to do in the nursery school. She looks at books, plays in the domestic corner, paints pictures, rides the tricycles, builds with the blocks, and puts puzzles together like an old pro. But she usually leaves the scene when another child

Carla cries constantly for her mother and begs to go home.

comes to play. Her mother is worried because Jennifer doesn't play with other children. Jennifer's nursery school teachers frequently try to involve her in activities with other children, but to no avail. Jennifer will engage in lively conversation with her teachers but seems reluctant to talk to the other children in the group.

These examples of child behavior in the prekindergarten are real. But more important, they are not unusual or extraordinary examples of child behavior. Similar incidents are taking place every day in hundreds of prekindergarten groups.

BEHAVIOR AND THE ENVIRONMENT

Your effectiveness as a teacher is measured by the behavior changes that occur in the children you teach. *Behavior is your basic source of information.* This is why we emphasize behavioral objectives when making lesson plans. Behavior gives you clues as to what, where, when, and why to teach. You can get this information by carefully observing the behavior of the child and the consequences of that behavior (that is, what happens immediately following each act).

Let's take another look at the three situations described at the beginning of this chapter and try to determine the observable behavior and its consequences.

Crying (the observable behavior) was the focus in the incident about *Carla.* Her crying was frequently followed by attention from the teacher (the consequences of crying), such as looking at the child and telling the child about interesting activities in the classroom.

Brad, on the other hand, exhibits such inappropriate behavior as pushing children out of swings, knocking over block structures, and painting the furniture instead of easel paper (the observable behavior). Brad's behavior is usually followed by a scolding from one of his teachers (the consequences of the behavior).

Brad seems to be stirring up trouble more often than not.

Jennifer, though she keeps involved in the various activities available at nursery school, engages only in activities where no other children are involved (observable behavior). Her social isolation is followed by conversation with the teachers, who attempt to help Jennifer play with other children (consequences of the behavior).

Note that in each case when the child engaged in inappropriate or undesirable behavior, that behavior was followed by some type of verbal or nonverbal attention from the teacher (consequences). If these teachers had been more aware of specific child behavior and the consequences that followed, they might have been able to determine some alternative consequences that could have changed the inappropriate or undesirable

Jennifer doesn't play with other children.

behavior to appropriate and desirable behavior. For example, the teacher could have given attention to Carla when she was *not* crying, rather than when she was crying.

The principle here is that *a child's behavior is followed by consequences in the environment. These consequences determine the future frequency of the behavior that precedes them.* For example, Carla's crying was followed by the consequence of teacher attention, verbal and nonverbal. The crying continued. Since consequences of behavior affect the frequency of that behavior, simple observation would reveal that the consequence of teacher attention maintained Carla's crying behavior. This idea will be easier to understand if we look at different kinds of consequences and their effects on behavior.

BEHAVIOR AND ITS CONSEQUENCES

The consequences of behavior can be classified into five different categories:

Presentation of Pleasant Consequences

Some behavior is often followed by the *presentation* of *pleasant* consequences, either tangible or intangible. Such pleasant consequences include such things as eye contact with another person, a smile, verbal approval, candy, good grades, and money. These consequences are called *rewards* or *positive reinforcers*. These rewards or reinforcers tend to *increase the behavior that precedes them.* Various forms of attention such as eye contact, a touch of the hand, or verbal praise are usually powerful reinforcers for young children. Apparently even negative forms of attention such as criticism and threats are reinforcers for the behavior of some children.

The simple test of a reinforcer is to look at the frequency of the behavior it follows. If the frequency of that behavior is maintained or increases, the consequence following the behavior is a reinforcer or a reward. For example, if a child is threatened with something uncomfortable if he continues an undesirable behavior, that threat may be a reinforcer, as determined by the behavior increasing in or remaining at the same level of frequency (which is usually what happens with such threats). A child uses his "indoor" voice to address his mother, after which his mother comments, "Thank you for remembering to use your indoor voice." If the child in later situations uses his "indoor" voice to address his mother, the approval from the mother can be identified as a reward or reinforcer because the behavior that precedes it increases in frequency or is maintained.

Presentation of
Unpleasant Consequences

Some behavior is often followed by the *presentation* of *unpleasant* consequences, either tangible or intangible. Such unpleasant consequences include loud noises, frowns, pain, and verbal criticism. If the frequency of the behavior that precedes these unpleasant consequences *decreases* or if the behavior *stops* altogether, the unpleasant consequence is called a *punisher* and the process of presenting such unpleasant consequences following these behaviors is *punishment*. If a young child touches a hot iron, that behavior is followed by pain, an unpleasant consequence. The likelihood that the child will reach for an iron in the near future is doubtful. That is, the frequency of the behavior (reaching for the hot iron) preceding the unpleasant consequence (physical pain) will decrease in frequency and perhaps even stop altogether (depending on the child's age and the length of his memory for pain). Punishment has some important side effects and implications, which will be discussed later. The test of whether or not the presentation of an unpleasant consequence is a punisher is to look at the future frequency of that behavior.

Removal of Pleasant Consequences

Some behavior is followed by the *removal* of a *pleasant* consequence, either tangible or intangible. The removal of pleasant consequences includes removal of certain privileges—food, money, prized possessions, and so forth. If the frequency of the behavior that precedes such removal of pleasant consequences *decreases* in frequency or *stops* altogether, that consequence is also called a *punisher*. The process of applying the consequence is called *punishment*. For instance, a member of the family who usually arrives late for dinner has his TV privileges taken away for a week. If TV privileges are important to him, his late behavior may decrease and even disappear. If this happens, the consequence of removing his TV privileges is called a punisher. Again, the simple test of whether or not the removal of a pleasant consequence is a punisher is to observe the frequency of the undesirable behavior. If the behavior decreases or stops altogether, the consequence is called a punisher.

Removal of Unpleasant Consequences

Some behavior is followed by the *removal* of *unpleasant* consequences, either tangible or intangible. The removal of unpleasant consequences includes the termination of threats and criticism, loss of pain, increasing the temperature in a cold room, and so forth. If the frequency of the behavior that precedes the removal of unpleasant consequences tends to increase in frequency, the removal of such consequences is called a *negative reinforcer* ("negative" because something was removed). However, to avoid the confusion between punishment and negative reinforcement, it is easier simply to call such consequences *reinforcers* because they tend to increase the frequency of the behavior that precedes them. An example would be a child cleaning up his room or putting away his toys to stop the scolding he is receiving from his mother. The consequence of cleaning the room or picking up the toys is the absence of scolding. Some children will increase the frequency of such behavior to remove unpleasant consequences. However, it is risky to assume that children will engage in appropriate behavior simply to avoid unpleasant consequences, especially if such unpleasant consequences take the form of verbal disapproval from adults. Verbal disapproval is a form of adult attention and the *presentation* of such disapproval may actually increase inappropriate behavior. The removal of the unpleasant consequences probably should be considered the last resort when attempting to change a child's behavior.

Withholding Any Kind
of a Consequence

Behavior can be followed by neutral consequences, which essentially are no consequences at all. In such cases useful consequences are neither presented nor removed. Any noticeable kind of consequence is simply *withheld*. Technically, there is always some type of consequence following a behavior, even if it is a minor change in the movement of air around an individual; such consequences are considered neutral because they are virtually unnoticed by the individual.

If noticeable, useful consequences are *withheld* following a behavior, especially pleasant ones, that behavior often tends to *decrease* in frequency. *Ignoring* behavior is the most frequent form of withholding a consequence. If the behavior in question decreases in frequency or stops altogether following continued withholding of pleasant consequences, that result is called *extinction* of behavior. For example, if a child uses naughty words in the presence of his mother and is ignored by his mother rather than receiving the expected scolding or threat (noticeable consequences that typically maintain such behavior), the behavior eventually will decrease in frequency.* Thus the withholding of any consequences is said to have extinguished the behavior.

Table 6-1 summarizes these five consequences of behavior.

*Behavior that is followed by neutral or extinguishing consequences tends to get worse before it gets better. Implications of extinction are discussed on pages 181–182.

Table 6–1.   Behavior and its consequences.

Description of the consequence	Name of the consequence	Effect on the preceding behavior
presentation of a pleasant consequence	reward or (positive) reinforcer	increases
presentation of an unpleasant consequence	punisher (by hurt)	decreases
removal of a pleasant consequence	punisher (by loss)	decreases
removal of an unpleasant consequence	(negative) reinforcer	increases
withholding of all consequences	extinction	decreases

Here are some exercises to help you assess your learning about behavior and its consequences.

---

1. Write the *description* of each category of behavioral consequences below:

    (a) _____

    (b) _____

    (c) _____

    (d) _____

    (e) _____

You were correct if you wrote the following:

(a)   presentation of a pleasant consequence
(b)   presentation of an unpleasant consequence
(c)   removal of a pleasant consequence
(d)   removal of an unpleasant consequence
(e)   withholding of all consequences

2.   In each space provided, write the *name* of the behavioral consequence described:

(a)   presentation of a pleasant consequence.

_____

(b)   presentation of an unpleasant consequence.

_____

(c)   removal of a pleasant consequence.

_____

(d)   removal of an unpleasant consequence.

_____

(e)   withholding of all consequences.

_____

You were correct if you wrote the following:

(a)   reward or (positive) reinforcer
(b)   punisher (by hurt)
(c)   punisher (by loss)
(d)   (negative) reinforcer
(e)   extinction

3. For each consequence listed below, write the results in frequency of the behavior that precedes that consequence:

   (a) reward or (positive) reinforcer_____
   (b) punisher (by hurt)_____
   (c) punisher (by loss)_____
   (d) (negative) reinforcer_____
   (e) extinction_____

   You were correct if you wrote the following:

   (a) increases
   (b) decreases
   (c) decreases
   (d) increases
   (e) decreases

4. Fill in the blank:

   Consequences determine the _____ of the behavior that precedes them.

   You were correct if you wrote: frequency.

5. Fill in the blank:

   The simple test of a reinforcer is to look at the _____ of the behavior it follows.

   Again, you were correct if you wrote: frequency.

6. A child uses his "indoor" voice to address his mother, after which his mother comments, "Thank you for remembering to use your indoor voice."

    (a) What was the consequence in this episode?
    (b) What would be the probable result in the future frequency of the child's behavior?

    You were correct if you wrote:

    (a) The mother's comment to the child was the consequence.
    (b) The child's use of his "indoor" voice will probably increase in frequency.

7. Write the name of each of the following consequences:

    (a) removal of privileges _____
    (b) ignoring a naughty word _____
    (c) a smile _____
    (d) pain _____
    (e) loss of pain _____
    (f) termination of a threat_____
    (g) loud noises _____

The above consequences would be named as follows because of the effect they usually have on the behavior that precedes them:

(a) punisher (preceding behavior will probably decrease in frequency as the result of the removal of pleasant consequences)

(b) extinction (preceding behavior will probably decrease in frequency as the result of withholding useful consequences)

(c) (positive) reinforcer or reward (preceding behavior will probably increase in frequency as the result of the presentation of a pleasant consequence)

(d) punisher (preceding behavior will probably decrease in frequency as a result of the presentation of unpleasant consequences)

(e) (negative) reinforcer (preceding behavior will probably increase in frequency as the result of the removal of unpleasant consequences)

(f) (negative) reinforcer (preceding behavior will probably increase in frequency as the result of the removal of unpleasant consequences)

(g) punisher (preceding behavior will probably decrease in frequency because of the presentation of an unpleasant consequence)

8. Write in each space provided specific consequences in your own
    life that fit each of the following categories:

    (a)   presentation of pleasant consequences:

    _____

    _____

    (b)   presentation of unpleasant consequences:

    _____

    _____

    (c)   removal of pleasant consequences:

    _____

    _____

    (d)   removal of unpleasant consequences:

    _____

    _____

    (e)   withholding of all consequences:

    _____

    _____

9. Write in each space provided specific consequences in the life of a typical prekindergarten child that fit each of the following categories:

    (a)   presentation of pleasant consequences:

    _____

    (b)   presentation of unpleasant consequences:

    _____

    (c)   removal of pleasant consequences:

    _____

    (d)   removal of unpleasant consequences:

    _____

    (e)   withholding of all consequences:

    _____

GUIDELINES FOR CHANGING BEHAVIOR

A very simple but important principle can be inferred from the preceding discussion of behavior and its consequences. *If you wish to change a child's behavior, you must change the relationship between the behavior and its consequences so that desirable behavior is rewarded (or reinforced) and undesirable behavior is not rewarded.* The two consequences of behavior that will aid you most in changing a child's behavior are *presentation of pleasant consequences (reinforcement)* and *withholding pleasant consequences (extinction).* The following guidelines will help you determine what behavior to change and how to change it.

1.   Before you can change behavior, *the behavior must be defined in specific and observable terms,* rather than in general and unobservable terms. For example, defining a child's behavior as "aggressive toward others" will not help you determine what behavior to reward and what behavior not to reward because "aggressive toward others" is too vague. If the aggressive child's behavior can be made specific and observable, such as "physically attacks other children" or "takes objects away from other children," then a plan can be developed to reward the more appropriate and desirable behavior and to eliminate rewards for the inappropriate and undesirable behavior.

Teachers normally wish to maintain in high frequency child behavior that contributes to pleasant interpersonal relationships in the classroom and indicates the child is growing in intellectual ability and physical skills. Some examples of this kind of behavior are: offers to assist other children who need help; asks questions of other children; answers questions asked by the teacher; follows simple directions from the teacher ("Put a napkin by each glass on the table"); looks at books when they are available and asks questions about them; participates in group movement experiences and tries new skills with his body; takes his turn on outdoor equipment when several children wish to use it at the same time; talks enthusiastically with peers who are engaged in the same activity; successfully completes each task during small group sessions in such content areas as language, music, movement, and art; asks for help when he needs it; and so on.

Examples of specific behavior that teachers wish to reduce in frequency and eliminate altogether are: verbally threatening other children; physically attacking other children; taking objects away from others; engaging in activities alone; crying; refusal to try new movement activities; refusal to use outside play equipment; constantly standing or sitting near a teacher, touching a teacher, requesting praise or approval from a teacher, or talking exclusively to the teacher; leaving a task uncompleted; yelling or screaming in the classroom; complaining; and so forth.

    Decisions about behavior that should be increased or decreased in frequency are based on the attitudes and values of the person responsible for making those decisions, such as the teacher or the parent. This concept of value judgment related to instructional behavior decisions is discussed later in the chapter.

    2. Once the behavior has been defined in specific, observable terms, you can then *count the number of times the behavior occurs and determine the usual consequences of the behavior observed.* It is easy to brand a child *aggressive* because he's "always hitting other children." However, the term *always* may be a generalization that is unsupported by the evidence. Highly visible and disruptive behavior, such as hitting other children, can be so distasteful that teachers become blind to other behavior in the child's repertoire that may be very desirable and appropriate. By counting how often a specific behavior occurs you can get some idea of how often the behavior occurs and under what circumstances it occurs.

    An easy procedure for counting behavior is to indicate on a time chart every occurrence of the behavior. For example, every ten seconds a check can be made if the child being observed engaged in the behavior during that segment of time. Figure 6–1 is a 12-minute record of Carla's crying in the prekindergarten one morning three days after she had entered the class for the first time. Each box represents ten seconds. Each block of six boxes represents one minute. During this 12-minute period, Carla cried 10.5 minutes. Just as important as a count of Carla's crying behavior, however, are the consequences of her crying. Each circle around an X indicates some form of attention from the teacher or the teaching assistant. This attention consisted of such teacher behavior as looking at the child, putting her arms around the crying child, or verbally attempting to attract the child's attention to one of the activities in the nursery school. At least one form of teacher attention was noted for each continuous segment of Carla's crying. The results of observation showed that Carla spent a high percentage of her time in nursery school crying (over 90%) and that this crying was resulting in a high incidence of teacher attention. Pleasant

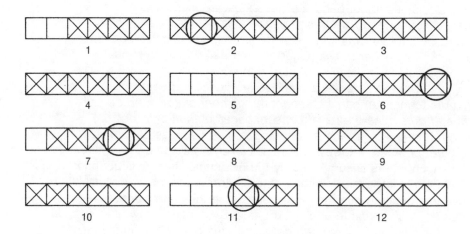

Figure 6–1.   Counting behavior. A 12-minute record of Carla's (age 3) crying in the prekindergarten. Each box represents 10 seconds. Each block of six boxes represents one minute. An X in the box indicates crying took place during that 10-second interval. A circle around an X indicates some form of teacher attention.

consequences occurred four times during crying episodes in the 12-minute period whereas no pleasant consequences occurred during the noncrying episodes. In other words, noncrying behavior was never reinforced.

Counting and recording behavior can take the complete attention of the person doing the counting. So if you are going to spend part or all of a class period counting and recording a child's behavior, someone will need to fill in for you. Better still, an assistant such as a volunteer or student trainee could be trained to do the counting and recording of the behavior inasmush as *your* behavior may be contributing to the maintenance of the child's behavior and, therefore, should be recorded as it occurs naturally related to the child's behavior. A stop watch or watch with a second hand is necessary for such observation. Elaborations of this system of counting behavior have been developed by Bijou and his colleagues (1969).

3.   When you know the specific behavior you wish to change and how often it occurs, you are ready to *change the consequences of the behavior. If you wish the behavior to increase in frequency, you reward or reinforce it. If you wish it to decrease in frequency, you prevent rewarding or reinforcing consequences from occurring following the behavior.*

4.   It is easy to get caught in the trap of looking only for the undesirable behavior in a child. If a child is engaging in inappropriate behavior, the better plan is to *reinforce behavior that is appropriate and desirable and ignore behavior that is not appropriate.* In other words, ignoring undesirable behavior is important but usually doesn't decrease inappropriate behavior unless desirable behavior is being rewarded as well. Desirable behavior should replace undesirable behavior. For example, Carla's crying can be ignored and at the same time any noncrying behavior can be rewarded, such as Carla's quietly looking at what another group of children is doing or looking at a book or listening to a story with the other children. Hart and her associates (1964) describe a similar case. Brad's disruptive behavior can be ignored, but any time he converses with a child without disrupting the play or participates cooperatively in a music experience, he can be rewarded. Jennifer can be ignored when playing alone but can be reinforced whenever she makes any kind of approach to other children, even if it is simply standing quietly nearby to observe them. Allen and associates (1964) describe a case similar to Jennifer's. Emphasis preferably is on the rewarding or reinforcing of desirable and appropriate behaviors.

5.   *The best way to determine if a consequence is a punisher or extinguisher or a reinforcer is to note how often over a period of time the behavior occurs following the consequence.* If Carla's crying eventually decreases and stops when ignored, ignoring her crying behavior is an extinguisher. If Jennifer's approaches to other children increase when she is given attention and approval for doing so, attention and approval can be considered reinforcers for Jennifer. Behavior does not immediately decrease or increase in frequency as the result of certain consequences. It is necessary to

observe the occurrence of behavior over a period of time before determining the nature of particular consequences.

6. *Often a consequence that a teacher assumes is unpleasant and therefore punishing is really a reinforcer.* For instance, verbal criticism of Brad when he attacks children or disrupts ongoing activities will probably result in increased frequency of his inappropriate behaviors. In such a case, verbal criticism turns out to be a reinforcer rather than a punisher, even though the crtiicism is thought to be the presentation of an unpleasant consequence. Verbal criticism is frequently used by adults in the sincere belief that the application of such unpleasant consequences will decrease the frequency of a particular behavior. Often adults fail to realize that their criticism of a child is really a means of relieving fear, anger, frustration, or guilt on the part of the adult. But often this "unpleasant consequence" is really a "pleasant consequence" to the child. It is a form of adult attention. Any form of adult attention is highly rewarding to most children. Remember, it is the individual child who determines his own reinforcers, not his teacher.

7. *A consequence that is reinforcing to one child may not have the same effect for another child.* Each child is unique in the particular consequences that are rewarding and punishing for him; no two children have exactly the same sets of reinforcers. For example, adult silence is a form of reward to some children who are frequently criticized by adults (Crandall, 1963; Crandall, Good, & Crandall, 1964). Silence is interpreted by the child as a form of assent or permission (for example, "If Mom isn't saying anything, I guess it's all right"). Yet some children (probably most children) consider silence on the part of an adult a form of disapproval or dissent. This is possibly one reason why consistently ignoring undesirable behavior is often effective in decreasing the frequency of the behavior.

8. *Some reinforcers are more reinforcing than others.* Each person has his own hierarchy of reinforcers, with the ones he likes most at the top of the list and the less effective ones at the bottom of the list. For instance, a pat on the back may be more rewarding to some individual children than being verbally praised for something they have done well. Older children and adults usually know their own reinforcement hierarchies. However, with prekindergarten children it is usually a matter of careful observation to

determine what each child's reinforcers might be. Your effectiveness as a teacher depends largely on how well you know each child's most effective reinforcers and how you dispense these reinforcers. Knowing that adult attention is reinforcing to a child isn't enough. You will be more effective if you know which form of adult attention is reinforcing, such as smiling at the child, telling the child you like something he did, putting your arms around the child, or standing near the child. To most children, however, each of these forms of adult attention is reinforcing.

9. *There are three convenient categories of reinforcers* (Tharp & Wetzel, 1969): *(1) activity reinforcers* (such as riding a tricycle); *(2) material or tangible reinforcers* (candy or trinkets); *(3) people or affective reinforcers* (a teacher giving praise, a child putting his arm around another). When teaching new behavior, material or tangible reinforcers are usually most effective in maintaining the desired behavior, especially when helping children with learning disabilities. For example, Lovaas and his associates (1966) use food such as sugared cereal to teach beginning speech to autistic children. They are careful, however, to pair the presentation of the food with verbal praise and physical affection from the therapist when the child makes an appropriate speech sound. Eventually the tangible rewards can be dropped because the verbal praise and physical affection become strongly reinforcing to these children.

To the average prekindergarten child, people or affective reinforcers are highly reinforcing. Simple verbal praise or a touch on the hand are enough to maintain desired behavior. In a study designed to test the effectiveness of two different methods of training on various cognitive skills (such as language and reading) in prekindergarten children, some of my colleagues used M & Ms as initial reinforcements for correct responses by the children. At the same time, they gave verbal praise such as "very good," "that's correct," "good thinking." They discovered that verbal praise was sufficient reinforcement for these children, even when learning new skills. Incidentally, if you decide you wish to use tangible rewards to teach some behavior, be certain that *each* child in the group has the same opportunity as any other child to receive similar rewards for specific appropriate behavior. Remember, the reward, regardless of its kind, must always be made contingent on appropriate behavior—that is, reward or reinforcement must *always* be preceded by the specified appropriate behavior. No cheating or you end up cheating the child in the long run!

For most children, engaging in certain kinds of activities is highly rewarding. Working a puzzle, riding the seesaw, swinging in the swing, digging in the sandpile, drawing at the easel, and other desired activities can be used as reinforcers for other appropriate but less probable behavior. More about this in the next guideline.

These three kinds of reinforcers—activity, tangible or material, people or affective—are often interrelated. For example, a "people" is usually attached to the presentation of a tangible reward and the reward is seldom given without some type of verbalization. Activities are seldom engaged in alone and usually involve something tangible, such as a shovel, a paint brush, a puzzle, or a book, even though these tangibles may not be consumable in the same way an M & M would be.

10. *For any given pair of responses, the more probable response can be used to reinforce the less probable response.* This is known as the Premack principle (Premack, 1965). This means that any behavior can be used as a reinforcer for any other behavior that has a lower probability of occurring. Children often receive instructions from their parents to "Eat your spinach" (less probable response) "and then you can have dessert" (more probable response) or "Practice the piano" (less probable response) "and then you can play outdoors" (more probable response).

An adaptation of the Premack principle is the use of the "reinforcement menu" (Daley, 1969). This can be effective in a prekindergarten class where the teacher has listed a "menu" of high probability behaviors, such as talking to a friend, coloring, drawing at the easel, looking at a book, listening to a record, hugging someone, dancing, walking, drawing on the chalkboard, working a puzzle, jumping, drinking water out of the fountain, singing, and looking out the window. The menu can be posted on a large chart in the reinforcement area of the room. Each activity listed on the menu is represented by a simple ink-line drawing of the activity. The child looks at the menu before starting a task to be learned and is allowed to select an activity from the menu. On completion of the task, the child returns to the reinforcement area where his selection is made available for him immediately. After a specified time at the activity, the child selects another activity (or the same one again), then returns to a learning task, completes it, and returns for the reinforcement he has selected. This procedure can be followed during the entire class period. It can be used with small groups of children as well as with individual children. This program is a particularly effective one when learning tasks are made explicit and when they take into consideration the child's length of task attention before reinforcement is required. The length of time between reinforcements should be short to begin with and then gradually lengthened. Many prekindergarten children have learned to attend a learning task for as long as 30 minutes at a time using the "reinforcement menu." An effective reinforcement period for prekindergarten children following low probability behavior is about two minutes.

11. *When a new behavior is being taught, that behavior should be reinforced every time it occurs.* For instance, Jennifer can be ignored and receive no adult attention while playing alone in the prekindergarten. However, *every time* she plays in the same area with other children she should be reinforced (if "playing with other children" is the desired behavior). Brad can be ignored when he is "stirring up trouble" but should receive a reinforcer *each time* he engages in some form of cooperative or nondisruptive play. Carla's crying can be ignored and reinforcement given *each time* she quietly watches or participates in a group activity.

12. *As a new behavior becomes consistent in its increased or desired frequency, reinforcement following that behavior can be presented less frequently.* Any behavior must receive *some* reinforcement if its frequency is to be maintained. However, once a behavior is learned, intermittent (occasional) reinforcement is necessary to maintain the behavior at the desired level of frequency. After Jennifer has learned to spend most of her class time in activities involving other children, reinforcement can be withdrawn gradually until only occasional reinforcement is given for such desirable activity. After Brad learns to spend his class time in cooperative social activities or other nondisruptive activities, his reinforcement can occur only once in a while to maintain his new behavior. Carla, once she has learned to be involved in activities with the other children, can be reinforced intermittently only. Children gradually can learn to wait longer before being reinforced for appropriate behavior. Thus they begin to learn delay of gratification and self-control.

13. *Reward (or punishment) is most effective when it immediately follows the act.* When Carla stops crying, she should receive reinforcement *immediately,* not at some other more convenient time for the teacher. Jennifer's social activity should be reinforced as soon as it begins. If you wait beyond the moment the appropriate response occurs to present the reward, the reward is likely to be related to a response *other* than the one you wish to reinforce. After all, humans are engaged in one activity after another. Most child behavior occurs in short intervals rather than long intervals; "strike when the iron is hot" applies to reinforcement.

Although our emphasis here is on teaching desired behavior, a common example relating to punishment might be helpful. Perhaps you have heard a distraught mother threaten her recalcitrant child with something like, "You just wait until your father gets home and he'll spank the tar out of you!" When Dad gets home from work, he receives the wifely complaint, "I can't do a thing with that child. I told him you would take care of the matter." Dad finds the child quietly and attentively at work on a design with his erector set. Dad, being a dutiful husband who wants to keep peace in the family, spanks his child who had erred earlier in the day. Possibly he guiltily confesses as he lays on the hands, "This is hurting me more than it's hurting you." The child runs into his room, slams the door, and howls his head off. Two days later he does the same thing he was spanked for two days before. The mother had great faith that the corporal punishment conferred by the father would hurt enough to stop the undesirable behavior in her child. The father, though perhaps less fervently, has the same sincere faith in the results of the dire consequences. But the behavior didn't stop. Why? The point is the punishment occurred long after the undesirable act had occurred. What's worse, the punishment occurred immediately following a *desirable activity.* Therefore, if the spanking was punishing at all, the act that probably decreased in frequency was the *desirable* one! (See p. 183 for further implications of punishment.)

14. *When giving positive reinforcement, it is wise to avoid overdoing the reinforcement. Otherwise, the reinforcement may backfire.* For example, if a teacher walked up to Brad while he was engaged in cooperative activity with another child and said, "I'm glad you're playing so well with other children now," Brad would probably revert to his old pattern of disruptive behavior.

Low-keyed, inconspicuous reinforcement is adequate to maintain the desired behavior. Conspicuous, overdone reinforcement tends to call more attention to the inappropriate behavior than to the desirable behavior (Vance, 1969; Varenhorst, 1969).

15. *When a new behavior is being taught, reinforcement should occur when an approximation of that behavior has occurred. Gradually, reinforcement then can be given for closer approximations of the desired behavior.* This principle is called *shaping.* An example of this is a child's learning to talk. When the child begins to make sounds like "ma-ma" ("mother"?), he is reinforced with all kinds of verbal praise and hugs and kisses from his adoring parents. At first the child is very indiscriminate in his use of those two sounds. He uses them with Daddy, Mommy, brother, sister, Grandma, Grandpa, the neighbor, or anyone else who happens to be standing near his crib. The results are the same: adoring smiles and verbal praise. Gradually, as the newness and excitement of the "word" wear off, baby gets reinforced only for saying the word in the presence of Mommy and Daddy. Still later, he is rewarded only when the sounds are *clearly* "mama" and mean only the person who *is* his "mama."

Jennifer's playing alone probably will not shift into full-scale activity with other children until she has taken some in-between steps and has been rewarded for them. Perhaps a first step for Jennifer simply will be watching a group of children at play. As her observing behavior becomes more frequent, the rewards then can be given only for physical approaches to the area where other children are engaged in activity. Then she can be rewarded for engaging in the same activity as the other children, though not saying anything to them. Eventually she can be rewarded only when she talks to children near her or gives them assistance. In similar fashion, Allen and her colleagues (1964) trained a prekindergarten child whose typical behavior pattern was isolate behavior to engage in frequent social activities with her peer group in the prekindergarten.

16. *When teaching new behavior to children, set up situations where the desired behavior can occur.* The situation should be of a nature that the child can experience *frequent* success with the behavior. Setting up a situation where a desired behavior can occur is called *prompting, priming,* or *pacing.*

Children will play together only if equipment and materials are available that "invite" them to play together cooperatively. Most prekindergartens have enough blocks, puzzles, books, records, art materials, domestic play equipment, and outdoor play equipment to allow several children at a time to engage in the same activity. Activity centers should be of sufficient variety and interest to attract even the most shy children. Children respond to attractive colors, pleasant sounds (and lack of noise), comfortable "child-size" equipment, a physical environment of order with a place for everything, and room in which to appropriately use the learning materials available.

One problem with a totally "free-play" environment is that some children, if not all, miss out on the opportunity for *systematic, consistent success experience*—that is, the opportunity to engage in desired behavior followed by frequent reinforcement. Directed learning situations can be rewarding to children and help them increase their sense of competence and self-worth ("I can do well; therefore, I am good"). Let's examine the case of Mark.

Four-year-old Mark was seated at a small table with four other children engaged in a counting game with their teacher. The teacher placed objects such as block cubes, toy fruits, and colored plastic shapes in groups of various numbers and asked each child to count the number of items in each group. Not once in all his counting attempts did Mark count the correct number. The four other children were more successful than Mark. Finally, Mark refused to count when asked by his teacher and started to poke the child next to him. That child poked Mark back. Then the two began to laugh. The teacher suggested that Mark find something else to do in another part of the room and leave the children in the group alone to finish their counting game. Mark wandered off to briefly observe two or three other groups of children. Then he stopped in the block corner, quickly built a block tower, knocked it down, and left the blocks for someone else to put away.

Obviously Mark was not having a successful experience with counting. The situation apparently had not been set up with Mark's problem in mind, nor had a method been planned to help him succeed (no assessment of preinstructional behavior). Mark did what could be expected of any child in a similar frustrating situation: he tried

something he *could* be reinforced for doing—that is, he poked the child next to him and started a disruptive scene that was followed by teacher attention (some form of attention is better than none!). Mark was instructed to leave the group, where he then wandered aimlessly before half-heartedly engaging in block play. It is probably safe to say that Mark's disruptive behavior will increase in frequency unless the situation changes.

But what could the teacher have done? The objective of the lesson in the group apparently was that each child would count correctly the number of objects in a given set of objects when asked by the teacher. In this instance, each time Mark was asked to count the number of objects indicated by the teacher, he was given a different set and number of objects from those used by the other children. Therefore, Mark didn't have any opportunity to hear and see the correct answer to his questions before he was asked the question. Mark's first incorrect answer could have given the teacher the clue to his problem. She then could have asked the *same* question of another child whom she knew could give the correct answer, and then immediately have returned to Mark again with the same question. Mark, having just heard the correct answer and seen the appropriate way to count the items, could then have given a correct answer. If the correct answer then could have been followed by verbal praise, such as "Good counting, Mark" or "You are correct," Mark would have been more likely to try an answer again, paying attention to the correct examples being provided for him. It might have been necessary to begin by giving Mark encouragement simply for *attempting* an answer, such as "Good try, Mark. Allen, can you help him?" (See guideline 15.) When we know a child is guessing and we don't show him the appropriate responses or allow him to practice them, we are failing the child. Mark's problem is one of poor teaching. Mark can be a good learner if his teacher provides him with many opportunities for success experiences through adequate prompting, priming, or pacing.

The following exercises will help you assess how well you understand the guidelines for changing behavior.

---

10. Before you can change behavior, the behavior must be stated in specific and observable terms. Which of the following statements specifies observable behavior?

     (a) aggressive toward others
     (b) takes objects away from other children

- -

     (b) is correct because it states a specific, observable behavior. The behavior described as "aggressive" in (a) is stated in an abstract, general way; it is, therefore, impossible to determine what to change.

---

11. By _____ how often a behavior occurs,
    you can get some idea of how often the behavior occurs
    and under what _____ it occurs.

---

counting
circumstances

---

12. Observe a prekindergarten child and select a behavior
    that seems typical for that child that is observable and
    countable. Using a stop watch, count the occurrence of
    the behavior in a 20-minute period using 10-second
    intervals for recording (see guideline 2). Count how often
    the behavior occurred in that 20-minute period.
       After performing this exercise, write your reactions to
    the experience, including what went well and what you
    would change to make this a more successful experience.

---

13. Once you know the specific behavior you wish to change
    and how often it occurs, you are ready to change the
    _____ of the behavior.

---

consequences

---

14. If you wish the behavior to increase in frequency, you
    _____ it. If you wish it to decrease in
    frequency, you prevent _____
    _____ from occurring following the behavior.

---

reward or reinforce
rewarding or reinforcing consequences

15. _____ behavior that is correct or appropriate and
desirable and _____ behavior that is not correct,
appropriate, or desirable.

reinforce
ignore

16. Carla's crying behavior should be _____
while her noncrying behavior should be _____.

ignored
reinforced

17. The best way to determine if a consequence is a punisher, an
extinguisher, or a reinforcer is to

_____

_____ .

note how often over a period of time the behavior occurs following
the consequence.

18. If Jennifer's approaches to other children increase when she is
given attention and approval for doing so, attention and approval
can be considered _____ for Jennifer.

reinforcers

_____

19. Often a consequence generally considered to be
     unpleasant, and therefore, punishing is really a
     _____.
- -

reinforcer

_____

20. Though both of the following consequences are
     considered unpleasant and, therefore, punishing, which
     one is more likely to be a reinforcer for many
     prekindergarten children?

     (a) verbal criticism
     (b) sudden pain after touching a hot stove
- -

     (a) is more likely to be a reinforcer because it is a form
          of attention.

_____

21. A consequence that is reinforcing to one child may not
     _____ for another child.
- -

have the same effect

_____

22. Adult silence is a form of_____
     to some children who are frequently criticized by adults.
- -

reward or reinforcement

_____

23. Each person has his own _____
    of reinforcers, with the ones he likes most at the top of the
    list and the less effective ones at the bottom of the list.

---

hierarchy

---

24. Name the three convenient categories of reinforcers:

    (a) _____

    (b) _____

    (c) _____

    (a) activity reinforcers
    (b) material or tangible reinforcers
    (c) people or affective reinforcers

---

25. For each of the reinforcers in the list, indicate whether it is
    (a) an activity reinforcer; (b) a material or tangible
    reinforcer; or (c) a people or affective reinforcer:

    _____1. "that's correct"
    _____2. drawing at the easel
    _____3. physical affection
    _____4. food
    _____5. trinkets
    _____6. riding a tricycle

---

    1. (c)   4. (b)
    2. (a)   5. (b)
    3. (c)   6. (a)

26. For any given pair of responses, the _____ probable response can be used to reinforce the _____ probable response.

   ---

   more
   less

27. In the following instruction to a child by his mother, which is (a) the more probable response and which is (b) the less probable response?

   "Eat one more bite of peas, and then you can eat more hamburger."
   (a) *more probable:*
   (b) *less probable:*

   (a) *more probable:* "Eat more hamburger"
   (b) *less probable:* "Eat one more bite of peas"

28. The "reinforcement menu" consists of _____ probability behaviors in children.

   ---

   high

29. When a new behavior is being taught, that behavior should be reinforced _____
   _____.

   ---

   immediately, every time it occurs

30. As a new behavior becomes consistent in its increased or desired frequency, reinforcement following that behavior can be presented _____ frequently.

   less

31. Intermittent reinforcement means that behavior is reinforced:

   _____(a) every time it occurs
   _____(b) occasionally

   (b)

32. Intermittent reinforcement (is/is not) necessary to maintain a behavior at the desired level of frequency.

   is

33. Reward (or punishment) is most effective when it _____ follows the act.

   immediately

34. When a new behavior is being taught, reinforcement should occur when _____ of that behavior has occurred.

an approximation

35. Setting up a situation where a desired behavior can occur is called _____, _____, or _____.

---

prompting, priming, pacing

36. Discuss in class or with your fellow teachers at least one example drawn from your own experience to illustrate each of the 16 guidelines in this section.

37. Discuss in class or with your fellow teachers at least one example in the lives of prekindergarten children to illustrate each of the 16 guidelines in this section.

Extinction

It's important to be aware of some probable side effects and limitations of extinction (the elimination of a behavior by ignoring or not reinforcing it). A side effect that teachers are usually unprepared for is the often sudden increase in the frequency of the behavior they wish to extinguish when extinction procedures are begun. There is a simple explanation for this increase in the frequency of the undesired behavior. Whenever an expected consequence of our behavior is not forthcoming, we try even harder to get that expected consequence. Sometimes we keep on trying hard for quite a while before our trials begin to drop off. If our expectations are unfulfilled over a long enough period of time we abandon the behavior entirely (*note:* the number of trials to extinction differs for each individual).

Another possible side effect of extinction procedures is *highly emotional behavior* in the child. He may whine, cry, tease, and even go into tantrums when expected consequences of his behavior do not occur. It is just such emotional behavior that frequently convinces parents and teachers that they are using the wrong procedures with a child. So the usual result, unfortunately, is a return to the old way of doing things, often reinforcing the child for inappropriate behavior. It often takes a good bit of intestinal fortitude to stick consistently to the extinction procedure; regardless of the provocation, ignore the behavior.

It is also important to recognize that *the more inconsistently a behavior has been reinforced, the longer it will take to extinguish that behavior.* If a behavior is intermittently reinforced on some sort of random basis, which is the typical reinforcement pattern for most human behavior, it is maintained at a strongly consistent level and is difficult to extinguish. It is possible that patience will not outlast the undesirable behavior.

Closely related to this point is the fact that a positive reinforcer, no matter how accidental, will prolong the occurrence of the behavior that is the focus of extinction. Williams (1959) describes the case of a young child whose tantrum behavior at bedtime was extinguished by his parents only to have his grandmother enter the picture, provide positive reinforcement for tantrum behavior, and necessitate starting the procedure all over again. Incidentally, behavior may be extinguished in one setting but occur in another setting as the child tests out other possible sources of reinforcement. This is one reason why some children may behave in a different way in prekindergarten than they do at home.

Because of the side effects and limitations of extinction, it is wise to *use extinction only in combination with positive reinforcement of appropriate alternative behaviors to that being extinguished.* While Carla's crying, Brad's disruptive behavior, and Jennifer's isolate behavior are being ignored, desirable alternate behaviors should be reinforced immediately and often (see guideline 4). This allows us to teach appropriate and desirable behavior and lessens the focus on undesirable behavior. As a matter of fact, extinction *works* more often if it is combined with the teaching of desirable behavior.

Punishment

Punishment, like extinction, has its side effects and limitations. The following are general conclusions about punishment you may wish to take into consideration before you use punishment as a teaching technique:

1.   As a general rule, punishment should be used only in emergency situations *when behavior must be stopped quickly.* For example, a young child reaching up to touch a hot stove has his hands slapped hard as Mommy shouts, "No, no!"

2.   Punishment usually must be *severe* in order to be effective in stopping behavior. People not prepared to be severe had better not use punishment *at all.* They may reinforce the behavior they mean to stop.

3.   The effects of physical punishment, if it has been painful at all, tend to last beyond the point of punishment and, therefore, *may generalize to appropriate behavior* as well.

4.   *Punishment does not teach new and more desirable behavior.*

5.   The child who is punished may develop *fear responses toward the person who punishes him.* This person may, thus, lose his reinforcing qualities.

6.   *Punished behavior is likely to pop up again when the punisher is not around.* For example, children may say "naughty words" to each other when the punishing parent or teacher is not nearby.

Social Imitation and Modeling

Any discussion of principles of behavior change would be incomplete without a description of the principle of social imitation and modeling. The role of example in shaping behavior has been recognized for centuries.

Bandura and Walters (1963) assert that *rapid* development of behavior is often a result of the child or adult imitating what he has seen others doing. Largely because of studies during the past decade, there are several generalizations about social imitation and modeling that can be suggested.

       A child tends to imitate those people who control his rewards. A child's parents usually control more of his rewards than anyone else. But other people become important to the child as he grows older because of their role in providing his rewards. His prekindergarten teacher can become one of these important people. If you observe the child as he talks and acts, you will soon discover who his most important social models are. The child usually gives his own unique imaginative twist to something he has heard someone say or seen them do, but often to the amusement or embarrassment of an observing adult such imitation is an exact replication of what was heard and seen.

       A child tends to imitate the behavior of those whom he sees receive rewards for their behavior. Children are constantly observing what is going on around them. If they see others being rewarded for certain behavior, they tend to engage in the same behavior, even if the behavior is inappropriate. A child who sees other children in the prekindergarten getting rewards for such actions as asking questions, following instructions, talking with other children, or attempting to solve problems will tend to engage in those same acts.

       A child tends to imitate behavior that is distinct and stands out from other behaviors. Our attention tends toward the most stimulating parts of our environment. If a person shouts in a room where everyone else is talking in a normal tone of voice, our attention is drawn to the shouting voice because it stands out above the others. We notice the brightest or most contrasting colors on a person or in a room. We notice two children fighting with one another rather than engaging in the quieter activities in the classroom. A child also notices the behavior that stands out in a class or in the neighborhood or at home. He tends to imitate the behavior that stands out above the others. Perhaps this explains why children often imitate aggressive behavior they see in their daily surroundings, including television, more frequently than other less distinct behaviors. There is a challenge here for parents and teachers, who are models for children, to make certain the desirable behavior they wish children to imitate stands out or is distinct in nature.

The child tends to perform adult behavior he sees performed consistently.   A parent or teacher who wishes a child to use words such as *please* and *thank you,* to eat everything on his plate, to close the door quietly, to share possessions with others, and to help other children who need assistance should consistently model these behaviors himself.

If there is inconsistency between what an important person tells a child and what he actually does, the child will tend to imitate the action rather than the telling.   Too many adults tell a child to do something but turn around and do what they have just told the child not to do. A parent tells a child he can't have a piece of cake before he goes to bed; then the parent has a piece of cake after the child has gone to bed. A child is told to use his voice instead of his hands when he is angry with someone; then a parent spanks that same child when the child does something inappropriate. Parents and teachers tell children to "look for the good" in the other person and yet verbally criticize someone for doing something wrong. If children see inconsistencies in what we tell them and what we actually do, they will tend to imitate what we do, not what we say.

A child tends to imitate more frequently if he is reinforced for imitating.

SOME LINGERING QUESTIONS

Up to this point we have discussed some principles of behavior change that are based largely on mechanical repetition and probably do not require the child's permission or conscious recognition in order to be effective. These are universal principles and include each one of us as we learn and grow and develop higher and more complex forms of behavior. At this point, two questions may arise. First, aren't these principles, if effectively used, manipulative and underhanded? Second, how can we take into account the individual's feelings and his ability to use language and control his own behavior?

Let's begin by tackling the first question about the possibility that the use of such principles may be manipulative and underhanded. It is important to recognize that the principles of behavior change do not comprise a value system. They are simply a set of principles that exist. These principles do not stipulate the specific behavior that should be taught. Society does that. The values of a particular society and culture, to a large degree, dictate the desired behavior. We do not ask the child's permission to teach him social skills, to control his wants when they conflict with those of others, to explore and be curious about his environment, to grow up free from race or religious prejudice. As teachers, we are prepared to teach certain behavior. These principles of behavior change are simply *tools* that can be employed to bring about desired changes in behavior.

The idea that the behavior of an individual can be controlled and manipulated by other individuals is so abhorrent to some people that they can't even think about it. Such people ignore the fact that such principles are part of their everyday lives. They assume that people in positions of power use these principles for evil purposes only. However, the use of such principles for purposes of good or evil is entirely in the hands of the individual and society. Labeling these principles of behavior change *underhanded* or *manipulative* does not change their nature or whether or not they operate in everyday life. The fact remains that everyone uses these very principles to influence the lives of those around him daily, usually without knowing it.

Let's turn now to the second question about *feelings, one's use of language, and self-control.* Certainly one prized goal of both parents and teachers is to help the child learn to control his own behavior. Mommy, Daddy, teacher, or some other authority figure cannot always be nearby to tell a child what to do and to provide the appropriate reinforcement at just the right moment. The younger the child, the less he is able to understand reasons for things. Therefore, parents and teachers and other adults must make all the decisions regarding the control of his behavior. As he grows older, has more experience, and develops a greater understanding of language, he can be told reasons for things. He can be told why he is receiving certain reinforcers. He can be told what the consequences of various behavior will be. Thus he can begin to make his own choices and learn to accept the responsibility for his own actions. He can be aided in planning his own behavior and its consequences, but he needs to experience considerable control from adults until he has learned the necessary social lessons. The more opportunity the child has to verbalize and consistently experience the consequences of his actions and to make choices based on his knowledge of these consequences, the better able he will be to take control of his own behavior.

And now let's turn to feelings. The feeling side of life is a very important aspect of learning that is often ignored in our planning for teaching. Let's examine some ideas related to feelings.

First, every behavior a person engages in has a feeling attached to it. A child who has just finished what his teacher has instructed or who has just given an appropriate response in a problem-solving situation probably feels a sense of accomplishment. The crying child probably is feeling lonely and frightened and bewildered. The child who hits another child probably is feeling angry. There are many kinds of feelings and they are always related to behavior of some kind.

The child who can verbally identify the nature of his present feeling at any given moment is in a position to select behavior that will result in desirable feelings, such as feeling happy, worthwhile, affectionate, and so forth. However, the young child needs help identifying his feelings because of his inadequacy with language, Therefore, it is important that you frequently verbalize to a child how he might be feeling in any given situation. For example, you can say to the child who has entered prekindergarten skipping enthusiastically with a big smile on his face, "Jimmy, you act as though you are feeling so happy." To the child who is hitting another child because that child took the block he was using you can say something like, "I know you're feeling very angry with Tommy because he took your block. I can't let you hit him. But you can tell him you're feeling very angry with him and that you want the block back." The teacher labels the feeling and acts as a model of the appropriate way to deal with the feeling. Much problem behavior in young children stems from the fact they don't know how to verbalize their feelings, particularly strong feelings. When children learn to identify their feelings, they then can learn to identify behavior that will help develop desirable feelings.

Adults can help children handle their feelings appropriately if they first accept the child's feeling for what it is. Telling a child that he should or shouldn't feel a certain way or denying the child's label for his feeling doesn't change the nature of the feeling. Strong feelings are not unusual in young children, and the undesirable ones can get out of hand because the child has too little verbal skill to recognize the feeling for what it is. Condemning a child for his feelings often leads to frustration behavior, added guilt feelings, and denial by the child of his own feelings. If we help the child verbally identify his feeling in a nonjudgmental manner, we then can find out if he wants to change the feeling and help him look at some alternative actions that could help him feel the way he would like to feel. A child will not find it necessary to act out undesirable feelings (or deny them) if he is helped to recognize them and to find appropriate ways to deal with them.

SUMMARY

Behavior is your basic source of information. The effectiveness of your teaching is measured by the desired behavior change that occurs in the children you teach. Behavior changes according to the consequences that follow it. Desirable behavior can be taught by setting up situations where such behavior can occur and following that behavior with rewards or reinforcement. At the same time, inappropriate or undesirable behavior can be ignored. Guidelines related to these principles have been discussed.

REFERENCES

Allen, K. E., Hart, B., Buell, J. S., Harris, F. R., & Wolf, M. M. Effects of social reinforcement on isolate behavior of a nursery school child. *Child Development,* 1964, **35,** 511–518.

Bandura, A., & Walters, R. H. *Social learning and personality development.* New York: Holt, Rinehart and Winston, 1963.

Bijou, S. W., Peterson, R. F., Harris, F. R., Allen, E., & Johnston, M. S. Methodology for experimental studies of young children in natural settings. *The Psychological Record,* 1969, **19,** 177–210.

Crandall, V. C. The reinforcement effects of adult reactions and nonreactions on children's achievement expectations. *Child Development,* 1963, **34,** 335–354.

Crandall, V. C., Good, S., & Crandall, V. The reinforcement effects of adult reactions and nonreactions on children's achievement expectations: A replication study. *Child Development,* 1964, **35**(2).

Daley, M. F. The "reinforcement menu": Finding effective reinforcers. In J. D. Krumboltz & C. E. Thoresen (Eds.), *Behavioral counseling: Cases and techniques.* New York: Holt, Rinehart and Winston, 1969. Pp. 42–45.

Hart, B. H., Allen, K., Buell, J. S., Harris, F. R., & Wolf, M. M. Effects of social reinforcement on operant crying. *Journal of Experimental Child Psychology,* 1964, **1,** 145–153.

Lovaas, O. I., Berberich, J. P., Perloff, B. F., & Schaeffer, B. Acquisition of imitative speech by schizophrenic children. *Science,* 1966, **161,** 705–707.

Premack, D. Reinforcement theory. In D. Levine (Ed.), *Nebraska symposium on motivation.* Lincoln: University of Nebraska Press, 1965. Pp. 123–188.

Tharp, R. G., & Wetzel, R. J. *Behavior modification in the natural environment.* New York: Academic Press, 1969.

Vance, B. J. Modifying hyperactive and aggressive behavior. In J. D. Krumboltz & C. E. Thoresen (Eds.), *Behavioral counseling: Cases and techniques.* New York: Holt, Rinehart & Winston, 1969. Pp. 30–33.

Varenhorst, B. B. Reinforcement that backfired. In J. D. Krumboltz & C. E. Thoresen (Eds.), *Behavioral counseling: Cases and techniques.* New York: Holt, Rinehart & Winston, 1969. Pp. 49–51.

Williams, C. D. The elimination of tantrum behaviors by extinction procedures. *Journal of Abnormal and Social Psychology,* 1959, **59,** 269.

Chapter 7

Evaluating Outcomes of Instruction

Instructional design is not complete until you have evaluated the outcomes of your instruction. First, it is important that you evaluate the lesson you have planned before you attempt to instruct the children. Second, you should find out if the prekindergarten children you instructed have learned what you planned they would learn.

EVALUATING THE LESSON PLAN

At this point in the book you have read instructions related to and have practiced the following steps in instructional design: determining the focus of instruction, determining instructional objectives, assessing preinstructional behavior, determining learning activities, and determining reinforcement procedures. You may not feel like an expert, but you have the necessary resources to check out the stops in the instructional design process.

For any given lesson you plan, you now should be able to evaluate what its weaknesses and strengths are and to make desired revisions before you actually use the lesson in an instructional period with the children. The checklist in Table 7–1 has been prepared for you as a convenient method of checking the instructional suitability of any lesson. The checklist is a summary of the major ideas related to each of the steps in the instructional design process. (Note that reinforcement procedures are included under the heading "Learning activities.")

Table 7–1. Checklist for instructional design evaluation.

I. The focus of instruction
_____1. The content area of the curriculum has been determined.
_____2. The specific subdivision (subject) of a particular content area has been determined.
_____3. The subdivision (subject) of focus is logically related to the one used in a previous lesson plan.

II. Instructional objectives
_____1. Each objective states a desired, specific, observable behavior.
_____2. Each objective states the conditions or circumstances under which the behavior is expected to be performed.
_____3. Each objective includes a statement of how well the child is expected to perform.
_____4. The type or classification of a given objective has been identified (single neuromuscular response, motor-sequence, complex-skill, naming, serial-memory, component-memory, concept-learning, rule-learning, or problem-solving).

III. Assessment of preinstructional behavior
_____1. Provision has been made in the lesson for review of the previous lesson's behavioral objective(s) in that same content area of the curriculum.
_____2. Provision has been made at the beginning of the lesson to assess how well the children perform the new objective(s).
_____3. Behavior characteristics of each child in the class have been determined by (a) studying the principles of child development, and (b) determining the unique behavior patterns of each child in the group through observation, conversation with the child, and discussions with parents and others who know the child.

IV. Learning activities

_____1.   An appropriate *show* step has been planned for each objective wherein provision is made for each child to see, hear, touch, taste, and/or smell through (a) direct contact with actual objects, people, places, or events (firsthand experience) or (b) vicarious or simulated experience as close as possible to the real object, people, places, or events.

_____2.   An appropriate *discuss* step has been planned, related to each show step, in which provision is made for each child (a) to put into words his thoughts and feelings about the show step; (b) to respond to questions requiring recall as well as reason, judgment or problem solution, or imagination; and (c) to practice the desired behavior.

_____3.   An appropriate *apply* step has been planned to determine how well a child can perform a given objective.

_____4.   Provision has been made to *reinforce* desired behavior in each child.
   (a)   Provision has been made to reward desired behavior with verbal or tangible reinforcers.
   (b)   Provision has been made to reward desired behavior *immediately.*
   (c)   Provision has been made to reinforce behavior that approximates the desired behavior when the desired behavior is being learned for the first time.
   (d)   Situations have been planned where the desired behavior can occur often and be reinforced often.

V. Evaluation of outcomes of instruction

_____1.   An appropriate test has been planned to evaluate whether or not a specific desired behavior has been learned related to a given type of behavior (single neuromuscular response, motor-sequence, complex-skill, naming, serial-memory, component-memory, concept-learning, rule-learning, problem-solving).

_____2.   Periodic tests have been planned that appropriately sample previous behavioral objectives in a given content area of the curriculum.

EVALUATING INSTRUCTION

The words *test, achievement,* and *evaluation* often have an unpleasant connotation for teachers of prekindergarten children. This may be due to the common idea that testing means subjecting the child to a long battery of verbal and/or written exercises to find out how "smart" he is in relationship to other children his same age and grade level. Such tests are heavily weighted with cognitive-behavior requirements. This is called *norm-referenced* testing or evaluation because the child's performance is compared to that of the other children in his same age group. Children soon get caught in a competitive struggle with their peers when such evaluation takes place.

Contrasted with the norm-referenced test is the *criterion-referenced* test. With criterion-referenced testing, the word *test* should be looked upon as any attempt on the part of the child to demonstrate a desired behavior. The child's present performance is compared with his own past performance. Competition with others can be reduced because the successful performance of a desired behavior is not dependent on how well the rest of the children in the group perform. When a child "achieves" in a criterion-referenced test, it means he has accomplished the specific, observable, desired behavior that was asked for in the lesson plans.

There are three basic and simple ways to evaluate the performance of prekindergarten children. The first, a type of posttest, occurs during the apply step of the instructional period. This learning activity is for the purpose of allowing each child to demonstrate how well he has learned a desired instructional objective. If each child can demonstrate the desired level of performance, you can move on to the next lesson in the series. If one or more children cannot demonstrate the desired objective, you need to re-evaluate that particular lesson in terms of the steps in the instructional design outlined in the preceding chapters and summarized in Table 7–1. You might ask yourself such questions as the following:

Does the child have the prerequisite behavior for this particular objective?

What were his responses to the instructional materials during the show and discuss steps? Did he use more than one of his senses to explore the materials? Did he talk about his interpretations and feelings related to the materials? Did he practice the desired behavior along with the other children?

Did he respond eagerly and voluntarily during the lesson or did he act withdrawn or bored?

Did he receive any reinforcement for appropriate behavior during the lesson? If so, what kind and how often?

Did I do most of the talking?

Did I feel prepared enough to give the lesson without reference to the lesson plan?

The answers to these questions can help you determine how to help any individual child achieve the desired objective. You may need to revise the lesson plan and teach it again.

The second way to evaluate the performance of the children you teach, also a posttest, is to review the apply steps from the preceding lesson before beginning the new lesson. That is, you provide a review session at the beginning of each instructional period in each of the areas of the curriculum each day. For example, if you teach a naming and a serial-memory objective in music on Tuesday, you should test how well the children do these objectives on Wednesday before you teach a new music objective, such as a concept-learning objective. A child who can perform the desired behavior immediately following practice may forget how to do that behavior the following day because of the effects of interference by intervening experiences. If a child is unable to do an objective the following day, he can be given additional learning experiences to help him accomplish the objective. Remember that learning is a fairly permanent change in behavior that occurs in spite of intervening experiences.

A third way to evaluate the outcomes of instruction is to provide periodic posttests in each area of the curriculum. These posttests should be made up of a wide sampling of desired behavioral objectives taught since the last posttest in a given area of the curriculum. You may wish to give such a posttest every fifth day, tenth day, or fifteenth day of instruction. For example, you could give a posttest every fifteenth day in music and every tenth day in reading. You may wish to spend an entire instructional period of 15 minutes on a given day administering a posttest to review behavioral objectives that you have taught in one area of the curriculum since the last posttest. In other words, on the day a posttest is scheduled in music, no new music objectives will be taught. It's a good idea to space the posttests in each content area to avoid the possibility of spending an entire day on posttests in each area of the curriculum.

Posttests can include a variety of types of behavior. This means you can have such combinations as a complex-skill, a naming, a serial-memory, a concept-learning, and a problem-solving objective in the same subtest. Be sure, however, when you plan tests of complex cognitive behavior (concept learning, rule learning, problem solving), that you use examples that were not used during the instructional process. Otherwise you will be testing memory, not complex cognitive behavior.

A simple record-keeping method for posttests is illustrated in Table 7–2. Make several copies of this form with spaces to fill in the name of the content area of the curriculum, subtopic focus, and behavioral objective. Include space for each learning group's number or identification symbol, dates tested, and names of the children in each group (grouping the names of the girls together and the names of the boys together helps you determine immediately if there are sex differences in performance). A separate form can be filled out for each behavioral objective taught. The symbol X has been used to indicate the child accomplished the objective on a given date. The symbol O indicates the child did not accomplish the objective on a given date. You may wish to use other coded symbols such as + and −. Such a chart is a simple way for you to evaluate each child's progress and determine the need for further posttests.

You may wonder what to do if a child is unable to do all the items in a posttest. The answer is the same regardless of when evaluation occurs: teach the child the behavior again. The purpose of

Table 7–2.   Sample behavioral objective posttest record.

File No. 3.2.2. Obj. No. 4

Content area of the curriculum: Living in a world of people
Subtopic focus: Rooms in a home
Behavioral objective: When shown a model of a home he has never seen before, each child will be able to correctly point to the kitchen, the bedrooms, the bathroom, the living room, and the dining room (Concept learning).

Group 1

Dates tested	Ann	Linda	Michele	David	Ronald	Joel	Comments
1/15	X	X	O	X.	O	X	
1/16	X.	X	X	O	O	X	
1/26	X	X	X	X	X	X	
2/10	X	X	X	X	X	X	

Group 2

Dates tested	Bonnie	Robin	Jane	Wally	Les	Joe	Comments
1/15	X	X	X	X	X	X	
1/16	X	X	O	X	X	X	
1/26	X	X	O	X	X	X	
2/10	X	X	X	X	X	X	

Group 3

Dates tested	Colleen	Ellen	Shauna	Nathan	Frank	George	Comments
1/15	X	X	O	X	X	O	
1/16	X	O	X	X	O	X	
1/26	X	O	X	X	O	X	
2/10	X	X	X	X	X	X	

instruction is to change behavior. If the child is unable to perform a desired objective, instruction has not been successful. You may need to revise a lesson or possibly go back to some earlier lessons. Perhaps you will need to plan some additional new lessons related to specific objectives in a given content area.

Periodic posttests will help you determine how to group the children in your class for instruction. Any child can learn. However, no two children in the same class have the same *rate* of learning. Some children learn quickly whereas others need more time to learn the same things. Posttests will help you determine which children learn at approximately the same rate so you can group them according to rate or speed of learning. Such grouping means the learning activities will be less likely to bore some children in a group while stimulating others. However, groups need not remain the same all year. The rate of learning for any given child will vary from week to week and month to month. In addition, the rate may vary from one content area to another. Posttests can help you determine when and how to change groups. (Additional information on how to group children is found in Chapter 8.)

Evaluation should occur throughout the entire instructional-design process as well as during each instructional period each day in the prekindergarten. A simple rule to follow is "a little bit of instruction, a little bit of evaluation."

---

1. This chapter discusses three basic kinds of evaluation.
   Name them:

   (a) _____

   (b) _____

   (c) _____

You should have written something like this:

(a) evaluation of the lesson plan before you teach it
(b) evaluation of how well each child performs desired objectives following instruction
(c) evaluation of how well each child performs desired objectives preceding instruction

2. The checklist in Table 7–1 is designed to help you:

_____(a) evaluate a lesson plan before you teach it
_____(b) evaluate child performance following instruction

(a) is correct

3. A criterion-referenced test:

(a) compares the child's performance with the performance of other children his same age
(b) compares the child's present performance with his own past performance
(c) is an intelligence test
(d) both (a) and (c)

(b) is correct

4. Name the three basic ways to evaluate the outcomes of instruction:

   (a) _____

   _____

   (b) _____

   _____

   (c) _____

   _____

   (a) test how well the children perform the objective during the apply step of the instructional period
   (b) review the apply steps from the preceding lesson before beginning the new lesson
   (c) provide periodic posttests in each area of the curriculum

5. A periodic posttest:
   (a) can include several types of behavioral objectives from the same content area of the curriculum
   (b) should include a wide sample of behavioral objectives taught since the last posttest
   (c) should be about 15 minutes in length
   (d) can help you determine how to group children in your class for instruction
   (e) all of these
   (f) both (a) and (d)

   (e) is correct

SUMMARY

The focus of the preceding chapters has been instructional design in the prekindergarten. Instruction is a process based on the principles of learning. By now you should have some basic skills related to this process.

Part 2 of the book focuses on curriculum. Curriculum is the content used in instructional design. In other words, instructional design is the "how" and the curriculum is the "what."

Part 2

The Prekindergarten Curriculum

Chapter 8

The Prekindergarten Curriculum: Basic Guidelines

At this point you are probably saying, "That's all fine and good, but *what* do I teach?" In other words, you may want some specific help in each of the content areas of the prekindergarten curriculum. The focus of this second part of the book is the content of the curriculum. Part 1 was the "how." Part 2 is the "what." This chapter will provide basic guidelines related to the prekindergarten curriculum. Chapters 9 through 16 will furnish information on the individual content areas of the curriculum.

CONTENT AREAS OF THE PREKINDERGARTEN CURRICULUM

Each content area of the curriculum has been organized in a logical sequence for use in teaching prekindergarten children. If you use the steps you have practiced in Chapters 2 through 7, these topics can help you plan the instructional design. The topical outlines for each content area, found at the end of each chapter, also can aid you in planning lessons in appropriate, small-step-by-small-step sequences.

The content areas of the prekindergarten curriculum, in alphabetical order, are as follows:

Graphic arts
Health and safety
Living in a world of people
Mathematics
Movement: The child's natural language
Music: The universal language
Our world
Reading

The content area *living in a world of people* is similar in content to that known as the social sciences in the elementary curriculum. The *movement* area of the curriculum has some relationship to physical education and dance but, as discussed in this text, has unique characteristics that precede traditional physical education, and other movement curricula. There are two separate content areas of the prekindergarten curriculum that are related to the fine arts—*graphic arts* and *music. Our world,* on the other hand, is related to the physical and biological sciences.

It is recommended that daily lesson plans be prepared in *each* of the content areas with the possible exception of *reading, mathematics,* and *health and safety.* Some teachers prefer to develop lesson plans in reading or mathematics or health and safety so that they can be taught less frequently. One satisfactory plan is to have mathematics one day, reading the next, health and safety the third, and then start the sequence over again.

The lesson plan should not be too long or too short. A lesson plan that takes about 15 minutes to teach has been found most successful. In this time period children have an opportunity to learn at least one concept or idea. Fifteen minutes is short enough that children in a group can have a great variety of learning experiences in other content areas of the curriculum as well. A sample lesson plan designed for a 15-minute presentation is included at the end of each of the chapters that follow.

THE DAILY SCHEDULE

Table 8–1 is a suggested daily schedule for a typical prekindergarten day of 2½ hours. Such a prekindergarten would have a head teacher and two teacher aides or one head teacher, one teacher aid, and one prekindergarten teaching intern from a nearby college or university. A prekindergarten group of 16 to 20 children would be divided into three groups of five to seven children each. The head teacher and each of the aides would teach one of the three groups during each 15-minute period, after which the children would rotate to the next group. That is, three groups would be going on at the same time. At a given signal, such as that of a cooking timer, the groups would rotate.

Table 8–1.   A daily schedule.

1 hr.	15 min.	Free choice
	15 min.	Graphic arts
	15 min.	Living in a world of people
	15 min.	Movement
1 hr.	15 min.	Math, reading, or health and safety
	15 min.	Snack
	15 min.	Story or sharing time
	15 min.	Our world
½ hr.	15 min.	Music
	15 min.	Free choice

Assign children to groups at random to begin with, mixing girls and boys, until you find out how the children work in the groups. Then you can change the groups according to the best working combinations you can organize. Children are best assigned to groups according to their learning rate, not IQ or some other test score—that is, children should be grouped according to how quickly they progress. This means that those who progress at a slower rate will not be pushed by those who learn at a faster rate. The faster ones, in turn, will not get bored.*

Groups can be assigned a color that can be used on a symbol chart to help the children learn the order of activities for their particular group. A symbol can be devised on the chart for each area of the curriculum, such as a palette and paint brush for graphic arts; a boy and a girl for living in a world of people; a child jumping over an object for movement; some math symbols, letters of the alphabet, and a toothbrush for math, reading, health and safety; some birds and flowers for our world; and a musical instrument for music. These symbols could be placed on the chart in different colors for each group and according to the sequence of daily lessons for each group as illustrated in Figure 8–1.

It is suggested that the children select activities in any one of several learning centers during the free-choice periods. One learning center could have manipulative learning games, another could have well-chosen children's books that are frequently rotated; another could have a record player and a small selection of frequently rotated records and a few musical instruments; another a carefully selected group of unit blocks and wheel toys; and another a domestic area with child-size cupboards, sink, table and chairs, dress-up clothes, dolls, doll bed, broom and mop, and so forth.

Behavior is being acquired during free-choice time as well as during the directed learning activities in each content area. Free-choice time is an ideal time to observe and count various types of social peer interaction. It is just as important to plan behavioral objectives for the free-choice period as it is to plan objectives for directed learning periods. These objectives could revolve around interaction skills such as how to enter a group of children who are already involved in a play situation, how to ask for help, how to give help, how to tell someone you like or don't like what he is doing, how to convince someone to try your ideas, or how to take someone's suggestion about how to do something. This means that learning centers could be set up that would invite peer interaction. For example, there should be enough chairs and table space so that more than one child can engage in the same activity. There

*This method of group assignment is discussed on p. 198.

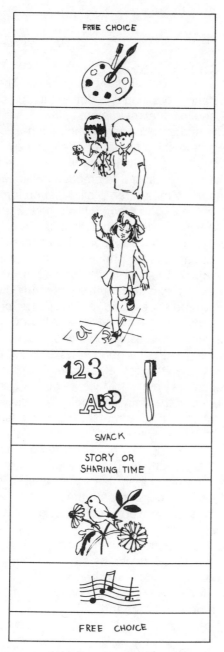

Figure 8–1. Daily schedule symbol chart.

should be several wheel toys and blocks in the block corner. There should be more than one set of clothes and more than one doll in the domestic corner. There should be more than one musical instrument in the music corner. As you count behavior in individual children during free-choice time, it will become apparent which social interaction skills need to be learned by individual children. You then can plan learning activities during this time to help individual children learn the desired social interaction skills. Free-choice time is not synonymous with free time or free play. Most children can engage in free play at home and in the neighborhood. Free-choice time provides opportunities to choose learning activities and to learn important social interaction skills needed in a densely populated society.

It is important that children in the prekindergarten have a simple snack in the middle of their school day. This snack should be high in protein, vitamins, and minerals (for example, cheese, milk, fresh fruit juices, celery, carrot sticks, peanut butter, apple slices) and low in sugars, or "empty calories" (such as cookies, crackers, cakes, pastries, soda pop). In addition to proper nutrition, snack time also provides experiences in conversation, sharing body skills (like pouring juice), and other good ways of living together.

Children enjoy a favorite story for relaxation—one that is not necessarily related to a lesson plan but is told just to be enjoyed. Therefore a story period has been included in the daily schedule. These stories can be children's books, flannelboard stories, or dramatizations. Occasionally, such as once a week or once every three days, the children in each group can share with the rest of the children something they have learned during the past few days in one of the areas of the curriculum. This helps the children to develop the ability to "do" and "say" in front of their peers and reinforces individual lesson experiences. The head teacher can plan these "sharing times" in advance so that a variety of lesson concepts and ideas can be presented from a variety of curriculum areas.

If the children are in a prekindergarten group that has longer hours, such as a day-care center, the schedule can be adjusted to fit the longer hours. More free-choice periods can be interspersed between planned lessons in the content areas, periods for outdoor play can be scheduled, and a lunch period as well as a rest or nap period can be added.

The suggested daily schedule is for the typical prekindergarten designed to supplement the home. The suggested curriculum is one that could not be provided in the average home and neighborhood. Long periods of free play are characteristic of children at home, out of school. A repetition of this same routine in the prekindergarten with peers does not seem a wise expenditure of time, effort, and money.

HELPS FOR LEARNING ACTIVITIES

You will recall that the steps in the instructional design process include determining the focus of the lesson, planning the instructional objectives, assessing preinstructional behavior, and then planning the learning activities related to the focus of the lesson and the instructional objectives. The learning activities consist of show, discuss, and apply steps. It is important that you learn to use a variety of learning activities suitable for these steps.

Media or Instructional Aids

Ideally a show step should be direct contact (a firsthand experience) with the real object, person, place, or event. When the real thing is not available, try to find something that comes as close to the real thing as possible. That is, if you are teaching a lesson on animals in the zoo, you could arrange for a visit to a real zoo where the children can see, possibly touch, hear, and smell the animals and their homes. But if a real zoo is not within traveling distance, you can provide a three-dimensional model of a zoo using toy animals and blocks and possibly some sand or dirt for the ground and branches for trees and shrubbery. You are using media whether you are providing a firsthand experience or a vicarious experience by means of a scale model. By the way, if a firsthand experience is not available, it might be a good idea to consider dropping a lesson on that topic.

Often teachers associate the words *media* and *instructional aids* with films, slides, overhead transparencies, and the hardware to display them, or pictures, flannelboards, flannel figures, chalkboards, chalk, and erasers. It is true that each of these items falls into the category of media or instructional aids. However, these are far down the list of vicarious experiences, especially for prekindergarten children. There are other more effective media. Use the world around you to provide firsthand experiences and effective vicarious experiences for the children in the prekindergarten.

How to select appropriate media for a given behavioral objective is a challenging topic that is too broad for coverage in this book. You may wish to look at a booklet by Merrill and Goodman (1971), which outlines teaching strategies and selection of media related to most of the 12 categories in Table 3–1 on page 43. Their booklet is oriented toward the older child and young adult. However, the same principles are applicable to your teaching in the prekindergarten.

Language Development

You may have noticed that there is no separate area of the curriculum in this book entitled language development, contrary to many other curriculum patterns for the prekindergarten. The child is developing his knowledge of and ability to use language in *every* area of the curriculum. For example, the child can learn concepts of color, shape, form, and quantity in the *graphic arts;* labels for occupations, kinds of money, and various behaviors of people in *living in a world of people;* concepts of spatial relationship, direction, level, speed, and bodily skills in *movement;* labels for sensory phenomena, biological and physical processes in *our world;* and concepts of rhythm, melody, dynamics, and tone quality in *music. Reading* and *mathematics* are basically language curricula.

Many prekindergarten children have trouble with prepositions such as *on, beside, at the side of, above, below, in between;* polar opposites such as *high-low, tall-short, fat-skinny, long-short, loud-soft;* plurals such as *men, leaves, dresses, knives;* and pronouns such as *his, its, ours, yours, theirs.* Be sure that each child understands the meaning of these terms before you use them in questions, directions, stories, and so on.

Questions

The various types of questions that can be used when conducting discussions with prekindergarten children are discussed in Chapter 5. Question-asking is an effective means of obtaining verbal or motor responses from the children. Don't expect responses to questions to be lengthy, especially from 3-year-olds. You can expect a high frequency of one-word replies.

Young children have a tendency to give answers that seem irrelevant, but don't be misled. Their "irrelevant" responses often indicate a misunderstanding of the question or the best answer the child can give with his present vocabulary and degree of experience. All too often a teacher asks the children a question and then fails to listen to the reply. In many cases—if not most cases—better discussions would occur in groups of prekindergarten children if the teacher listened and responded to the replies of the children.

Role-Playing and Pantomime

Role-playing includes both speech and action when the child plays the role of someone other than himself, such as a parent, a younger or older child, a community helper, a doctor, and so on. When the child demonstrates a concept or an idea or even plays the role of another person by action only, he is *pantomiming.* No words are used. Pantomime and role-playing are effective learning activities as either show or apply steps; they are subdivisions of the movement curriculum that are suitable in each of the content areas of the prekindergarten curriculum.

Pantomime and role-playing are typical patterns in the free play of young children. These form the "pretend" areas of the child's play. It is through these "pretend" activities (and others) that abstract concepts may become concrete. For instance, a group of children had been discussing birthdays. One young child told of his recent birthday party. The teacher asked the child who was at the party, what happened at the party, what food was served at the party, and other questions that helped to form a picture of what the party was like. After the child had told the class all about it, the teacher asked the children if they would like to "pretend" the same birthday party. She helped each child choose who he was going to be at the party (someone new played the role of the guest of honor) and decide what he was going to do at the party. A very few props were used, such as some dishes from the play cupboard, some napkins used at snacktime, and a multicolored box for cake. The children acted out their parts in the pretend party, encouraged by carefully selected questions from the teacher such as, "Then what did Billy do?" "Who brought in the cake?" "And then what happened?" After the short role-playing session, the teacher asked each child what he felt like at the party and how he thought the child who was having the birthday felt. Thus, through movement and some speech, an abstract event became more concrete to a group of 3-year-olds. In addition, such a learning activity totally involved each child.

The possibilities of role-playing and pantomime are endless. Although they are effective in each area of the curriculum, they are particularly effective in the content area *living in a world of people*.

Children's Literature and Storytelling

Children can have the opportunity to enjoy a book or story for its own sake. For this reason, provision is made in the daily schedule for storytelling. However, books and stories can be effective show steps in any area of the curriculum.

There are excellent children's books available to reinforce concepts in every area of the curriculum. Guidance for the selection of such books can be found in texts such as Pitcher, Lasher, Feinberg, and Hammond (1966), Hildebrand (1971), Taylor (1970), and Todd and Heffernan (1964) and in periodicals such as *Horn Book* and *Saturday Review*.

Stories also can be told using flannelboard figures, stand-up figures, pictures, and three-dimensional objects. Stories can be those written by someone else or those written by the teacher. It is important that the story be well illustrated, told or dramatized in an unhurried fashion and in words the children understand, and told in such a manner that the teacher has eye contact with the children.

Stories and books can be effective secondary experiences after the child has had a firsthand experience with a concept or an idea, but they should not be used to introduce a concept or an idea.

When reading a book or telling a story during a lesson presentation, give the children something to look for, such as, "Listen carefully because I'm going to ask you _____ later." When the story is finished, ask the children some questions about the story, particularly questions that relate to the lesson concept or idea. This question technique can be overdone, however. For example, I probably would not ask questions following a story told during story and sharing time.

Graphic Arts

A special area in the prekindergarten curriculum is reserved for the graphic arts, with the focus on the exploration and use of various art media. However, objectives in other curricular areas can also be demonstrated through graphic arts activities. For example, an objective in a lesson about birds might be that each child will draw with crayons or paint with tempera paint his idea of a bird. Objectives from other content areas of the curriculum can be correlated to art activities so that the graphic arts curriculum one day can be set up to accomplish the objective in another area of the curriculum. Such objectives are referred to earlier in the book as expressive objectives.

Songs

Singing is a music skill that can be learned during lessons in the music area. This, however, does not mean that songs should be sung exclusively during music time. Songs are appropriate learning activities in other areas of the curriculum. Suggestions for using songs in learning activities other than music are discussed in Chapter 14.

REFERENCES

Hildebrand, V. *Introduction to early childhood education.* New York: Macmillan, 1971.

Merrill, M. D., & Goodman, R. I. *Selecting instructional strategies and media: A place to begin.* Instructional Development Institute, National Special Media Institutes, 1971.

Pitcher, E. G., Lasher, M. G., Feinburg, S. G., & Hammond, N. C. *Helping young children learn.* Columbus, Ohio: Merrill, 1966.

Taylor, B. J. *A child goes forth.* (2nd ed.) Provo, Utah: Brigham Young University Press, 1970.

Todd, V. E., & Heffernan, H. *The years before school.* New York: Macmillan, 1964.

Chapter 9

Graphic Arts

The narrator in *The Little Prince* (de Saint-Exupery, 1943) reports an experience at age 6 when he became intrigued by the fact that some snakes swallow their prey whole. He attempted to draw his concept of such a phenomenon that ended up looking like this:*

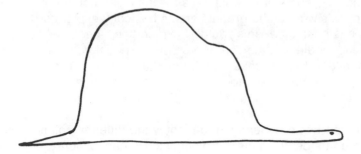

Adults said it was obviously a hat. So the young artist was forced to explain that it was a picture of a boa constrictor who had swallowed an elephant. He then drew a picture of the inside of the boa constrictor in

*Reproduced by permission of the publisher from *The Little Prince* by Antoine de Saint Exupery, copyright 1943, 1971, by Harcourt Brace Jovanovich, Inc.

order for grown-ups to understand what the picture was all about. Finally he was advised to stick to subjects people could understand, such as geography and history. The would-be artist thereafter confined his efforts to those things people could understand because grown-ups "always need to have things explained."

Grown-ups are sometimes paradoxical in their attitudes about the graphic arts. They believe that in graphic arts an individual can find a natural means of creative expression. On the other hand, creative expression must be an understandable product. That is, the goal must be to *produce something*.

There are two basic problems presented by such grown-up logic when we consider the work of young children in the graphic arts. First, creativity in the graphic arts is a result of the knowledge of and ability to use the elements of art and the various art media. The elements and media of art can thus be combined in novel and clever combinations. But an individual who does not have this knowledge and skill with a variety of alternatives is limited in his ability to create. Therefore, young children need an opportunity to learn about the elements of art and the various art media. This means that much if not most of a young child's work in the graphic arts is basically exploratory.

Perhaps it is best to call this "guided exploration," because the teacher provides the media and the verbal prompts and reinforcements that motivate the child to try out ideas with the media, to discover the properties of the media, and to talk about his ideas and feelings. Otherwise exploration by the child may be simply "going through the motions."

The child can begin by learning to identify the different colors and shapes and then to identify their combinations. He can explore ways of combining them. He can identify and use the various media of the graphic arts, exploring what his body can make the media do and what kinds of feelings and ideas he can express with each medium.

This brings up the second problem of the grown-up view of graphic arts. When a child is exploring with elements of art and the media used for their expression, he is not necessarily producing "something." *The process takes precedence over any product.* The process is basically exploratory in nature. The child may label his explorations, but these labels can be very fluid, starting as a horse, then becoming a river, then becoming the sky, depending on how the medium looks to the child as his body makes changes in that medium. Or the child will label what he is doing because he has learned that labels please adults immensely.

Even when a child makes a conscious attempt at making "something" in one or more art media, we must remember that children perceive the world around them very differently from adults. They also have less body control than an adult. Therefore, even when their art productions are made to "represent" something, that something may be quite different from that expected by an adult. The 6-year-old's drawing illustrated at the beginning of this chapter is one child's perception of an abstract concept. The representation of that perception in the drawing shows good body control because the contours of the "snake" and the "elephant" are basically those that could be expected if such a phenomenon actually existed. The average prekindergarten child could come up with the same concept of the elephant-snake phenomenon but represent it in media with a simple line interrupted by a hump, such as this:

In other words, the prekindergarten child may not have the body control or skill that would allow him to include the artistic detail of the 6-year-old artist. Nevertheless, he may recognize that his art work can *represent* something he has perceived or conceptualized. Thus a 5-year-old could say in the wisdom of childhood, "Drawing is easy; you just think your thought and draw your think!" (Pitcher et al., 1966).

THE ROLE OF THE PREKINDERGARTEN
TEACHER IN THE GRAPHIC ARTS

There are two basic areas of the graphic arts curriculum in the prekindergarten—the elements of art and art media. These are outlined on page 237. The purpose of the graphic arts curriculum is to teach the child to understand and to use the elements of art and the art media singly and in all of their possible combinations.

It is very easy for a prekindergarten teacher to carefully prepare the clay and put a lump at each place at a table, mix the paints and put them at the easel with some paper, or prepare the fingerpaint and set it in the middle of the table without helping the children understand what the substance is and what its possibilities for use are. Then the children simply choose to dabble in any one of these media. The teacher thus becomes a maintainer of rules ("Keep the fingerpaint on the table" or "Keep the brush in its own color") or a busy supplier as children ask for more of this, a different color of that, and so forth. It is true that rules must be maintained to avoid chaos, and children need materials if they are to learn ideas and skills and feelings in the graphic arts. But "teaching" involves much more than this.

Graphic arts is a language curriculum as well as a skills curriculum. In other words, children can be given the opportunity to identify colors, shapes, the art media, what they are doing with them, and how they think and feel about what they are going to do or what they are doing. For example, before the children start a fingerpainting experience, the teacher can help them identify the materials such as the fingerpaint and the fingerpaint paper. He can ask questions such as, "What colors of fingerpaint are on the table? What is the fingerpaint made of? What do you think it feels like? What do we use it on? What are some rules we need to remember?" If the children have learned what colors can be produced from the combinations of other colors, the combining of colors could be discussed, motivated by such questions as, "How can you make the color brown?" Ways to use the fingerpaint can be discussed, beginning with such questions as, "How do you fingerpaint? What part of the body do you usually use to fingerpaint? What other parts of the body can you use to fingerpaint?" The teacher might ask each child what he would like to do with the fingerpaint. If the fingerpaint lesson is being used to demonstrate an objective in another part of the curriculum, each child could state what he would like to fingerpaint related to that lesson. When the children start fingerpainting, the teacher encourages the children and motivates discussion with such comments as, "Tommy is using his whole hand in his fingerpaint," "Sally has mixed blue and yellow fingerpaint to make green," "I'm glad you remembered how to keep the fingerpaint on the table." The teacher thus helps the children to develop their art skills through trial and encouragement.

Avoid questions that assume the child is making "something." Two examples of questions that can stop exploration with the media entirely are "What is that?" and "That looks like a house; is that your house?" One 4-year-old replied to the question "What is that?" with the comment "I don't know. I haven't finished yet." If you wish to know about the child's art work, you can make open-ended statements and questions such as, "I like the way you've used the color blue," or "That's an interesting picture. Would you like to tell me about it?"

Teachers frequently ask what they should do when a child makes comments such as "Draw a jack o' lantern for me, teacher; I can't do it," or "You make one. I don't know how." Such comments could mean, "I'm afraid to try because pictures should be just the way the teacher does it. And the teacher won't like me if I don't do it the way he does." So the child asks for a model so his own drawing can be "just the way the teacher does it." Thus the child learns to imitate but seldom learns anything about the elements of art.

Another possibility is that the child doesn't know what can be done with the media or the various ways his body can respond to the media. This would indicate the child needs some help identifying some of the elements that make up a piece of artwork and exploring ways he can use these elements in the media. Let's take the example of the child who wanted his teacher to draw a jack o' lantern. Some teachers have learned to say something similar to, "I like the way you draw. *You* try drawing a pumpkin." This response *may* motivate the child to go ahead and draw on his own. A more successful approach, however, would probably be an attempt by the teacher to help the child think through and solve the problem. The teacher could say:

> What color is a pumpkin? Yes, can you find that color? What shape is a pumpkin, round or square? How would you make something round? [Child tries drawing a circle.] Yes, that's a good big circle. Now what else does the pumpkin need to become a jack o' lantern? [Child suggests eyes, a nose, a mouth.] What shape would you like his eyes to be, a circle, a square, or a triangle? [Child says a circle.] That's fine. Where do you think the eyes would go on the pumpkin? [Child points to two spots across from each other.] Now you can make two round circles where you pointed. [Child draws two circles.] Good work. Now where would the nose go? [The child points between the eyes.] That's almost correct. Look at your own nose. [Child looks in mirror.] Is your nose right between your eyes or is it between and a little bit below the eyes? [Child says the latter.] Show me where that could be on your pumpkin. [Child points to appropriate spot.] That's very good. Do you want the nose to be a circle or a triangle? [Child says triangle.] All right, draw a triangle where you pointed. [Child draws nose.] Now, does the jack o' lantern need anything else? [Child says it needs a mouth.] That's right. Where could you put the mouth? [Child points.] That's a good place. Do you want the mouth to smile or frown? [Smile.] How would you draw a smile? [Child draws a smiling mouth.]That's a very good jack o' lantern. And you did it all by yourself. [Child says he wants some teeth in the jack o' lantern's mouth.] That's a good idea. You can draw the teeth wherever you want them to go. [Child draws three teeth.] Now, aren't you proud of your jack o' lantern? [Child smiles and hangs it up on the wall with the teacher's help.]

In this example the teacher has helped the child to examine some specific alternatives, one step at a time. The task that seemed overwhelming to the child at first became a success experience—that is, he created something on his own. The teacher gave continuous reinforcement as the child tried each step. Near the end of this episode the child had gained enough confidence to suggest his jack o' lantern needed something else—some teeth. In other words, the child was beginning to use his problem-solving ability without the teacher's help. This ability to solve problems independently will lead to greater creativity in the graphic arts.

The following two sections of this chapter discuss the two basic divisions of the graphic arts curriculum, the *elements of art* and *art media*. An outline of the graphic arts curriculum is found on page 237. The idea for the subdivisions of art media comes largely from the chapter on art in the book by Pitcher and her associates (1966).

ELEMENTS OF ART

The five basic elements of art suitable for study in the prekindergarten are *color, shape, line, form,* and *texture.* Virtually everything in the graphic arts consists of these elements, whether it be a painting, a collage, a ceramic, or a sculpture. To begin with, learning the elements of art is basically a language process. That is, the child can learn the names of the various colors and shapes, identify examples of each color and shape, and identify examples that are *not* a given color or shape (this is concept learning, discussed in Chapter 5).

Prekindergarten children can learn every color in the color spectrum. They can also learn what combinations of colors make other colors, such as blue and yellow make green. When teaching colors to children, be sure you give several examples of each color in different media. If a child sees the color red in different sizes of blocks or balls only, it is likely that he will learn that red can be only a block or only a ball. But if the child sees red demonstrated with a ball, a block, a piece of paper, a piece of furniture, the carpet, and so on, he can learn that the common attribute in each of these media is "redness." The same principle applies to the learning of shapes. A given object itself is not the shape but, rather, an attribute of a particular object is the shape. For example, a ball is a ball, not a circle. "Circleness" (or "roundness") is one attribute of a ball among others such as a particular color, the capacity to bounce, something to play with, and so forth.

Children can learn to name and identify a wide variety of shapes, including squares, circles, rectangles, ovals, crescents, parallelograms, stars, pentagons, and trapezoids. They can learn to identify a shape by its definition, such as "a square has four sides exactly alike" or "a triangle has three sides" (this is rule learning, discussed in Chapter 5).

When children are skilled in naming and identifying the shapes and colors, they can learn how shapes are combined and the different colors that are used in various two-dimensional and three-dimensional media. For example, the child can look at his own face and determine what kinds of shapes he sees, such as the roundness or ovalness of the whole head, the ovalness of the eyes, the triangle of the nose, the crescent or oval of the mouth, the oval of the ear, and so on. Thus children will begin to note the shapes in the food they eat, the toys they play with, the houses they live in, and the growing things they see outside. They then can combine shapes in the various art media.

Line, form, and texture are elements of art easily overlooked in the prekindergarten. However, the child who performs desired objectives related to these three elements can expand his creative or expressive ability with the various art media.

Whenever you look at a picture, notice the direction of its various elements. Trees basically have an up-and-down or vertical line as do people standing up. This line can be described as stately. Other lines such as

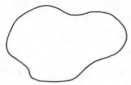

in a picture of ocean or water, for example, can be described as restful. A curved line such as

can be described as feminine or soft, whereas diagonal lines such as

that give the impression of movement are often described as masculine. A line can also be the outline of something, such as a child tracing around his hand and fingers with a crayon. Children can learn to express their feelings in lines, such as, "Draw a happy (or sad or angry) line."

Form is the way something actually is—that is, what it looks like in reality. Let children look at pictures and pick out what they see in the pictures. Don't overlook the importance of exposing children to art masterpieces in museums or to good art borrowed from an art gallery or local art-lending library. Many fine paintings have been prepared in prints of excellent quality that can be permanently displayed in the prekindergarten.

Texture in art is of two kinds. The first, implied or simulated, can be seen in a piece of linoleum that looks like a specific texture or a painting that expresses the quality of texture in the way the colors, shapes, lines, and forms have been combined. Some wallpaper looks like, or simulates, brocade but is smooth in actual texture. The second form of texture, actual or tactile, is demonstrated by real objects such as fur (smooth, soft), sandpaper (rough), wood (course, smooth), silk (soft, smooth), fingerpaints (slippery, wet, smooth), clothes (such as wool pants that itch), food, rubber, and so on. Firsthand experience is essential when you are teaching objectives related to actual or tactile texture.

As the children learn objectives related to the elements of art, they can apply them to their learning in the use of the various art media. They also will begin to notice and label various colors, shapes, lines, forms, and textures in the real objects they experience in the world around them.

ART MEDIA

Art media are the materials used in the graphic arts. These materials determine to a large extent the techniques or type of activities used in creating something or exploring in the medium. For example, potter's clay lends itself to manipulation by the hands, and poster paint lends itself to stroking with a brush. Reversing the techniques would be ridiculous in most cases.

Drawing Media

Materials that lend themselves to drawing are crayons, chalk, oil-base pastels, and felt-tip pens and markers.

Crayons are probably easier for the prekindergarten child to handle if they are about one-half inch in diameter. Provide a wide variety of colors and enough crayons for all children to select from and use freely. Children can be taught how to tear back the paper when the crayon wears down. Crayons that have reached the stump stage need replacing.

Chalk can be purchased in the one-half inch or one-inch kindergarten size. Children can explore drawing with chalk when it is wet as well as when it is dry. Wetting the paper is usually a more pleasant experience than wetting the chalk. Chalk smears easily, particularly dry chalk. Spraying the child's finished chalk drawing with shellac is one effective way to prevent most smearing of chalk.

Oil-base pastels are a cross between crayons and chalk. They provide an intriguing new sensory experience for children when they draw. However, they are usually more expensive than crayons or chalk.

At one time the cost of felt-tip pens and markers was prohibitive for use in the prekindergarten. However, the price is now more reasonable and such items are plentiful on the market. But they are still expensive compared to chalk and crayons and, therefore, probably should not be used as frequently in the curriculum. They come in two varieties—waterproof and washable. The waterproof pens can be exciting to use on fabrics.

Painting Media

The basic materials necessary for painting are the paints and the brushes. Paper will be discussed later.

Powdered tempera paint must be mixed with water before it can be used for painting. The most effective way to mix it is to make a paste of the paint powder and a little bit of water in the container. Then add more water to the desired consistency. The paint should be bright and fairly thick for most effective use so be cautious when you dilute the paint paste. Incidentally, paint extenders can be used with the pigment powders to aid in getting the proper consistency.

Bottled prepared paint is more expensive but is easier to handle inasmuch as it requires no mixing or adding of water. However, it is of such a consistency that you may wish to add some water before the children use it. It is less expensive when purchased by the gallon.

Both the powdered and bottled paints can be used for easel painting, fruit or vegetable printing, and other miscellaneous painting and printing purposes.

Paint containers can be purchased commercially or can be made from frozen fruit juice cans or baby food bottles. For food and miscellaneous printing and painting, shallow plastic dishes can be used.

Easels are convenient for children to use when painting but they are not absolutely necessary. Newspapers or oilcloth or plastic can be spread on the floor or pinned on the wall as background for painting papers. Even a table can be used if the space provided is large enough for the child to move comfortably.

The most satisfactory easel brushes have long handles and a bristle wide enough to make a path at least three-fourths of an inch wide. Such a brush allows for greater freedom of movement in the young child. It's a good idea to have some extra paint containers and brushes available for the children to use in mixing various colors of paint.

Fingerpainting Media

Fingerpainting is done with the hands and/or the fingers, but also with bare feet (footpainting?). Children enjoy an occasional stroke with an elbow, an arm, or a chin. There are several varieties of fingerpaint, each with its unique texture and consistency.

Homemade fingerpaint can be made in several ways. One popular homemade fingerpaint includes soap flakes and dry laundry starch:

Homemade Fingerpaint

½ cup linit starch
1½ cups boiling water
½ cup soap flakes
1 tablespoon glycerin (optional)
Food coloring or powdered paint
Mix enough cold water in starch to make a smooth paste.
Add starch paste to boiling water.
Cook until smooth and fairly clear.
Add soap flakes to hot mixture, stir thoroughly.
Add glycerin, if desired, and food coloring or powder paint (food
    coloring is the more desirable of the two).

Soap bubble fingerpaint can be produced by making a paste out of soap powder or flakes and water and then whipping the paste into a stiff foam with an egg beater. Food coloring or paint powder can be added. Other suitable homemade fingerpaint recipes can be found in Pitcher (1966) and Taylor (1970).

Fingerpaint is available in jars commercially but, of course, is more expensive than homemade fingerpaint. Wheatpaste (wallpaper paste) can be mixed with a little warm water to form a fingerpaint of an interesting texture.

When the children use fingerpaint, the fingerpaint paper should be wetted with a sponge. But children also enjoy fingerpainting on the tabletop itself.

Food-Printing Media

Children enjoy dipping various kinds of fruits and vegetables cut in half into paint and printing designs on different kinds of paper. Vegetables that can be used for this purpose are carrots, green peppers, and potatoes. Fruits that serve the same purpose are lemons and oranges.

Miscellaneous Printing Media

There is no end to the number of other materials that can be used for printing. Some of these miscellaneous printing media are sponges, keys, paper clips, hair rollers, pieces of paper towel, corrugated cardboard, empty film spools, empty sewing spools, leaves, sticks, and so on.

Papers

Most graphic arts processes involve paper. A variety of papers can be made available in the prekindergarten for use in the graphic arts. Unprinted newsprint is by far the least expensive of all the art papers. It is available not only plain but in pastel shades. Newsprint is most satisfactory for use when cut to the size of 18″ × 24″. It is an excellent easel paper also.

Construction paper is always popular. It is available in all colors and should be purchased in a size that can be cut to any desired size. It can be purchased in sheets 18″ × 24″.

Specially prepared fingerpainting paper can be purchased for the prekindergarten but is expensive. Butcher paper is a suitable substitute.

Other papers that can be used in graphic arts activities in the prekindergarten include poster paper (comes in a variety of colors), cellophane, rice paper, sandpaper, contact paper, shelf paper, tissue paper, paper towels, salvage and remnant papers.

Children occasionally enjoy cutting paper. Blunt scissors especially for use by children are the most satisfactory.

Collage Media

A favorite art activity of prekindergarten children is making collages with a variety of materials. Paper scraps and fabric scraps can be collected in special containers. Various kinds of dried beans and most noodle products also make interesting three-dimensional collages, especially if the noodles have been colored and dried beforehand. Other collage materials include sand and colored salt. With the children, make a design on the paper with paste and then sprinkle the sand or colored salt on the design. Excess sand or salt can then be poured off the paper.

Pastes and Glues

It's a good idea to have plenty of paste and glue for the children to use in making collages and engaging in other pasting activities. Homemade paste is the least expensive. One method is to mix one-half cup flour with enough cold water to form a creamy consistency. This mixture can then be brought to a boil, stirring constantly. Then cool and add a few drops of wintergreen for a pleasant odor and retardation of spoiling. This can be stored in covered jars preferably in the refrigerator. Other homemade paste recipes can be found in Taylor (1970).

White library paste is less expensive when purchased by the gallon. It can be made thinner by stirring.

Some pasting activities require white all-purpose glue. These glues can be used directly from the container or a little poured onto a piece of paper or a miniature paper cup for each child.

Paste brushes are available for use by young children and often are more satisfactory than the use of fingers alone. Some children need help learning how to use paste, whether with their fingers or with a brush.

Linear Three-Dimensional Media

A number of miscellaneous items can be used for a variety of painting, pasting, and modeling purposes. These include string, thread, yarn, rick-rack, bias tape, colored sticks, toothpicks (plain or colored), pipe cleaners, tongue depressors (wood), and Q-tips.

Tapes

Various tapes can be used for a variety of purposes in the graphic arts. These include cellophane, masking tape, and vinyl and holiday tapes.

Modeling or Sculpture Materials

The list of graphic arts media would not be complete without modeling or sculpture materials. These come in a variety of interesting forms.

Modeling doughs are inexpensive and easy to make. One of the most popular modeling doughs is salt-flour dough.

Salt-Flour Dough

1 cup salt
3 cups flour
Water
Food coloring
Mix the salt and flour together.
Add food coloring to 1 cup water. Add to salt and flour.
Mix salt, flour, and colored water with bare hands, adding more
    water to make a soft, pliable dough.
Add about 1 tablespoon cooking oil to retard drying of the
    dough.
Store in the refrigerator.

Recipes for other modeling doughs can be found in Pitcher (1966) and
Taylor (1970).

Potter's clay, used by professional artists, can be purchased in
almost any art supply store. It is best stored in large pottery crocks.
Leftover clay can be returned to the crock. Punch holes in it with your
fingers, and sprinkle water over it. A damp burlap cloth over the stored
clay also helps to keep it moist. Large pieces of this clay (about the size
of two adult fists) should be provided each child in order for effective
exploration to take place.

Another commercial clay is Plasticene, which has an oil base
and therefore cannot dry out. However, it is not as pliable as potter's
clay or the various modeling doughs.

Children enjoy inserting objects into various kinds of bases
such as clay, soap, styrofoam, Plasticene, and small boxes. Materials
used for insertion into these bases would include wire, toothpicks,
straw, noodle products, beans, and pipe cleaners.

SAMPLE LESSON PLAN

Area of the curriculum: Graphic arts

Graphic arts focus: Fingerpainting media

Behavioral objective: Each child will make a design of his choice with the colored fingerpaints of his choice on the paper provided (problem solving, expressive).

To the teacher: This experience with fingerpaint will require the following materials:

Homemade fingerpaint (a jar of each of the three primary colors)
Fingerpaint paper (butcher paper will do, cut to 12" × 18")
A wet sponge
An available supply of water
Aprons for the children

It is expected that the children will already have learned to make a variety of shapes and to identify specific colors that result from various combinations of the primary colors. (See sample lesson plan on concept *red,* pages 128–129.)

Provide an apron for each child. Provide enough space at the table that each child can freely use his body with a 12" × 18" sheet of fingerpaint paper. Dampen the paper with a wet sponge before placing a heaping tablespoonful of the child's desired color of fingerpaint in the center.

Learning Activities:

Posttest   (behavioral objective from a preceding lesson). Each child will tell the correct name of each color of fingerpaint and each primary color pigment combination he has not seen before in instruction when shown by the teacher. (Concept learning.)

Pretest.   (The objective for this lesson can be tested during the planned learning activities.)

Show.   Have the fingerpaint paper at each place as each child, after putting on his apron, sits down. As soon as all the children are seated, sit down yourself where all the children can see you at one corner of the table. Put the three jars of fingerpaint on the table in front of you.

Discuss.   Ask the children : "What do you think this is in these jars? [If they have never seen it before, tell them it is fingerpaint.] What do you think you could do with it? [Lead the discussion to the idea that the fingerpaint is moved around on the paper with the hands and fingers.] What would happen if you mixed the yellow fingerpaint with the blue fingerpaint [makes color green—suggest other combinations as well]?"

Show, discuss, apply.   Dampen each sheet of paper with a wet sponge and put a heaping tablespoonful of the child's desired color in the center of each sheet. Encourage the children to try out with their fingers and hands what they just discussed. Encourage them to try straight and curved lines and different shapes. Help them to identify shapes and lines in each other's fingerpainting (for example, "Mark is making a shape with the side of his hand. What shape do you think he is making?"). Ask the children if there is another part of the body they could use to help them fingerpaint (lead to discussion and use of elbows and chins; some children may even wish to use the entire arm). As each child requests other colors of fingerpaint, ask him to tell what the resulting color is. If he can't tell, ask the other children to help him. Be sure then to ask the child who received help from the others to give the correct color after hearing it.

Posttest.   This is an expressive problem-solving objective where there is no known solution. However, children should be given the opportunity periodically to engage in a similar expressive problem-solving experience.

Caution: Avoid asking too many questions. Exploring the uses of fingerpaint and expressing oneself with the medium require some degree of silence and concentration on the "doing."

Graphic arts topical outline.

1.1   Elements of art
      1.1.1.   Color
      1.1.2.   Shape
      1.1.3.   Line
      1.1.4.   Form
      1.1.5.   Texture
1.2.   Art media
      1.2.1.   Drawing media
            1.2.1.1.   Crayons
            1.2.1.2.   Chalk
            1.2.1.3.   Oil-base pastels
            1.2.1.4.   Felt-tip pens and markers
      1.2.2.   Painting media
            1.2.2.1.   Powdered tempera
            1.2.2.2.   Bottled prepared paint
            1.2.2.3.   Easel brushes
      1.2.3.   Fingerpainting media
            1.2.3.1.   Homemade fingerpaint
            1.2.3.2.   Commercial fingerpaint
      1.2.4.   Food-printing media
            1.2.4.1.   Vegetables
            1.2.4.2.   Fruits
      1.2.5.   Miscellaneous printing media
      1.2.6.   Papers
            1.2.6.1.   Newsprint
            1.2.6.2.   Construction paper
            1.2.6.3.   Fingerpainting paper
            1.2.6.4.   Miscellaneous
      1.2.7.   Collage media
            1.2.7.1.   Paper scraps
            1.2.7.2.   Fabric scraps

1.2.7.3. Dry beans (various)
1.2.7.4. Noodle products
1.2.7.5. Miscellaneous collage materials
1.2.8. Pastes and glues
      1.2.8.1. Homemade paste
      1.2.8.2. White library paste
      1.2.8.3. White all-purpose glue
1.2.9. Linear three-dimensional media
1.2.10. Tapes
1.2.11. Modeling or sculpture materials
      1.2.11.1. Modeling doughs
      1.2.11.2. Potter's clay
      1.2.11.3. Plasticene
      1.2.11.4. Miscellaneous

REFERENCES

De Saint-Exupery, A. *The little prince*. New York: Harcourt Brace Jovanovich, 1943.

Pitcher, E. G., Lasher, M. G., Feinburg, S., & Hammond, N. D. Art for young children. In *Helping young children learn*. Columbus, Ohio: Merrill, 1966.

Taylor, B. J. *A child goes forth*. (2nd ed.) Provo, Utah: Brigham Young University Press, 1970.

Chapter 10

Health and Safety

The subject of health and safety is seldom dealt with directly in the average prekindergarten curriculum. Yet accidental injury is a top killer of young children in the nation today, and the health of the nation's children is nothing to brag about. It is true that the responsibility for the health and safety of young children is primarily that of their parents. However, it is likely that many health and safety problems could be avoided if children were taught explicitly how to care for their bodies and how to avoid accident and injury. The old adage is still a good one: "An ounce of prevention is worth a pound of cure."

It is not necessary to teach a lesson on health and safety during each class period in the prekindergarten. Probably a lesson once a week could be arranged to alternate with lesson materials in mathematics and reading. That is, a lesson in mathematics could be given two days a week, a lesson in reading two days a week, and a lesson in health and safety could be given on the fifth day. A list of subject headings for the health and safety curriculum is found on page 251.

CARING FOR THE BODY

The primary focus of the health curriculum is *caring for the body.* This involves many activities we take for granted that can be of great interest to young children.

The subject of *bathing* includes how to properly bathe oneself, where bathing occurs, when it occurs, and why it is necessary. Differences and similarities in the bathing routines of the various children can be discussed.

Washing occurs more frequently than bathing. The difference between bathing and washing can be examined. The children can learn when to wash, how to wash, and why it is necessary. Because most washing facilities in the average home are too high for the young child to reach, children can learn to find suitable and safe means for reaching the wash basin.

Care of the *teeth* is extremely important, even for young children. It is unfortunate that many parents take the defeatist attitude that prekindergarten children are too immature to take responsibility for the care of their teeth. And yet the patterns for the care of the teeth begun in these prekindergarten years can extend throughout a lifetime. Skills are involved, such as putting the toothpaste on the toothbrush and manipulating the brush in the mouth. The differences between electric and manual toothbrushes can be examined. In a day-care center where children attend all day, a routine can be established so that each child has his own toothbrush, his own place to store it, and a special time to use it, such as immediately following lunch. Dental caries do not occur exclusively in children from low-income families. Therefore, children can learn who the dentist is, what he does, and what his equipment and materials are like. A visit to a real dentist's office followed by some role-playing in the prekindergarten about the dentist and his work can plant some positive attitudes about visits to the dentist. What the teeth do can be examined. Their major function is to cut and chew food so that food can be more easily swallowed for use by the body. Some foods are good for the teeth, such as chewy vegetables and fruits like carrots and apples, and other foods are hard on teeth, such as soft drinks and candy.

The *eyes* need to be protected and guarded because they give us so much information about the world we live in. They help us when we cross the street and also when we walk to prevent us from stepping on something that will hurt. Children at Halloween often find themselves in dangerous situations because their vision is impaired by masks. They can learn how to wear clothing so it won't retard good vision.

Care of the *hair* can be another interesting subject for learning. The children can learn how hair is washed, what is needed to wash hair, and how to brush and comb it. Differences between hair care for boys and girls can be examined, such as the fact that many girls have longer hair than the boys and arrange their hair in different ways. The importance of clean hair should be emphasized. A visit to the beauty shop or barber can be arranged to show children how the hair is cut. Also different textures of hair can be noted. A point can be stressed that each person's hair is best for him. This is one way to teach appreciation for all features of different people regardless of race or national origin.

Prekindergarten children are not too young to learn about the kinds of foods that give them healthy bodies. They can learn how to identify foods in the four basic food groups: meats, fish, and poultry; fruits and vegetables; breads and cereals; and dairy products. As they eat snacks they can relate what they are eating to the basic four food groups. Children can occasionally be given the opportunity to select from the basic four foods those that would be the most nutritious for their snacks. This will help them to apply what they are learning about *nutrition.* Some children have developed a dislike for new foods, thus narrowing their range of food choice. New foods can be introduced during lessons on nutrition and children encouraged to taste the new foods. These new foods, then, can be gradually introduced as snack items along with other more popular foods. Children who try new foods can receive verbal reinforcement from the teacher while those who refuse to taste these same foods can be ignored. The encouragement that the "tasters" receive is usually sufficient in the long run to motivate the "non-tasters." Children can also learn how to serve themselves and take the amount of each food that they can eat. Manipulating a serving spoon and a pitcher of fluid is no easy task for young children. Ways to serve oneself can be demonstrated in lessons and then plenty of practice can be offered during snack time and lunch time.

Many prekindergarten children struggle with the skills involved in *dressing and undressing*. Buttons and zippers are major problems, but often the real problem is that the child has not learned the sequence of dressing and undressing and he thus becomes frustrated when faced by the whole task at once. Three-year-olds are especially susceptible to these problems of dressing and undressing. Lessons can be developed that help children to identify the various items of clothing and the order in which they are put on and taken off. Ways of putting on each item can be demonstrated and then practiced with real pieces of clothing. Special attention can be given to the manipulation of buttons, zippers, hooks, ties, and snaps. Even 3-year-olds can learn how to tie their own shoes. The appropriate times for dressing and undressing can be discussed as well as different types of clothing for different occasions such as going to church, going to school, going on a picnic, playing in the snow, or going to the beach.

Children become *thirsty* and can learn how to independently take care of their thirst. Cups and low water faucets or drinking fountains should be made available in the prekindergarten. The child can also learn how to get a drink for himself when he is at home, the type of container to use, how to turn the water on and shut it off, and so forth.

Most prekindergarten children, if they could write, could chronicle a long list of *illnesses and injuries* and all the experiences surrounding them. Prekindergarten children, especially, are susceptible to respiratory illness and infection. The list of bruises and cuts and broken bones in the average child makes one wonder how children survive childhood. They have become well acquainted with doctors, nurses, shots, salves, pills, thermometers, and bandages. These experiences with illness and injury often leave negative feelings in the child. The prekindergarten teacher can alleviate much of this problem by helping the children identify various illnesses and injuries, what needs to be done to treat them, and what to expect from parents, doctors, and nurses when an accident or illness occurs. A doctor and a nurse can visit the prekindergarten and show the children the instruments and materials they use and how they use them. An actual visit to a doctor's office can be planned as one important learning experience since so many children shy away from the doctor's office because of its association with pain. The doctor can help the children identify the materials and equipment in his office, what they are used for, and how they are used. It is also important to teach children how to stay well, including the idea that immunizations help children stay well.

Rest and sleep are essential to every human being but many children fight sleep or rest periods. Their days are so full of energetic activity that it is difficult to "turn off" for a nap or bedtime. Children can develop pleasant attitudes about naps and bedtime when they can learn together why they are necessary and when they occur. The desirable quiet routine before nap or bedtime can be demonstrated and different routines of the various children can be discussed. Many children enjoy demonstrating their favorite position on the bed or cot they rest or sleep on.

SAFETY

The emphasis in lessons on *safety* is on the positive, preventive side rather than the negative "look-what-happened" side. Children can learn the meaning of "This can hurt you," by seeing real examples of things that can hurt and learning what to do in each situation.

Open doors let out warm air and bring in cool air in the winter, making it very uncomfortable for the people inside. In some parts of the country at certain seasons of the year an open door is an invitation to an invasion by flies and other unsanitary and harmful insects. Children can learn to close doors to prevent these problems.

Spilled liquid can cause painful falls. Therefore when a child has spilled a liquid, he can learn how to clean it up with a sponge. Other children and the teacher can help him.

Some children need to learn how to turn off a *water faucet.* Faucets left on can cause water to spill over, possibly causing a painful fall. Or scalding water left on can possibly injure children and other members of the family.

Broken toys are a constant menace. Children can learn to identify broken toys and bring them to the teacher or parent for repair.

Broken glass can cause painful cuts. Children can be taught to tell a teacher or parent when something has been broken so it can be cleaned up. Children should never attempt to clean up broken glass, but they can learn how adults do it.

The number of injuries caused by *nails,* including those left exposed in boards, is legion. Children can learn how to handle nails, where they are kept, and what to do with nails they find, including boards with nails in them.

There are appropriate places to *walk* and *run.* It is usually appropriate to walk indoors (unless a child is in a gymnasium) and run outdoors. Sharp objects should be avoided. Running should be done in unobstructed areas and where a fall will not injure the child, such as on grass or in a field. Children can also learn that when lots of people are walking or running in the same area, they all go the same direction to avoid hurting others and themselves.

Occasionally *poisonous* substances used on the farm, in the yard, or in the home are left within reach of young children. Among the most common of these substances are fertilizers, insecticides, and cleaning solvents. The range of poisonous substances is so broad that it would be almost impossible to teach the prekindergarten child how to discriminate poisonous from nonpoisonous substances. It probably is best to teach the child to tell the nearest adult whenever he finds a bottle or container of any kind of powder or liquid. If he wishes to smell it or taste it, he should ask the permission of the adult.

Children can learn the appropriate uses of *knives* and *other sharp objects.* Then it is easier for them to understand why these objects are not suitable objects to use for play purposes.

For many young children *matches* hold a particular fascination. Again, children can learn the appropriate uses of matches before learning the rule that only adults handle matches. Some adults may wish to allow children to strike a match but only in the presence and under the supervision of an adult. *Fireworks* are included in this category.

Playing in the street may be quite safe and appropriate in some neighborhoods and quite dangerous in others. If you teach the children the various places suitable for play, then playing in the street probably will be no problem.

Crossing the street safely depends on the child's ability to discriminate colors on an electric traffic signal and to recognize what action is prompted by each color on the signal. Some streets have crosswalks but no electric signals. Children can then learn how to look for approaching traffic and when to cross the street. If children live in a community where traffic officers occasionally direct traffic, they learn stop and go signals and practice responding correctly to these signals.

Many fathers, relatives, or friends of prekindergarten children have *guns* in the home for use in sport activities. Some family members are officers of the law such as highway patrolmen or local policemen. Children should learn that guns are handled by adults only.

Thousands of children every year are burned or scalded from cooking units or boiling substances on the stove or in the oven. Many of these accidents can be avoided if children are taught how *stoves and ovens* operate and how to respond to rules about stoves and ovens.

Adults often lower their safety standards during a *holiday* period, possibly due to the excitement of the festivities. During the Christmas or Hannukah season lighted candles are always a potential source of danger. During Halloween some children have received harmful objects and substances while out "trick-or-treating." Children should learn the rules pertaining to these potentially dangerous situations, with the accent on the positive rather than the negative.

Basically, lessons on safety revolve around rules regarding specific objects, people, or events. Additional safety rules would apply to kites, plastic bags, old appliances, safe places to play, strangers, climbing, electrical outlets, pushing others, throwing objects, water sports, and camping. The emphasis should be on what the child is *to do* in each case rather than on the dire consequences if he oversteps the bounds of safety.

ACCIDENTS

Regardless of how well children respond to rules of safety, accidents are bound to happen. Because of the unexpected nature of accidents, children often feel as frightened by the sudden occurrence of the accident as they do by the pain resulting from the accident. Discussions of some specific types of accidents such as *falling* or *injuries* that occur in the course of everyday activities and practice of what to do when an accident occurs can help to alleviate much of the fear generated by an accident.

SAMPLE LESSON PLAN

Area of curriculum: Health and safety

Health and safety focus: Washing

Behavioral objective: Each child will correctly demonstrate with soap, washcloth, water, and towel how to wash his face and hands. (Complex skill.)

To the teacher: The concept of washing is very familiar to some prekindergarten children and very unfamiliar to others, depending on whether or not washing is emphasized in the home. Many children accustomed to washing themselves still need help in using the soap, washcloth, water, and towel appropriately. The towel often gets used as the main soil-remover rather than as a means of removing water from the washed area. This lesson can help the children to appropriately use the washing facilities available and to take pride in their ability to wash themselves when needed.

Equipment and supplies needed for this lesson are:
Washcloth (wrapped in a package)
Bar of soap (wrapped in a package)
Hand towel (wrapped in a package)
Basin of warm water
A sponge (to wipe up excess water)
Bowl of water for each child

Seat the children around the table where they can see you and the supplies used in the lesson.

Learning Activities:

Posttest   (behavioral objective from a preceding lesson). Given a group of seven miscellaneous items not used before in instruction, each child will correctly select three items used in the washing process. (Concept learning.)

Pretest.   (If each child demonstrates he can accomplish the objective during the discuss step, further training beyond the discuss step may not be necessary. Posttesting will be necessary, however, at a later date.)

Show, discuss.   Place on the table in front of you three separately wrapped packages (one containing a washcloth, one a bar of soap, and one a hand towel). Say, "In each of these packages I have something I used this morning before I got ready to come to school. Each one of these is something you can use every day here in the prekindergarten." Have three children open the packages. As each package is opened, ask the children to name what was in the package. After each of the three packages has been opened, ask the children to tell you what you did with each article that morning. Ask each child to tell when he washes (when he gets up in the morning, before eating, and when he comes in after getting very soiled in outdoor play). Then help the children determine the steps in the washing process (wet face and hands with water, rub soap on face and hands, use washcloth to rub face and hands and rinse off with clear water, use towel to wipe off water from hands and face). As each step is discussed, have a child demonstrate that step with the appropriate washing article.

Show.   Have a child demonstrate the entire chain of washing responses as you name them. Then hand each child a bar of soap, a washcloth, and a towel. Put a bowl of water in front of each child. Say, "It's your turn to practice washing yourself. Remember to wet your face and hands with water, rub soap on your face and hands, use a washcloth to rub your face and hands, rinse off the soap with clean water, and use the towel to wipe off your hands and face just the way [Johnny] did."

Discuss.   As the children practice washing their faces, tell each child what part or parts of the performance he is doing well. If a child has trouble with any component, such as rubbing soap on his face and hands, have another child who can do this step demonstrate it for the child having trouble. Have the child try again, reinforcing him for what he does well and encouraging him as he gets better and better. "That's much better. You're getting the soap on your face and hands where it belongs," "You are rubbing very well," "Doesn't that feel good, now?"

Apply   (also posttest). Have the children wash their faces before snack or lunch the same day and on several days following the lesson. Continue to give occasional verbal praise to those children who master the objective. Give verbal prompts to children who still have trouble.

Health and safety topical outline.

2.1. Caring for the body
    2.1.1. Bathing
    2.1.2. Washing
    2.1.3. Teeth
    2.1.4. Eyes
    2.1.5. Ears
    2.1.6. Hair
    2.1.7. Nutrition
        2.1.7.1. New foods
        2.1.7.2. Serving oneself
    2.1.8. Dressing and undressing
    2.1.9. Illness and injury
    2.1.10. Thirst
    2.1.11. Rest and sleep
2.2. Safety
    2.2.1. Open doors
    2.2.2. Spilled liquid
    2.2.3. Water faucets
    2.2.4. Broken toys
    2.2.5. Broken glass
    2.2.6. Nails or boards with nails
    2.2.7. Running and walking
    2.2.8. Safety in the car
    2.2.9. Poisons
    2.2.10. Knives and other sharp objects
    2.2.11. Matches (including fireworks)
    2.2.12. Playing in the street
    2.2.13. Crossing the street
    2.2.14. Guns
    2.2.15. Stoves and ovens
    2.2.16. Medicines, drugs
    2.2.17. Holidays
    2.2.18. Kites
    2.2.19. Plastic bags
    2.2.20. Old appliances
    2.2.21. Safe places to play
    2.2.22. Strangers
    2.2.23. Climbing
    2.2.24. Electrical outlets
    2.2.25. Pushing others
    2.2.26. Throwing objects
    2.2.27. Water safety
    2.2.28. Camping
2.3. Accidents
    2.3.1. Falling
    2.3.2. Injuries from toys and other objects

Chapter 11

Living in a World of People

Living in a world of people is the title of a curriculum area better known as the social studies in the academic world. Social studies have been defined as " ... those studies that provide understanding of the physical environment and its effect upon man's ways of living, of the basic needs of man and the activities in which he engages to meet his needs, and the institutions man has developed to perpetuate his way of life" (Leeper, Dales, Skipper, & Witherspoon, 1968, p. 237). The academic subdivisions of the social studies are history, sociology, geography, economics, political science, psychology, anthropology, and education. These subdivisions have been translated into subject headings for a social-studies curriculum suitable for prekindergarten children on pages 263–266. This curriculum area is one of the broadest and most important in the prekindergarten program. The ten major subdivisions of this content area of the prekindergarten curriculum will be discussed in the sections that follow. Emphasis is on here-and-now experiences.

Living in a family. This subdivision of this area of the curriculum is the most extensive of all the subdivisions. The primary focus is on the traditional family, which includes a mother and a father and usually one or more children.

Occasionally grandparents and even aunts, uncles, and cousins become part of the immediate family, at least in terms of time spent together and feelings of companionship and friendship.

The traditional family is the basic unit of society. This basic unit is now under strong attack by many factions of society. But man has never found a suitable substitute for the basic family unit. It seems unjustified to exclude a study of the traditional family and what it is because some children in the prekindergarten are illegitimate, come from broken homes, live with relatives or friends, are adopted, or in any other way represent an exception to the rule. These special cases can be taken into consideration and shown that they, too, are special members of families.

Special occasions in the family help to cement the bonds of love and friendship existing within the family unit. These occasions, though practiced in one form or another, are unique to each family unit. Here children can learn some additional lessons in tolerance by learning that birthdays, weddings, reunions, family outings, and vacations are unique in each family. It is the uniqueness of special occasions that helps to build family tradition and thus family solidarity. Role-playing can be especially helpful as a learning activity in lessons about special occasions.

Most young children have never thought about what a *father* is and what a *mother* is. Mothers and fathers just *are*. Children need help to understand that "fatherness" or "motherness" means "*I* am a child of my mother and/or father." Mothers and fathers are often defined in terms of their function in the home, so learning activities can be planned to help children learn what mothers and fathers do in the home. Especially important are ways that individual parents show their love for their children. There is no one way to show love and each child can share what he feels are actions of his parents that help him to know his mother and his father love him. I know two children who were convinced the nightly "paddling" by their father was a sign of love. Love, like beauty, truly is in the eye of the beholder! Ways that parents show affection for one another in front of their children will be effective models for their children. The arm around the shoulder when encouragement is needed, the affectionate words, the hug and kiss before and after work—all help children to know their parents love each other.

Children form many of their sex stereotypes by watching roles played by their own parents over and over. They seem to learn that what is, is what *ought to be*. With a diversity of examples children can learn what other mothers and fathers do in their own homes. They then begin to learn that most activities of males and females, with the exception of giving birth to babies, are really a matter of preference and training. Mothers usually do the cooking, washing, cleaning, shopping, dishes, and chauffeuring in the family whereas the father goes off to work, mows the lawn, takes care of the car, and so on. Yet many fathers help with dishes, scrub the floors, do the shopping, and do much if not all of the cooking in some households. In homes where mothers work there may be a great deal of overlap in activities normally considered those of a man or those of a woman.

Most young children have older or younger *brothers* and *sisters*. Prekindergarten children can learn what brothers and sisters are, what they do in the family, and special things they can do because they are older or younger. Prekindergarten children can be helped to understand that increasing age brings with it differences in interests, privileges, responsibilities, and opportunities to move in an ever-widening geographical circle around the home.

Being a boy or being a girl is one part of the prekindergarten curriculum that deals with sex role identification in young children. Learnings include how boys and girls are alike and how they are different physically and behaviorally. A long sheet of butcher paper or plain newspaper can be put up along one side of the room where the height of each child can be measured and the children can compare heights. Some will be the same height, some will be different; boys and girls can be the same in height and they can be different. Children can also count parts of their bodies such as eyes, ears, nose, mouth, arms, legs and discover that each child has the same number of each regardless of whether he is a boy or a girl. Children can talk about the way they sit, bend their arms, walk, and run and find that everyone does each of these the same. Thus the children learn that most differences among people are due to something other than sex.

Babies are of special interest to young children. Most

prekindergarten children who have babies in the home take great pride in the things they can do for the baby. Jealousy occurs also, but emphasis should be on what babies are like, the care they need, and how various babies are the same in some ways and different in others. Prekindergarten children enjoy comparing what they can do with what the baby can do. This seems to build their own self-confidence and self-esteem because the differences are so visible. Hopefully real babies can be brought into the prekindergarten by their mothers during the lesson periods on babies, preferably from the homes of children in the group.

One of the *advantages of living in a family* is being able to live with someone who cares 24 hours a day. This doesn't mean that each person in the family is physically at home 24 hours a day. It means, rather, that when things occur that make us happy or sad, we've always got someone to share it with. In a family you learn from each other and learn how to get along with each other, regardless of age, secure in the knowledge that the family unit will not be disrupted at the first sign of trouble. Problems arise and there are ways of solving them. Some solutions are better than others and family members are committed to the family enough to find the solutions. Prekindergarten children can learn that they, too, are important members of the family and can contribute to a pleasant atmosphere in the home by the things they do and say.

Other family members include grandparents, aunts, uncles, cousins, and step-parents. Prekindergarten children have a difficult time understanding what it is that makes a grandfather or a grandmother, an aunt, an uncle, or a cousin. They learn these labels by association, by hearing them used in reference to these special members of the family. Probably no effort should be made during this age period to teach the children the real meaning of *grandfather, uncle,* and so on. The focus is on what these other family members do that is of special interest to these children.

Homes people live in. The focus of lessons on homes people live in should be on the homes of the children in your prekindergarten class. Pictures of each home can be displayed. The children can learn that there are many things about the homes that are the same, such as the fact that each home has a kitchen, usually at least one bathroom, a living room, bedrooms, and possibly a dining room. Lessons about the various types of furniture that go in each room are important. Homes are also different in the way they are shaped, the color of the paint or brick or wood, and the location. Four-year-old children may even be ready to learn how to get from one home to another on a walking or driving excursion.

Holidays. Holidays help a child to learn the traditions not only of his family and community but also of the state and country in which he lives. Lessons related to holidays are best scheduled just a few days before each individual holiday. Lessons can revolve around national holidays and special days, religious holidays, and special holidays and events.

Preparing foods. Food preparation lessons related to the child's culture provide important lessons in the prekindergarten. Young children enjoy preparing simple foods such as shelling and cooking peas, making applesauce or butter or cookies, preparing Jell-O, whipping cream, popping corn, mixing fruit salads, and many other kinds of food preparation. Again, firsthand experience is necessary and the children can be instructed in such a way that they can do most of the work in the preparation of a particular food. Children get bored easily if they "just watch." Watching is not participating. Lessons in food preparation require of the teacher great patience and tolerance of less than a perfect product.

Learning to live with others in the prekindergarten. This subdivision of the curriculum emphasizes learning to know others in the prekindergarten, learning the rules necessary in the prekindergarten, and learning how to identify feelings and channel them into appropriate behavior. These principles can transfer into the home and into the broader community.

It is important when children begin a new school year to learn the *names* of each child and adult in the group. It is easier for a child to feel at home in a group when he can call his peers and teachers by their proper names. Games, songs, and stories can be used in learning activities designed to help the children and adults get acquainted with one another. In addition, individual children can share with one another something special about themselves, such as a favorite food, a favorite playtime activity, or a pleasant experience they have had.

Rules are necessary in the prekindergarten to make learning together more pleasant. The rules should be as few as possible. The children can learn what the specific rules are and the consequences of keeping and breaking rules. Emphasis should be on the rewards that come from keeping the rules rather than on the aversive consequences if a rule is broken. When children are rewarded for keeping a rule (or suffer unpleasant consequences for breaking a rule), it is best to restate the rule and the reason for the specific consequences.

Lessons about *feelings* are an important part of the curriculum. Names for feelings can be discussed, such as joy, anger, sadness, and fear. Then the children can act out behavior that makes them think someone is feeling joyful, angry, sad, or afraid. The children can also discuss what makes them feel each of these emotions, such as ways people act toward them, ways they act toward other people, and events that make them feel a certain way. The next step is guidance in what to do about these feelings, especially strong feelings such as anger and excitement. The children can decide in a group the most desirable ways to handle these feelings.

Money.   Virtually every prekindergarten child has had some experience with money and its uses. Most young children think there is a never-ending supply of money in their families. You can provide learning experiences with real money that will help children to identify the various coins and pieces of currency used as money, to actually spend some money at a grocery store or bakery or other place in the community, and to learn how money is earned and who earns it. Role-playing experiences can be used effectively to supplement the firsthand experiences with money.

People and places in the community.   The prekindergarten child is growing in his ability to act appropriately in situations farther and farther from home. He can thus learn where various places such as the grocery store, the drugstore, the shoe repair shop, the restaurant, and others are located in the community. He can begin to sense the geography of his community and find his way about in this community space. Firsthand experiences are necessary for effective learning to occur in this subdivision of the curriculum.

Closely related to the places in the community are the people who work in each place. These places and their occupations have been classified as services, stores, medical and social services, recreation, transportation, and the military. There are specific places and occupations associated with each of these categories.

Some occupations are highly visible to young children while others are not. When young children are asked what they want to be when they grow up, they usually say a cowboy, a fireman, an astronaut, a pilot, or some person they have seen frequently on TV or in the neighborhood. Many children have no concept of what their fathers do other than "go to the office" or "he's at work." They probably haven't had the opportunity to spend some time at work with their fathers to find out what "work" and the "office" is all about. And yet interests that are developed in the early years tend to carry over into later years. Lessons can be planned that provide firsthand experience for the children with as many occupations in the community as possible. People in the occupations can visit class and the class can visit people at work where it is practical and safe. Opportunities to discuss what the children have learned from their visits and special visitors and to role-play and try out some of the occupations should not be overlooked. Some occupations are the same in every community, but there are occupations that are different in each community as well. Because the child is oriented to his experiences here and now, his learning experiences with occupations probably should include those in his own community, whether they include those listed on pages 263–266 or not.

Subcultures within the community.   If the children in your prekindergarten live in a community that has a highly visible ethnic or regional subculture, such as a large group of blacks, Mexican-Americans, or orientals, it might be a good idea to introduce the children to some of the more visible customs of this group such as dress, language, dialect, interest, and food. Emphasize similarities between the larger community and its subculture rather than the differences.

People in other countries.   Prekindergarten children in our modern society have traveled as far away as exotic foreign countries. Many were born in other countries because their fathers served overseas in industry or the military. Some children are immigrants from other countries. Therefore, it may be a good idea in those prekindergartens where such children attend to learn of people in other countries, particularly those countries represented by the children in the group. Similarities and differences in dress, food, money, interests, and language can be explored.

People of other times.   Lessons about people of other times can be prepared if the prekindergarten is located in an area where reference is frequently made to these early people. These people of other times include the early Indians, the pioneers, early settlers in any community, and the Pilgrims.

SAMPLE LESSON PLAN

Area of curriculum: Living in a world of people

Living in a world of people focus: Family

Behavioral objective: Each child will demonstrate that he understands the differences between *father, mother, brother,* and *sister* by selecting and putting on the flannelboard appropriate figures representing each member of his family. (Include grandparents, other relatives, a special child where applicable—Concept learning.)

To the teacher: Before giving this lesson, obtain from school records or from each child's parent the following information about his family: the name, age, and sex of each child in the family, whether or not both parents live in the home, and the names and relationship of other family members such as relatives or a special child. This list will help you to assist each child as he selects flannel figures representing each member of his family.

The children can be seated on the floor, on the rug, or in chairs in a semicircle where they can see you and work at the flannelboard.

Learning Activities:

Show. Place on the flannelboard figures representing a mother, a father, a brother, a sister, and a baby. As you place each figure, beginning with the father, say: "All of us come from families. A family has a father, a mother, and at least one child. Some families have just one child. Other families have lots of children. Some of the children are older. Some are younger. Some are babies." Put appropriate figures on the flannelboard to illustrate different sizes of families and different ages of people in the families. If appropriate to one or more children in your group, say: "Some families have no daddy or no mother [take off the appropriate figure from the flannelboard]; some families have a grandmother, a grandfather, an aunt, an uncle, or even a special child [such as a foster child] as part of the family [put on appropriate figures]."

Discuss, apply. (Posttest. Each child will tell the correct definition of a family.) As you point to each figure, ask the children as a group, or individual children, to tell whether the figure is a father, a mother, a brother, a sister, a baby, and so on. Then repeat: "A family has a father, a mother, and at least one child." Then say to each child, "What is a family?" Give each child an opportunity to repeat the definition.

Show. As you put appropriate figures on the flannelboard, describe to the children what your own family was like when you were the age of the children in the group. Then say: "Each of you comes from a family. I'm going to ask each of you to pick a flannel figure for each member of your family and put it on the flannelboard."

Discuss, apply. As the child puts appropriate figures on the flannelboard, have him tell the name of the person each figure represents and the age of each child. Before the child sits down, have him and the rest of the children in the group count out loud the number of people in the family as you point to each figure. Take the figures off the flannelboard. Then have another child come to the flannelboard and go through this same process. Give *each* child in the group a turn. Have your list of family members for each child with you in order to help each child select the appropriate figures for the flannelboard to represent his family. Some of the children may forget to select figures to represent themselves. This is not unusual for such young children. Simply remind the child that he is part of his own family and can choose a figure that stands for himself. Provide encouragement and verbal praise as the children perform this task.

Posttest. Follow the steps in this section one week later.

Living in a world of people topical outline.

3.1. Living in a family
    3.1.1. Family
        3.1.1.1. What a family is
        3.1.1.2. Who is in a family
        3.1.1.3. What a family does
        3.1.1.4. Special occasions in the family
            3.1.1.4.1. Birthdays
            3.1.1.4.2. Family outings
            3.1.1.4.3. Holidays and special days (see 3.3.)
            3.1.1.4.4. Reunions
            3.1.1.4.5. Vacations
            3.1.1.4.6. Weddings
    3.1.2. Father
        3.1.2.1. What a father is
        3.1.2.2. What a father does in the family
        3.1.2.3. How a father shows love for his children
        3.1.2.4. How a father shows love for his wife (the mother)
    3.1.3. Mother
        3.1.3.1. What a mother is
        3.1.3.2. What a mother does in the family
        3.1.3.3. How a mother shows love for her children
        3.1.3.4. How a mother shows love for her husband (the father)
    3.1.4. Differences between what mother does and what father does
    3.1.5. Some things that both mothers and fathers do
    3.1.6. Brothers and sisters
        3.1.6.1. What brothers and sisters are
        3.1.6.2. What brothers and sisters do in the family
        3.1.6.3. Special things brothers and sisters can do because they are older or younger
        3.1.6.4. How brothers and sisters show love for one another
        3.1.6.5. How brothers and sisters show love for their parents (mother and father)

3.1.7.   Being a boy or being a girl
        3.1.7.1.   Similarities between boys and girls
        3.1.7.2.   Differences between boys and girls
3.1.8.   Babies
        3.1.8.1.   When I was a baby
        3.1.8.2.   How babies are alike
        3.1.8.3.   How babies are different
        3.1.8.4.   Caring for a baby
        3.1.8.5.   What a baby does (how it differs from older brothers and sisters)
3.1.9.   Advantages of living in a family
        3.1.9.1.   Someone always there to be a friend and companion
        3.1.9.2.   People of different ages can live together and learn to get along
        3.1.9.3.   Opportunities to help others of different ages
        3.1.9.4.   Opportunities for family members to teach each other
3.1.10. Other family members
        3.1.10.1. Grandfather
        3.1.10.2. Grandmother
        3.1.10.3. Aunt
        3.1.10.4. Uncle
        3.1.10.5. Cousin
        3.1.10.6. Stepfather
        3.1.10.7. Stepmother
3.2. Homes people live in
    3.2.1.   Kinds of homes people live in (house, apartment, trailer)
    3.2.2.   Rooms in a home
        3.2.2.1.   The uses of each room
    3.2.3.   Furniture in each room
3.3. Holidays and special days
    3.3.1.   National holidays and special days
    3.3.2.   Religious holidays
    3.3.3.   Special holidays and events
        3.3.3.1.   Chinese New Year
        3.3.3.2.   Local holidays and celebrations
3.4. Preparing foods
3.5. Learning to live with others in the prekindergarten
    3.5.1.   Names of children and adults in the prekindergarten
        3.5.1.1.   Identifying each person in the classroom
        3.5.1.2.   Something about each person in the classroom

3.5.2. Rules
    3.5.2.1. What a rule is
    3.5.2.2. Rules in the prekindergarten
        3.5.2.2.1. Rules that protect property
        3.5.2.2.2. Rules that make people safe
        3.5.2.2.3. Rules for an orderly physical environment
    3.5.2.3. Choices and consequences
3.5.3. Feelings
    3.5.3.1. Words for feelings
    3.5.3.2. Feelings about others
        3.5.3.2.1. What makes children feel good
        3.5.3.2.2. What makes children feel bad
    3.5.3.3. Feelings about events
    3.5.3.4. Feelings about oneself
    3.5.3.5. Expressing strong feelings
3.6. Money
    3.6.1. What money is
    3.6.2. What can be done with money
    3.6.3. How money is earned
3.7. People and places in the community
    3.7.1. Services
        3.7.1.1. Post office—mailman
        3.7.1.2. Fire station—fireman
        3.7.1.3. Police station—policeman
        3.7.1.4. School—teacher, principal
        3.7.1.5. Barbershop—barber
        3.7.1.6. Gas station—gas station attendant
        3.7.1.7. Car repair shop—mechanic
        3.7.1.8. Shoe repair shop—shoemaker
        3.7.1.9. Bank—bank teller
        3.7.1.10. Beauty shop—beauty operator (hairdresser)
        3.7.1.11. Restaurant—waiter, waitress
        3.7.1.12. Drugstore—druggist
        3.7.1.13. Miscellaneous
    3.7.2. Stores
        3.7.2.1. Grocery store—clerk, butcher
        3.7.2.2. Bakery—baker, clerk
        3.7.2.3. Department store—clerk
        3.7.2.4. Ice cream parlor—clerk, waiter, waitress
    3.7.3. Medical and social welfare services
        3.7.3.1. Doctor's office, clinic, hospital—doctor, nurse

                3.7.3.2. Dentist's office, clinic—dentist, dental assistant

                3.7.3.3. Welfare office—social worker

                3.7.3.4. Community and volunteer services— VISTA volunteer, SCORE volunteer, CAP workers, Boy Scouts, etc.

       3.7.4. Recreation

                3.7.4.1. Swimming pool—life guard, instructor

                3.7.4.2. Park, woods—park or forest ranger

                3.7.4.3. Movie theater—usher, cashier

                3.7.4.4. Spectator sports—players in the various sports

                3.7.4.5. Theater and concert stage—actors and performers

       3.7.5. Tranportation

                3.7.5.1. Railroad station—engineer, porter, conductor, ticket agent

                3.7.5.2. Airport—pilot, stewardess, ticket agent

                3.7.5.3. Automobile salesroom—salesman

                3.7.5.4. Bus station—bus driver

                3.7.5.5. Truck freight company—truck driver

                3.7.5.6. Taxi stand—taxi or cab driver

                3.7.5.7. Subway—ticket agent

                3.7.5.8. Dock, seaport—sailor

       3.7.6. Military

                3.7.6.1. Army

                3.7.6.2. Navy

                3.7.6.3. Marines

                3.7.6.4. Air Force

3.8.   Subcultures within the community

       3.8.1.   Ethnic subcultures

3.9.   People in other countries

       3.9.1.   Unique dress

       3.9.2.   Unique food

       3.9.3.   Unique money

       3.9.4.   Unique interests

       3.9.5.   Unique language

3.10.   People of other times

       3.10.1. Indians (early tribes)

       3.10.2. Pioneers

       3.10.3. Early settlers

       3.10.4. Pilgrims

REFERENCE

Leeper, S. H., Dales, R. J., Skipper, D. S., & Witherspoon, R. L. *Good schools for young children.* (2nd ed.) New York: Macmillan, 1968.

Chapter 12

Mathematics

We live in a world of numbers. The world of mathematics involves the use of numbers in a rigorously defined, logical set of operations. Mathematics is basically a language process—a language process that deals exclusively with the form, relationship, and arrangement of numbers. The symbols used in mathematics are really shorthand forms of logical, precise statements or operations.

Unfortunately many adults shy away from the subject of mathematics because it is perceived as "difficult," requiring great intellectual ability to understand. But if a young child can speak his native tongue, he can develop great skill in the use of many mathematical concepts. Principal mathematical subjects that can be studied in the prekindergarten are outlined on page 281.

Most contemporary mathematics programs for young children are based on the child's understanding of the concrete world around him and of everyday language. Fundamental concepts about numbers and their relationships are taught while emphasizing these concrete experiences and language abilities. The suggestions in this chapter are based on the child's ability to use his concrete world and everyday language. If you teach disadvantaged children, it may be wise to consider in detail the program outlined by Bereiter and Engelmann (1966). They suggest:

> Because of the culturally deprived child's deficiencies in language skills and concepts, he is greatly handicapped in reality applications of arithmetic learning, but he is relatively less handicapped in the kind of arithmetic learning that involves a special and limited set of concepts and rules [230].

SETS

A set, according to Maertens (1971), is "... any grouping of objects or elements whose members have something in common." The child is surrounded by hundreds of sets. For example, there are sets of blocks, sets of dishes, sets of silverware, sets of furniture, sets of pillows, and sets of books. The number in a grouping or set does not always remain static. That is, a set of silverware in most homes consists of a knife, a fork, and a spoon, or a set of three. Each person at the table receives a "set" of silverware. For more formal occasions the set of silverware for each person may be a soup spoon, a dessert spoon, a salad fork, a main dish fork, and a knife, or a set of five pieces of silverware. A set of living-room furniture in one home may consist of a sofa, two upholstered chairs, a coffee table, two end tables (or a set of six), whereas a set of living-room furniture in another home may consist of a sofa, a coffee table, and one reclining chair (or a set of three). It's a good idea to identify for the children the number of items in a set of silverware. Then ask them if such combinations as a knife, fork, and a saucer or a spoon, fork, and a cup can be sets. Children thus learn what *is* and what *is not* included in a given set. The rules of mathematics consist of the relationships among "sets" of various kinds.

COUNTING

Basic to mathematics is the concept of counting. It isn't unusual to see a young child imitating a counting procedure where he "counts" a group of objects but fails to attach each number in succession to each object counted. In other words, he may say more or fewer numbers than the actual number of objects. Bereiter and Engelmann (1966) and Engelmann (1969) have made many practical suggestions regarding teaching young children to count out loud, count the number of objects in a group, count to and from a given number, and determine which number comes after a given number by counting.

Counting out loud. Children can learn the names of arabic numerals like 3 and 5 just as they can learn names for objects such as *doll* and *house.* You can begin with the children by clapping your hands five times and counting, "One, two, three, four, *five."* Emphasize the last number because it not only stands for the last clap counted, but also for the total number of claps. Then have the children count with you, clapping their hands as they count. You can state the rule: "To count to *five,* I must say 'five.' One, two, three, four, five." Ask the children, "Did I count to five?" Teach the children the signal at which they are to begin counting, such as, "When I say 'clap,' you begin: one, two ... " as you demonstrate. Be sure the children are counting only when they clap and that they are progressing correctly from one to however many you count. When children are beginning to count, use numbers under five. You can increase to ten after the children have mastered counting to five.

Counting the number of objects in a group. After each child has successfully learned to count out loud up to the number ten, he can begin to count objects in groups. Start with different sets of the same number, such as three oranges and three cups. Arrange the sets in separate rows. Ask each child to tell you how many are in each row. Then have him count the objects to confirm what he just told you. Ask him how both sets are the same (they both have three members). Do the same for sets containing under three members and containing more than three members but not more than ten. Have sets of varied sizes, colors, shapes. You can arrange some sets so that the members are closely spaced and other sets with members widely separated. Sets can be arranged in semicircles or designs other than straight rows.

Counting to and from a given number. Children can learn to count *from* a given number *to* a given number. For example, say, "Begin counting from three. All set? Begin. Three, four, five, six. Where did we start counting? Yes, we started at three. Do it again. Begin. Three, . . . " When starting such learning experiences, begin with a number under five.

As soon as the children have mastered counting from a given number, teach them to count *to* a given number. For instance, "Let's count to seven. One, two, three, four, five, six, seven. What did we count to?" Try this with several numbers under ten. Then you can combine counting from and counting to, such as, "Now we're going to count from two to six. Here we go. Two, three, four, five, six. Where did we start counting? Where did we count to?" Continue similar exercises with several combinations under ten.

Naming the number that comes after a given number. Occasionally a prekindergarten child can successfully count to ten as long as he starts with "one" and doesn't stop before a given number. Ask children the basic question, "What comes after _____?" For example, "What comes after three? Let's try it [clap]. One, two, three, *four*. Four comes after three." Then ask individual children, "What comes after three?" If they give an incorrect answer, count from one to four, emphasizing four, the number that follows three. You can do this with each number up to ten. Clapping helps the children identify the number with something—in this case a simple action.

Once a child has learned to count, he is ready for the more

complicated operations of mathematics, such as addition and subtraction.

NUMBER SYMBOLS

Children who have learned to count objects can learn to identify symbols used to represent numbers or sets. These number symbols can be related to the counting processes. The child has the two-fold task of identifying the meaning of that symbol. That is, he learns not only to identify 5 as the numeral five but also to relate that symbol to such processes as counting the fingers on one hand, counting five objects of any one kind such as blocks, or counting the five different objects in a particular group. Flash cards, numbers on the chalkboard, and flannel numbers can be used for teaching number symbols.

ADDITION

Addition is basically the operation of counting forward or joining sets. In order to understand addition, children need to learn the meaning of the concept zero, the meaning of the plus sign, and also the idea that equality is basically the end result of a counting or joining operation. An example of an effective program to teach addition operations to prekindergarten children is the Distar Arithmetic program published by Science Research Associates (1970).

Adding as counting and the joining of sets. A flannelboard and flannel figures consisting of varied sets can be very useful for teaching the principles of addition. You could put flannel figures of four horses in a row on the flannelboard. Then say, "These horses are eating hay in the pasture. Now three more horses come over to eat the hay [place three flannel horses in a separate row on the flannelboard]. Now how many horses are eating hay in the pasture? Let's count them. First we started with four horses. Then three more came. That's five, six, seven horses [pointing to each horse in the group of three]. Four horses and three horses make seven horses." If the children have mastered sets from one to ten, they will recognize that four horses plus three horses equals seven horses.

The meaning of plus.   Children can first learn the name of the plus symbol, +. Simply say, "This is a plus symbol. What kind of symbol is this?" Make certain every child can identify the symbol. Then say, "The plus symbol [point to it on chalkboard] means to 'get more.' " Put two balls on the chalkboard. "How many balls do I have?" Put the plus sign to the right of the balls (O O +). Point to the balls and say, "I have two balls. This plus symbol [point to +] says I must get more balls. So I get three more balls [draw three more balls: OO + OOO]. What did this sign tell me to do [pointing to +]? Yes, it told me to get more balls. How many more balls did I get?" Do this with other sets on the flannelboard or the chalkboard. Sets can include spoons, squares, bunnies, trees, or anything else you select. If the children have mastered the use of the number symbols from one to nine, these number symbols can then be included after you have had many experiences joining sets.

The equal sign and the rule of equality.   The children are now ready to identify the equal sign or symbol, =. Add the equal sign to the joined sets just discussed with comments such as, "This is an equal sign. What is this? Yes, it is an equal sign. This says we *end up with* something. Here we have two balls [draw them on chalkboard or place them on flannelboard]. This sign [draw a +] says we get more. So let's get three more balls. This sign says we end up with something. Let's count the balls and see how many we end up with. We started with two balls and we got three more balls. That's three, four, five balls [point to each ball in second set]. So we end up with how many balls? Yes, we end up with five balls [place five balls in a row to the right of the equal sign]. If we have two balls [point to set of two balls] and get three more balls [point to plus sign and set of three balls], we end up with [point to equal sign] five balls [point to set of five balls]." Do similar exercises with other sets of varied numbers under ten. Then use correct number symbols above each set. Eventually fade out the sets and use just numbers such as 2 + 3 = 5. Work with the basic question, "(Some number) plus (some number) equals how many?" Move on to each succeeding step only after the children have mastered the preceding step.

The meaning of zero. The concept *zero* should be introduced to children before it is used in addition problems. One way to do this is to hold up the fingers of one hand and say, "How many fingers do I have?" Then hold up a closed fist and say, "Now how many fingers do I have? I have none. I have *zero* fingers. When there aren't any we call that zero." Then have the children look around the room for such things as golf balls, blankets, old ladies with hats, and so on. Say to each question, "Count them. That's right. There are no (name of item). We have *zero* (name of item)s."

The next step is to identify the symbol for zero, 0. Draw it on the chalkboard and say, "This is a *zero*. What is it?"

Finally, the zero sign can be added to equations in the following sequence:

$$1 + 0 =$$
$$2 + 0 =$$
$$3 + 0 =$$
$$4 + 0 =$$
$$5 + 0 =$$

Then read the first statement, "One plus zero equals how many? One plus zero equals one." Do the same for the other equations in the sequence. Then ask questions such as, "One plus how many equals one?" and "One plus zero equals how many?" and so on.

SUBTRACTION

Subtraction is the operation of undoing addition (Maertens, 1971). In order to use this process, children need to learn to identify and demonstrate understanding of the meaning of the concept *minus* and the minus sign, and how to remove sets in a given problem. The Distar Arithmetic program (Science Research Associates, 1970) also includes the concept of subtraction.

The meaning of minus. While teaching the principles of addition, you can also teach the principles of subtraction. First, the children learn to identify the symbol for subtraction, the minus sign or −. This means "get less." If you started with four horses on the flannelboard and "got more" or "added" three horses, you would end up with seven horses. Now you can demonstrate that if you "take away" the set of three horses, you end up with four horses, or the same set you started with. As you demonstrate this with the children for any given pair of sets, be sure to use the appropriate symbols (+, −, and =) and refer to them appropriately ("get more," "get less," and "end up with"). After the children have mastered subtraction with sets, you can add the number symbol for each set, eventually fading out the sets entirely.

TIME

While learning the basic mathematical concepts of sets, counting, addition, and subtraction, the children can learn the concepts of time. There are many words and phrases in our language that refer to time, such as *today, yesterday, tomorrow, soon, right now, early, late, in a little while*, and *birthday*. Units of time are countable. Artifacts of time such as watches, clocks, and timers help us to count units of time. The child who can count can begin to look at units of time in the past (counting backwards), in the present, and in the future (counting forward). Units of time can be minutes, hours, days, weeks, months, or years; or designated periods of time throughout a day such as snack time, play time, lunch time, or the time father is home from work; or throughout a week such as a school day, a holiday, or the day to go to church. The abstract and rather nebulous concepts of time such as *early* and *in a little while* can be learned in terms of selected units of time. A watch, clock, or timer can help children count these units of time with something tangible.

MISCELLANEOUS MATHEMATICS CONCEPTS

There are many other words in our language that are really number concepts learned through counting various units. Distance can be counted in terms of inches, feet, yards, miles, or in terms of so many given objects. Height can be counted in terms of inches and feet or some other comparison measure such as a block, a piece of string, or someone else's height line. Weight can be measured in pounds or in terms of the number of items in a container. The concept *pair* is learned by counting items in two's. The concepts *big, small, little, full, empty, few, many, first, second* are basically counting concepts in relationship to a given unit used for counting.

Because mathematics is so much a part of the child's here-and-now world, he can be given sequenced learning experiences that help him to speak the language of mathematics with understanding. Many prekindergarten children can learn more complex mathematical operations such as multiplication, division, and algebraic processes if they have good backgrounds in counting, addition, and subtraction. Because mathematics is basically a logical and precise language and so much a part of the child's world, he can be given the opportunity to utilize its operations as soon as he begins to use language with meaning.

SAMPLE LESSON PLAN

Area of curriculum: Mathematics

Mathematics focus: The equal sign and the rule of equality

Behavioral objectives: Each child will:

1. Tell the correct name of the equal sign when asked by the teacher. (Naming.)
2. Tell the correct meaning of the equal sign when asked by the teacher. (Serial memory.)
3. Verbally and physically demonstrate his understanding of equality by correctly solving each addition problem presented by the teacher. (Rule learning.)

To the teacher: The following materials will be needed for this lesson:

Flannelboard
Felt sets of 15 each: dogs, leaves, balls, pine trees
Felt cutouts of several plus and equal signs

This lesson is the first relating to this area of focus in mathematics. The children should have mastered the principles relating to sets, adding as counting and the joining of sets, and the meaning of plus.

   The children should be seated near you on the rug or on chairs where they can see and point to items on the flannelboard.

Learning Activities:

Posttest (behavioral objective from a previous lesson). Given a set of five cards he has never seen before containing mathematics symbols such as +, − and =, each child will correctly select the two cards containing the symbol +. (Concept learning.)

Show. Place an equal sign on the flannelboard. Say, "This is an equal sign."

Discuss. Ask each child (pointing to the equal sign), "What is this?" Let each child respond to the question. If a child gives an incorrect response simply say, "No. This is an equal sign. What is it?"

Show. Say (pointing to the equal sign), "This says we end up with something."

Discuss. Ask each child (pointing to the equal sign), "What does this say?" Allow each child to respond. If a child gives an incorrect response, simply say, "No, it says we end up with something. What does it say?"

Show, discuss. Put three dog cutouts in a row on the flannelboard to the far left of the equal sign. Say, "Here are some dogs. How many dogs? Yes, we have three dogs." Add a plus sign and ask, "What is this? Yes, it's a plus sign. What does it tell us to do? It tells us to get some more. [Put two more dog cutouts in a row to the right of the plus sign.] Let's get how many more dogs? Two more dogs. If we have three dogs [point to set of three] and we get [point to plus sign] two more [point to set of two dogs], we *end up with* [point to equal sign] how many?" Then say, "If we have three dogs [point to set of three dogs] and get two more dogs [point to set of two dogs], we end up with [point to equal sign] five dogs—one, two, three [put three dogs in a row to the right of the equal sign, then pause before continuing to put down two more dogs in the same row], four, *five* dogs. Say it with me." Repeat what you have just said as you point to appropriate sets and symbols. Then ask each child, again pointing to appropriate sets and symbols as you ask each question, "If you have three dogs and you get two more dogs, you end up with how many?" Be sure each child responds. If a child responds incorrectly, give him the correct answer and have him repeat the answer.

Show, discuss.   Repeat the procedure with cutouts of leaves
and with cutouts of balls, using the same number in each set
(three and two and five). Then, using the same cutouts, change
the sets to three and four and seven respectively and follow the
same procedure a third time.

Show, apply.   Put the following configuration on the
flannelboard with pine tree cutouts:

Say, "Here we have three pine trees [point to set of three], we
get [point to plus sign] two more pine trees [point to set of
two], and we end up with [point to equal sign] how many
[say name of individual child]?" Allow child to respond
verbally and place an appropriate set of pine trees to the right
of the equal sign. If the child demonstrates incorrectly, ask
another child to help. Then give the same problem to the child
who answered incorrectly. Present a similar problem to each
child in the group, using sets of pine trees in the following
configurations at random: two and one and three; one and two
and three; two and three and five; three and two and five;
four and three and seven; three and four and seven. Also
randomly ask individual children as you point to the equal sign,
"What is this? What does it tell us?" Be sure that each child has
the opportunity to name the equal sign, tell what the equal sign
means, and solve an equation problem with sets of pine trees.

Posttest.   Repeat this procedure in a day or two, using figures
of rabbits or some other type of figure not used previously in
instruction.

Mathematics topical outline.

4.1. Sets
4.2. Counting*
    4.2.1. Counting out loud
    4.2.2. Counting the number of objects in a group
    4.2.3. Counting to and from a given number
    4.2.4. Naming the number that comes after a given number
4.3. Number symbols
4.4. Addition*
    4.4.1. Adding as counting and the joining of sets
    4.4.2. The meaning of plus
    4.4.3. The equal sign and the rule of equality
    4.4.4. The meaning of zero
4.5. Subtraction*
    4.5.1. The meaning of minus
4.6. Time
    4.6.1. Calendar
        4.6.1.1. Days
        4.6.1.2. Weeks
        4.6.1.3. Months
    4.6.2. Artifacts of time
        4.6.2.1. Clock
        4.6.2.2. Watch
        4.6.2.3. Timers
    4.6.3. Miscellaneous time concepts
        4.6.3.1. Today
        4.6.3.2. Yesterday
        4.6.3.3. Tomorrow
        4.6.3.4. Soon
        4.6.3.5. Right now
        4.6.3.6. Early
        4.6.3.7. Late (also "later")
        4.6.3.8. In a little while
        4.6.3.9. Birthday
4.7. Miscellaneous
    4.7.1. Distance
    4.7.2. Height (feet, inches)
    4.7.3. Weight (pounds)
    4.7.4. Pair
    4.7.5. Big—small—little
    4.7.6. Full—empty
    4.7.7. Few—many
    4.7.8. Ordinals (first, second, etc.)

---

*Derived from Bereiter, C., & Engelmann, S., *Teaching disadvantaged children in the preschool.* Englewood Cliffs, N. J.: Prentice-Hall, Inc., 1966; and Engelmann, S., *Preventing failure in the primary grades.* New York: Simon and Schuster, 1969.

REFERENCES

Bereiter, C., & Engelmann, S. *Teaching disadvantaged
      children in the preschool.* Englewood Cliffs, N. J.: Prentice-
      Hall, 1966.
Engelmann, S. *Preventing failure in the primary grades.* New
      York: Simon and Schuster, 1969.
Maertens, N. W. Who's afraid of modern math? *Parent's
      Magazine,* August 1971.
Science Research Associates. *Distar Arithmetic I and II.* 1970.

Chapter 13

Movement: The Child's Natural Language

Prekindergarten children move far better than they speak. Their movement vocabulary is larger than their speaking vocabulary. They have been moving longer than they have been speaking. Therefore they probably learn more effectively by movement than by the spoken word. Adults often forget that children learn most effectively by demonstrating what they know through movement. Perhaps this is because most adults have learned to depend on the spoken or written word as the best demonstration of what they have learned. And, too, adults often feel uncomfortable and embarrassed when they must describe something with their bodies rather than with their voices (note the problems some adults have playing the game of charades).

Young children are constantly moving. Even in deep sleep their bodies seldom seem to stop moving. When they talk, their language is usually punctuated with movements that reinforce and almost "repeat" what they say. Their movements reveal their feelings, such as the wide swinging arms and lunging walk of a happy 3-year-old or the arms pulled close to the body and the head turned to one side of the child who is shy and somewhat afraid. Sometimes their bodies are tense and rigid and poised for flight. At other times their bodies are relaxed and their heads and arms and hands seem to flow in space as they gently reach out to touch a loved person. Movement is their natural language.

THE BASIC MOVEMENT CURRICULUM

A basic movement topical outline is found on page 300. This analysis of movement is a modified form of one developed by Laban (1963). The basic movement concepts in the outline can form the basic movement learning experiences for children in the prekindergarten, and these learning experiences can form the movement area of the prekindergarten curriculum.

Basic movement learning forms the foundation of the movement vocabulary from which to draw for learning experiences in other movement areas such as games, sports, gymnastics, dance, pantomime, and role-playing. Basic movement can be likened to the trunk of a tree with the other movement areas forming the branches extending from the trunk, as illustrated in Figure 13–1.*

Some of the derivatives of basic movement, such as role-playing, pantomime, and dance, are used in other areas of the prekindergarten curriculum as important learning activities related to other concepts and ideas. Role-playing and pantomime are discussed in Chapter 8 and dance is discussed in Chapter 14. Games, sports, and gymnastics are generally too advanced for emphasis in the prekindergarten curriculum. As the children continue their movement experiences in the kindergarten and elementary grades, the relative emphasis on basic movement is decreased as greater emphasis is placed on basic movement derivatives, particularly games and sports.

In the basic movement curriculum the *problem-solving approach* is utilized in the learning activities. That is, the children are presented problems to solve in movement, and the solutions lead them to a discovery of the basic movement objectives desired. This approach

*Acknowledgment for the idea of basic movement is given to Carolyn Rasmus, Women's Physical Education Department, Brigham Young University.

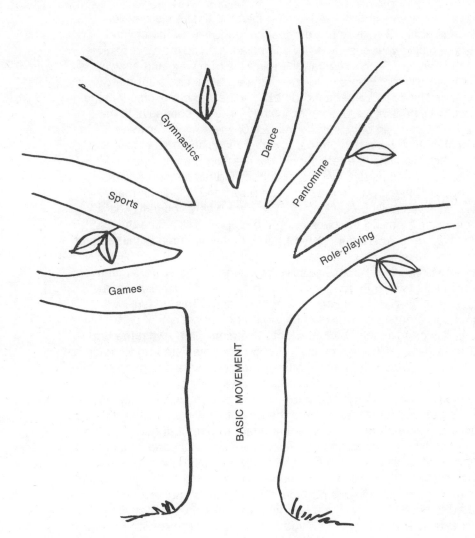

Figure 13–1. Basic movement and its derivatives.

seems more effective in terms of learning than the this-is-the-way-you-
can-do-it approach. For example, the teacher suggests to the children,
"Find some part of your body that you can balance on so that your back is
toward the ceiling." Each child can then find his own way, and his way
may be quite different from someone else's way, but it can still be a
correct way. Not every child has to do exactly the same movement at the
same time everyone else does it. For instance, the teacher says to the
children, "Put one part of your body in back of you so you can't see it."
Some children will put a hand in back, some a foot, some an elbow, and
so on. In the meantime, the teacher encourages children in their
differences by saying such things as, "Johnny hid his hand in back,"
"Suzy tried a different way; she used her elbow," and "I like the many
different ways you put a part of your body in back where you can't see it."
Children who are having trouble solving the problem will notice the
children who receive encouragement and usually will imitate these other
children. As these children imitate others, their basic movement skills will
develop. They will then be able to solve problems on their own. Whenever
these "imitators" begin to solve problems in new and different ways, they
can receive immediate reinforcement for their efforts. This, in turn, will
lead to a continuing success spiral in solving basic movement problems.

       Basic movement is divided into two main parts: what the body
does, and where the body moves. The sub-concepts listed under each of
these parts on page 300 form the basis of lesson plans designed to help
the child learn to move his body in as many ways as possible. These
sub-concepts can be combined into a variety of behavioral objectives
related to basic movement that help the child to know well what his body
can do and where it can move. It is important to point out here that the
emphasis of learning activities in basic movement is the *movement of the
child's own body as an end in itself,* not as a means to an end. When a
child is "flying like a bird" or "moving along like a truck," the movement
becomes a means to demonstrate the child's understanding of concepts
unrelated to his own body. Such learning activities are perfectly
legitimate for a lesson about birds and a lesson about trucks. But a lesson
about basic movement per se should help the child learn

something about *"how I move."* An illustration will help. A teacher
said to a group of children learning about the movement concept *flight*,
"See how you can fly like birds." The children went scurrying across the
floor wildly flapping their arms while some even made shrieking sounds
in an attempt to imitate birds. This wasn't what the teacher expected so
she continued, "See if you can fly higher," in a desperate attempt to
motivate the children to get their feet off the ground. But arms just flapped
higher while feet remained in steady contact with the floor. This teacher
would have been far more successful if she had left out the *birds* concept
and asked the children to "Show me how high you can get up off the
ground." She possibly could have added later, "Can you use your arms to
get higher?" Then she would have been putting the emphasis on the
child's own body movement related to the movement concept *flight*
rather than shifting the emphasis to *birds*.

     Some simple pieces of equipment are needed for basic
movement learning experiences. Logsdon and Barrett (1969) suggest the
following.

> *For each child:*
>   A seven to eight foot jump rope (made with #10 sash cord
>   with ends taped to prevent fraying)
>   Ball (6 to 8 inches in diameter)
>   Beanbag
>   Marker (bleach or detergent plastic bottles)
>   Plastic hoop (28 to 36 inches in diameter)
>   Yarn ball
> *For every three to five children:*
>   Wooden box (approximately 18" × 24" × 14")
>   Mat (4" × 6")
>   Balance beam (2 × 4 boards are suitable)
> *For each class:*
>   Tambourine or other percussion instrument to be used as a
>   signaling device

WHAT THE BODY CAN DO

The purpose of lessons in this section is to help the child become aware of the possibilities of movement with various parts of his body and his whole body as well as to develop greater facility in various body skills.

Body Awareness

Body awareness has to do with the conscious perception of what each body part is doing or can do and what the body as a whole can do. First the child learns what the parts of the body can do.

Adults take it for granted that young children know the various parts of the body. This isn't necessarily the case and, therefore, the children in the prekindergarten group could begin with a learning activity related to identification of the parts of the body. The parts of the body include the head, the neck, the chin, the forehead, the shoulders, the arms, the elbows, the hands, the fingers, the chest, the stomach, the back, the seat, the legs, the knees, the feet, the toes, the wrists, and the heels. You could start out by pointing to each of your own body parts and having the children name each one. Those the children miss can be labeled and the children can then repeat the names of the parts they didn't know until they can name them correctly. Then you can have the children point to their own body parts and name them as they point. Be sure that each child learns to name each part of his body.

Children may then be ready for a simple game, where you give them directions about various parts of the body and they move as you direct. For example, "Shake your head; put your hands on your feet, your knees, your shoulders; touch your chin; touch your knees with your elbows; grasp your left foot with your right hand; touch your right shoulder with your left hand." Another activity would be a game where individual children get under a sheet and hold up various body parts such as a foot, a knee, an elbow, a head to be named by the other children in the group.

(If there are children in the group who are afraid to go under the sheet, don't force them.) The music game "hokey-pokey" is a favorite of many prekindergarten children. The song is sung and the children follow directions: "Put your left foot in, put your left foot out; put your left foot in and shake it all about ... "

After the children have learned what the parts of the body are, they can learn to move these parts in *relationship* to other parts of the body, to other people, or to objects in space. The particular relationships to be learned would be *above, level, below, near,* and *far.* These concepts of spatial relationship are basic to all movement. If the children do not understand any of the spatial concepts, teach them the concepts before they use them in solving movement problems. For example, a problem could be, "While you move around the room, get your elbow as near to someone as you can without touching him." Here you are asking the child to move the body part *elbow* in a *near* relationship to another person. You could do something similar to teach the other relationships. For example, "Put your hands at the same level as the drum," "Get your chin higher than the chair while sitting on the floor," "Move your shoulder as far away from someone else in this room as you can." A child can also learn how to use one body part in relationship to another, such as, "Find a way to put your feet above your head," or "Get your forehead as far away from your knees as you can."

Parts of the body also can act as *body supports.* That is, they can support the weight of the body. Here the children could first discover what parts of the body will support the rest of the body (for instance, the seat, the back, the stomach, the feet, and the hands). As you discuss these points, let the children try supporting their bodies on these parts. For example, "Find some part of your body besides your feet that can support your body." After the single body supports have been discussed and practiced, you might help the children discover ways that combinations of parts of the body can be used to support body weight (for example, hands and knees, hands and feet, hands and seat, elbows and knees, and so on). Let the children solve body support problems, such as "Support your body on two body parts with your seat higher than your head." Such learning activities help the children to recognize that body parts can support the body in many other ways besides the usual ways of using the feet or the seat.

Body awareness also is developed through *whole body* activities. *Relationship* activities can be done with the whole body as well as parts of the body, such as moving the whole body as near to an object or person as possible without touching it /him, moving the body above or below an object, making the body level with something or someone else, and moving as far away from a person or object as possible. The body can also move *around, under, in, over,* and *through* in relationship to objects and people in space. For example, one activity children enjoy is walking through a simple chair maze, trying not to bump into any of the chairs.

The whole body can also curl and stretch, twist and turn, and make different shapes. To *curl* means to assume a position with the legs drawn up. To *stretch* is to lengthen the body or its parts by reaching as far as possible. To *twist* is to wind or coil the rest of the body while one part of the body remains still. To *turn* means the body can move around as a whole, rotate, or revolve. Children can learn to do each of these separately and then try to do them in sequences, such as, "Find a way to stretch your body and then twist it." Children also can learn the *shapes* their bodies can make. For instance, the body can form a circle (or at least an oval) by lying down on the floor and bringing hands and feet together while the back, seat, and stomach remain as rounded as possible. A triangle can be formed by standing on hands and toes and keeping the seat in the air. Three sides of a square (or rectangle) can be formed by sitting on the floor and extending hands and arms in front of the body. Body parts can also form shapes, such as the arms formed into a circle, the hands on the hips while standing, the elbows sticking out from the side forming a triangle, and so forth. Even the fingers can make circles, squares, triangles, ovals, and rectangles.

Body Skills

Basic body skills are involved in most basic movement experiences. Body skills are of three types—locomotor, nonlocomotor, and manipulative.

Locomotor skills.   Locomotor skills involve movement of the body from place to place. There are four main locomotor skills: walking, running, jumping, and hopping. Sliding is a derivative of walking. Leaping and galloping are derivatives of running. Skipping combines hopping and walking. Rolling is a hybrid all by itself.

Walking is the ability to advance on foot in step-by-step fashion without support. Virtually all prekindergarten children without physical handicaps can walk.

Sliding means to move in smooth, continuous contact with a surface. It can be in any direction. However, when sliding sideways, prekindergarten children have a tendency to cross their feet. Sometimes just calling this problem to their attention will solve the problem. Occasionally you might have to demonstrate a slide for the children before they learn how to slide sideways.

Running means to move on foot in such a way that both feet leave the ground during each stride. Most prekindergarten children can run.

Leaping means to spring forward off the ground with both legs, often with one leg extended in front of the other. One must be able to leap in order to participate in structured sport activities such as basketball, volleyball, and the trampoline in later years. It also is a basic skill in dance.

Galloping is the typical prekindergarten "skip." It means to move forward rapidly at a speed similar to running but with a syncopated rhythm, a type of leap-step, leap-step or long-short, long-short gait. The same foot always leads.

Jumping is springing off the ground by a muscular effort of the legs and feet and landing on both feet at once. Some prekindergarten children need extra help to develop this skill.

Hopping is taking off on one foot and landing on that same foot. It often gets confused with jumping. Hopping involves one foot whereas jumping involves two feet.

Skipping is a complicated skill that many prekindergarten children have not learned. It involves a hop and a step by each foot in alternating fashion. Most prekindergarten children gallop and call it skipping. Don't attempt to teach skipping if children can't skip in the prekindergarten. Just call it a gallop.

Rolling means to move along a surface by turning over and over. There are several ways to roll, such as rolling like a log from back to stomach or doing a somersault. A child might also roll from seat to shoulder to seat.

Once the children have learned the basic locomotor skills well, they can begin to combine them in sequences such as, "Find a way to move around the room by sliding, then hopping, then rolling." Start in sequences of two and then move to three skills in a sequence. Most prekindergarten children will probably have difficulty with sequences longer than three. Skills can also be combined with body awareness activities, such as "Gallop with some part of your body behind you" or "Roll in a curled position" or "Find a way to walk with your body in a triangle shape."

Occasionally it is a good idea to accompany skills activities with a rhythm instrument such as a drum, a suitable piano composition, or an instrumental recording. However, when children are first learning a skill and ways to combine skills, accompaniment may confuse them. Your own voice, the suggestions you make, and the verbal reinforcement you give will be adequate in most cases.

Pieces of equipment are useful when teaching skills because they enrich the learning environment. For instance, it is difficult to "go over" an object if an object is not available to go over. Objects such as boxes, plastic hoops, ropes, or long boards can be used in many ways as children develop their locomotor skills.

Nonlocomotor skills.   Nonlocomotor skills involve movement of the body while staying in one place. This type of skill includes pushing and pulling, swinging the body, and twisting and turning. For example, you can say, "Find a way to push your partner to the marker" or "Find a way to swing your body while you are standing still."

Manipulative skills.   Manipulative skills are movements involving controlled use of the hands and feet. These include grasping, opening and closing the hand, pointing, throwing, and catching. The manipulative skills of throwing and catching are not highly developed in prekindergarten children and it probably is not necessary to spend a great deal of effort teaching these skills. Larger objects for throwing and catching can be quite motivating for some children in a planned experience. These objects might include balls about the size of volleyballs and yarn balls. Small balls such as balls the size of baseballs, softballs, or golf balls are unsuitable because they travel at too high a speed and require visual motor control usually beyond the maturation level of the prekindergarten child.

WHERE THE BODY CAN MOVE

Children who have explored what their bodies can do in terms of body awareness and body skills can begin to explore movements related to *where* the body can move. This includes an exploration of direction, level, and pathway in relationship to movement. The whole body as well as parts of the body can move in various *directions*. These directions include forward and backward, upward and downward, and sideward. Some possible instructions for direction would include, "Gallop forward as far as you can and then walk backward until you get to me" or "Curl up into a tiny ball and grow up as tall as you can and then come down as low as you can."

The body can also move at various *levels*. These levels can be high or low or somewhere in between. A movement can only be at a certain level, high or low or in between, as it relates to another part of the body, an object, or a person. Some possible instructions would be, "Find one part of your body that can move higher than any other part" or "Move your body so nothing you move is higher than your belt."

There are various *pathways* for movement in space. *Floor patterns* can be straight or curved. A straight pathway is one that moves in a straight line, like a ruler or a board. A curved pathway bends and winds like a snake. *Shape in space* refers to the shape of the body and its parts as it moves through space. Sample instructions related to pathway might be, "Walk and run in a straight line as far as you can go" or "While two parts of your body make a circle, leap across the room in a curved line like the rope on the floor."

The purpose of learning what the body can do in terms of movement and where it can move is not only to participate in and enjoy these movement skills for their own sake but also to provide a broader vocabulary of movement through which the child can communicate what he perceives, thinks, and feels.

PLANNING AND TEACHING
BASIC MOVEMENT LESSON PLANS

When teaching a basic movement lesson, it's a good idea to let the individual children be the *show* steps rather than the teacher. For example, in a lesson relating to the concepts of speed and pathway, one objective could be, "Each child will run continuously at a given signal, changing his pathway at least two times." In earlier lessons the children have demonstrated that they understand the meaning of pathway. So the teacher begins the lesson by talking to the children in a group. He suggests that he would like to see if the children can run and change their pathways at least twice while they are running. He asks one child to demonstrate. While the child demonstrates, the other children watch and the teacher encourages the volunteer child (show step). After the demonstration the teacher asks the children in the group whether or not the child was running, how they could tell, what pathways he used and whether or not he had at least two pathways while he was running (discuss step). After the discussion the teacher asks all the children to find a way to run using at least two pathways. As the children apply the suggestion of the teacher, the teacher provides verbal encouragement to the children, such as, "Rob is running in a straight line now and Aaron is running in a curved line" and "I like the way Susan is running without touching anyone else" (reinforcement). Sometimes the whole group can act as a show step with the teacher giving the children a movement problem to solve (show step) and then bringing them back into a group to discuss what they did (discuss step) before having the children try it again (apply step). Examples of such problems would be, "Find a way to twist your body while your body is in one place" and "Show me one way to turn while your body is moving."

If the teacher demonstrates the movement patterns for the children, the demonstration tends to restrict the imagination of the children. Because the teacher is an authority figure—just because he's bigger and older if for no other reason—the children seem to feel they must do exactly what the teacher does and nothing else. However, when children demonstrate for one another, they tend to be free and imaginative in discovering new ways to move. The teacher can label the movement of the children and provide encouragement as the children move their bodies. In general, the teacher who is bounding around the room with the children is abdicating his role as careful observer and encourager.

For an interesting change of pace when the weather is good, basic movement lessons can be held outside. You will need a space that is flat and at least as large as the space used indoors. When you teach these lessons outdoors, be sure you discuss with the children a few necessary rules, such as where the boundaries of your movement space will be, objects or materials to be used for the lesson, and so on.

If possible, children should be allowed to have bare feet while participating in basic movement instruction. This allows greater freedom of movement.

The size of the group of children you work with depends a great deal on the amount of free floor space available. Many elementary schools have gymnasiums where groups of 12 to 15 children can work at one time. In most prekindergartens, however, the ideal group size would probably be between five and eight children. It is not a good idea to work with the entire prekindergarten class, even if the space is available. This would prevent you from giving individual attention to each child in the group.

SAMPLE LESSON PLAN*

Area of curriculum: Basic movement

Basic movement focus: Body awareness: Relationships

Behavioral objectives: Each child will:

1. Demonstrate with his body a minimum of three different ways to go over and three different ways to go under the objects provided. (Complex skill.)

*Acknowledgment for this lesson idea is given to Carolyn Rasmus, Women's Physical Education Department, Brigham Young University.

2. Demonstrate his awareness of his total body by moving under and over an object without touching it with any part of his body. (Complex skill.)

To the teacher: Before beginning the lesson, set up the equipment in a semicircle as illustrated in the following diagram:

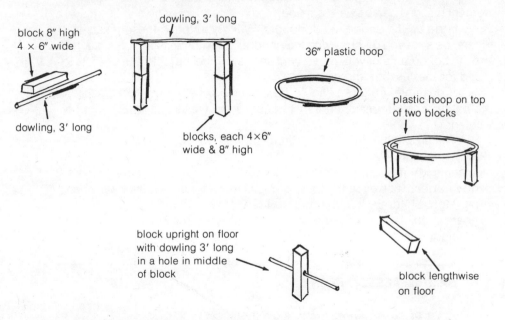

block 8″ high
4 × 6″ wide

dowling, 3′ long

dowling, 3′ long

blocks, each 4×6″ wide & 8″ high

36″ plastic hoop

plastic hoop on top of two blocks

block upright on floor with dowling 3′ long in a hole in middle of block

block lengthwise on floor

Learning Activities:

Posttest   (behavioral objective from a previous lesson). When shown a film clip of children using movement equipment, each child will correctly select the three instances where children go over and the three instances where children go under equipment. (Concept learning—this is also a pretest for this lesson.)

Show.   Say to children, "Go to a piece of equipment and show me how you can go over it and under it." (Children demonstrate.) Call children back to the group on the floor.

Discuss.   Ask each child to tell how he went over and how he went under. Point out as the children talk that there are different ways to go over and go under, using as many examples from the children's demonstration as possible. These different ways include crawling under, jumping over, leaping over, moving backwards or forwards with the stomach toward the ceiling or the floor, and so on.

Apply.   Now tell the children that they can choose three different ways to go *under* an object. Let the children try while you encourage their efforts. Then tell the children to choose three different ways to go *over* an object, again encouraging their efforts.

Show, discuss.   Call the children back to the group and tell them you are going to ask them to do something that is a little bit different now. Select one of the children to choose an object and go under that object without touching it with any part of his body. As the child goes under the object, have the rest of the children watch to see if he touches it. If he touches it, have the children decide which part of his body touched it. Have another child go under an object a different way (such as his stomach toward the floor instead of the ceiling). Discuss his movement the same way.

Apply: After the two demonstrations, have each child in the group go under an object without touching it with any part of his body. Verbally encourage the children as they do this exercise.

Posttest.   One week later have the children perform both objectives again.

Basic movement topical outline.

5.1. What the body does
    5.1.1. Body awareness
        5.1.1.1. Parts of the body
            5.1.1.1.1. Body relationships
            5.1.1.1.2. Body supports
        5.1.1.2. Whole body
            5.1.1.2.1. Relationships
            5.1.1.2.2. Curl—stretch
            5.1.1.2.3. Shapes
            5.1.1.2.4. Twist—turn
    5.1.2. Body skills
        5.1.2.1. Locomotor skills
            5.1.2.1.1. Walk
            5.1.2.1.2. Slide
            5.1.2.1.3. Leap
            5.1.2.1.4. Gallop
            5.1.2.1.5. Jump
            5.1.2.1.6. Hop
            5.1.2.1.7. Skip*
            5.1.2.1.8. Roll
            5.1.2.1.9. Run
        5.1.2.2. Nonlocomotor skills
            5.1.2.2.1. Push—pull
            5.1.2.2.2. Swing—sway
            5.1.2.2.3. Twist—turn
        5.1.2.3. Manipulative skills
            5.1.2.3.1. Throw
            5.1.2.3.2. Catch
5.2. Where the body moves
    5.2.1. Direction
        5.2.1.1. Forward—backward
        5.2.1.2. Upward—downward
        5.2.1.3. Sideways
    5.2.2. Level
        5.2.2.1. High
        5.2.2.2. Medium
        5.2.2.3. Low
    5.2.3. Pathway
        5.2.3.1. Floor pattern
        5.2.3.2. Shape in space

---

*Most prekindergarten children do not skip.

Vance

Oct 1   Ch 1, 2

" 8   3, 4, 7

" 15   16

" 22   —

" 29   —

Nov 5   12

" 12   15

" 19   11

" 26   9, 14

REFERENCES

Laban, _____ ... _____ onal Dance (2nd ed.) London: MacDonald and Evans, Ltd., 1963

Logsdon, B. J. & Barrett, K. R. Ready? Set ... Go! (Teacher's _____ ... Course) Bloomington, Ind.: National Instructional _____ vision Center, 1969

Chapter 14

Music: The Universal Language

Music has been called the universal language. Cultural anthropologists have even suggested that some melodies are universal in children and, therefore, possibly inherited, such as this childhood chant:

Yah-yah- yah-yah   yah- yah;   yah-yah- yah-yah   yah- yah.

But whether or not music is an "inherited" universal language, it is obvious to anyone who lives and works with young children that music is an important part of the experience of the growing child. Infants in their cribs each have unique patterns of rhythmic movement accompanied by patterns of sounds that vary in pitch, in dynamics, in tempo, and in tone quality. These are some of the elements of music. These elements of music continue to be apparent as the child increases in verbal and motor skill. It isn't unusual to hear a toddler or prekindergarten child punctuate his play with "mood music" of his own creation. The words of his thoughts in play may be coupled with a familiar tune.

Or words and melody can be made up as the moment, mood, and thought dictate.

Music has been defined as "forms moving tonally" (Hanslick, quoted in Aronoff, 1969). Children are less esoteric in their definitions; to them, music is:

... nice sounds
... making nice sounds go together
... singing how you feel [Aronoff, 1969, p. 26]

The elements of music are rhythm, tempo, melody, tone quality, dynamics, harmony, and form.* But music is not created in a vacuum. Skills are necessary if music is to be made. Music skills include listening, singing, moving, playing instruments, creating, and reading. Prekindergarten children can develop all of these skills.

Because the structure of music is made up of unique elements as well as skills, it qualifies as an area of study in itself. Music skills and music elements are outlined on page 335. The music area of the curriculum can be one of the most effective areas for the provision of firsthand experiences, frequent application, and successful experiences for the young child.

The prekindergarten child who experiences a wide variety of carefully sequenced learning experiences related to specific music elements and skills will be more likely to enjoy and participate in many kinds of music activities throughout his lifetime. His musical tastes will broaden, and he will have the freedom to select musical experiences that deepen and enrich all areas of his life.

This chapter is designed to help you plan lessons related to music as a field of study in itself. However, music activities can and should be important learning activities to enrich lessons in other areas of the curriculum also. For example, a song about a doctor could enrich a lesson on the idea, "The doctor is a special kind of helper;" a recording of two contrasting tempos could be used to help the children think about and create different kinds of

*Acknowledgment for many ideas in this chapter is given to Frances Aronoff, author of *Music and Young Children* (N. Y.: Holt, Rinehart and Winston, 1969); to Mrs. Kent (Patricia) Nielsen and Dr. D. Evan Davis, Brigham Young University.

fingerpaintings during a lesson in the graphic arts; a song about the wind could enhance a science lesson revolving around the concept of air. The suggestions in this chapter for planning lessons related to music can also help you plan music activities in other curriculum areas.

MUSIC SKILLS

It is easy to assume that prekindergarten children know how to listen and what to listen for in music, that they know how to sing, to move, and to create their own musical experiences. It is true that most 3-year-old and 4-year-old children have most of these skills; movement is as natural as breathing and the other skills seem to be learned by imitation of others if by no other means. However, it is important to provide the child with a wide variety of experience in the prekindergarten so he can practice his musical skills and broaden his use of these skills. In addition, these skills are necessary in order for the child to learn the elements of music. Let's take a closer look at the music skills outlined on page 335.

Listening

The skill of listening is the foundation on which all the other music skills are developed. A child cannot move to musical sounds unless he has first learned to listen. He must listen before he can create his own musical experiences.

When teaching children to listen, be sure to give some focus for their listening. You could play a series of three or four short compositions on the piano or record player and ask the children to choose which music they would like to accompany these activities:

Rock a doll to sleep
Fly like a bird
Run down a grassy hill
Jump on a large inner tube

You could have children listen to a record or to someone singing a song or playing an instrument and tell you how it makes them feel inside. Children also can listen to you hum a tune or play a record in order to identify a familiar tune or a familiar rhythm. When children listen with their "inner ears," they pantomime or do only the actions to a song, singing only a specific part of it out loud. Brothers and sisters, parents, or local musicians can bring their instruments to class to perform for the children and help them to identify the name and type of instrument by its sound. It is recommended that only instruments the children can see and hear firsthand should be used for such listening experiences. Any music skill you teach should always begin with a similar listening experience.

Singing

Every child who can talk can sing. Contrary to what you might believe, it is impossible for a person to sing in a monotone. Some children will take longer to learn the melody or words (or both) than others, but each child is capable of singing. Children who have developed a broad repertoire of songs can use these songs to enrich many everyday activities. There is probably a great deal of truth in the statement, "The singing child is a happy child."

In order to sing a song, a child must be able to do more than say the words to the song. Saying words is a language experience, but singing includes the ability to hear and produce an appropriate series of musical tones together with the words that accompany them. This is a complicated skill, but it is within the ability of virtually every prekindergarten child. If you enjoy the songs you sing, your enthusiasm will carry over to the children. They will enjoy the repetition of songs as they practice singing appropriate words and tones. When you set the model, they are likely to follow. However, learn to watch and listen to individual children as they sing in a group. If children are not singing appropriate words or melody, it is quite possible the words and music are not distinctive enough. You may have to slow down the singing, reduce or eliminate the accompaniment, or sing the song alone several times before the children learn to sing it well. Here are some suggestions that may help you when teaching a song to prekindergarten children.

1.   When introducing the song for the first time, *play it or sing it from beginning to end.* Be sure that the words and the melody are clear and distinct. It isn't always necessary to put the words and the music together when first learning a song. You can hum the song and then have the children hum it with you. You can have someone play the melody on the piano or other musical instrument and ask the children what kind of song they think it is. Then you can put the words with the music and have them listen to find out if the song is what they thought it would be. Often the best way to teach a short song is to sing it with simple accompaniment several times, suggesting that children join you when they are ready to do so. Teaching a song by line or phrase is frustrating to children and prevents them from perceiving the whole song as an entity. Singing thus becomes a chore instead of a happy experience.

2.   *Motivate the children to learn the song by presenting a picture, an object, a story, or a problem to solve.* For example, when teaching the song "Popcorn Popping on the Apricot Tree" (Groesbeck, 1968), you could bring a bouquet of apricot blossoms to class and ask the children what they are, what they look like, how they smell, where they're found, and so on. Then suggest that the song they will be learning has something to do with these blossoms.

3.   *Give the children something to listen for.* For instance, after you have talked about the apricot blossom bouquet, ask the children to listen carefully to the song "Popcorn Popping on the Apricot Tree" so they can tell you the words that talk about the apricot blossoms. Then sing the song:

*Popcorn Popping on the Apricot Tree**

(Line 1)   I looked out the window and what did I see?
(Line 2)   Popcorn popping on the apricot tree!
(Line 3)   Spring had brought me such a nice surprise
(Line 4)   Blossoms popping right before my eyes.
(Line 5)   I could take an armful and make a treat,
(Line 6)   A popcorn ball that would smell so sweet.
(Line 7)   It wasn't really so, but it seemed to be
(Line 8)   Popcorn popping on the apricot tree.

After singing the song, ask the children to tell you what words they heard in the

*Groesbeck, 1968. Copyright, Deseret Book Company. Reprinted by permission.

song that tell about the apricot blossoms. They may not say the words exactly as they were sung in the song, but give them encouragement for coming close to the correct words. Sing the song again while the children listen for the same thing. They will begin to select more correct words the second time and even more the third time.

You also can introduce songs by having the children listen for other special things, such as, "Listen carefully while I sing the song and be ready to tell me how it made you feel" or "What special person do the words tell us about?" or "What kind of sound do the words tell us about?" or "What are the boys and girls in the song doing?"

4. *Use pictures or gestures to remind children of the words.* After the children have selected the words in the song that relate to the real apricot blossoms bouquet, you could show a series of pictures or flannelboard figures that relate to the ideas in the song. Mix these pictures and say to the children, "On the flannelboard are some pictures of things in this song. I've got them all mixed up. So listen carefully. I'm going to ask one of you to put these pictures in the right order—that is, the way they come in the song." After you sing the song, choose a child who would like to try to put the pictures in order. The pictures could include a child looking out the window (line 1), a tree in bloom (lines 2 and 4), a bouquet of blossoms (lines 4 and 6), popcorn popping in a popper (line 8). Rather than correcting the child if he makes a mistake in ordering the pictures, tell the children to listen to the song again to see if the pictures are in the right order. Then let another child try to correct the order if necessary. It might even be necessary to sing a song the third time before the children put the pictures in the correct order. When the pictures have been put in the correct order, have one of the children point to each picture in the appropriate place as you sing the song again. Don't worry about repeating the song too many times. Repetition helps children learn the song. This technique with pictures or flannel figures is especially useful when teaching a long song.

Another way to help children remember a song is to let the children decide on some gestures that represent various parts of the song. As you sing each line of "Popcorn Popping on the Apricot Tree," the children could decide what gesture they would use for that line. For example, the children might suggest the following:

Line 1: Hands to eyes as though peering out the window
Line 2: Jump like popcorn or hands jump like popcorn
Line 4: Open eyes wide as though in wonder
Line 5: Hold out arms as though full of bouquets of flowers
Line 6: Smell a "pretend" bouquet
Line 8: Jump like popcorn popping

5. *Vary the approach when you return to a song the children are learning.* Children enjoy hearing and singing songs over and over again, but they also enjoy variety. Therefore it's a good idea to try something different the second and third time you return to a song the children are learning. One effective technique is to use a tape recorder and let the children hear the song sung by another group of children. If you have children of your own, they might enjoy recording the song for the prekindergarten children to hear. Also, children this age seldom hear men sing children's songs. It would be a delightful experience for the children to hear a man sing the song on the tape recorder. After the children hear the song on the tape recorder, they can sing along with the voice or voices on the tape.

Other ways of varying the approach when the children are learning a new song is to let them clap a special rhythm or sing one place where the words and melody repeat. Or they can raise their hands high when the melody goes up and put them down toward the floor when the melody goes down. You can also vary the accompaniment that you use with the songs, one time using an autoharp, another time the piano, another time a guitar. Children can also sing fast, then slowly or sing loudly, then softly.

Once children have learned a new song, they need opportunities to sing the song often. As the children's song repertoire grows, they can have special choosing times at the beginning or end of a lesson in the music curriculum or as a self-selected activity in the music learning center in the classroom. Interest can be increased during song-choosing time by preparing visual aids that enhance song selection. For example, you could make a clown out of paper holding a batch of paper balloons of different colors and prepare it for flannelboard or corkboard. Children could choose "balloons" from the board. On the back of each paper balloon would be written a song the children know well.

Another motivating device is a paper "nest" (for a duck or a chicken or some other bird) pasted onto poster board, with a slit in the nest into which paper "eggs" have been placed. On the back of each paper egg is the name of a favorite song. The children can choose eggs from the nest and sing the song indicated on the back of the egg.

Some children who have difficulty learning to sing prekindergarten songs can learn to sing with the group by participating in the singing of favorite radio and TV commercials. Children often learn TV and radio jingles and commercials long before they learn songs that are written for young children to sing because the tunes are catchy and the words are simple. Therefore the children can be successful frequently with attractive tunes and words. Children who enjoy singing are those who have had frequent successful singing experiences.

The singing skill includes the following characteristics: (1) singing the correct melody; (2) singing the correct tempo; (3) singing the correct rhythm; (4) singing with appropriate dynamics; and (5) singing with appropriate tone color. These characteristics are discussed separately in the section on elements of music. Singing is a skill all children can learn and enjoy.

Build a broad repertoire of songs you can sing with the children. If you enjoy the song, the children are likely to learn it well and enjoy it too. There are many kinds of songs suitable for learning activities in the music curriculum as well as in other areas of the curriculum.

Action songs are songs that invite the child to move his body in various ways to express the meaning of the song. Some examples of action songs include:

Clap Your Hands (Seeger, 1948)
Hey, Betty Martin! (Landeck, 1950)
If You're Happy and You Know It (McLaughlin & Schliestett, 1967)
Join Along Josie (Seeger, 1948)
New River Train (Landeck, 1950)

The Paw-Paw Patch (Landeck, 1950)
Where is Thumbkin? (Tune: Are You Sleeping?) (McLaughlin &
Schliestett, 1967)

Some songs can be used to teach a *concept or idea*. For example:

Colors
(Tune: The Paw-Paw Patch, Landeck, 1950)
Children wearing red, please stand up.
Children wearing red, please stand up.
Children wearing red, please stand up.
So we can see your colors.
(Introduce enough colors to include all children and all the colors the
children are wearing.)

Animals
Old MacDonald's Farm (Lloyd, 1966)

Occupations
Ten Little Indians (Beattie, 1954)
(Can select other occupations such as spacemen, policemen, firemen,
pilots, etc.)

Growing Things
Popcorn Popping on the Apricot Tree (Groesbeck, 1968)

Numbers
By'm By (Landeck, 1950)

Some songs such as "Old MacDonald" and "By'm By" were originally written
about a concept or idea. Other tunes such as "The Paw-Paw Patch" and "Ten
Little Indians" can be adapted to teach a particular concept. Concept or idea
songs usually are to be sung as learning activities in other parts of the
curriculum. However, when children are learning the song for the first time,
especially the original tune, it can be learned as part of the music curriculum.
Humorous or nonsense songs are favorites with children as well as

adults. Some examples are "I Know an Old Lady Who Swallowed a Fly" (Winn, 1966) and "Fooba-Wooba John" (Winn, 1966).

Personal songs are effective in helping children become involved in the singing process because they apply to something about the individual child. Such songs include "Hello Ev'rybody" (Bailey, 1955) and "Mary Wore a Red Dress" (Landeck, 1950). Favorite songs can be adapted to include names of individual children, something they are wearing, activities they enjoy, and so forth. Such songs are as unlimited as your imagination.

Singing games are popular with children. If the singing game involves a great deal of structure, prekindergarten children learn little and lose interest. A singing game should be fun (isn't that what games are all about?) and allow for some creativity and even elements of surprise. Two songs suitable for singing games are "The Muffin Man" (Landeck, 1950) and "Punchinello" (Landeck, 1954).

Some songs become favorites of young children because of an *appealing melody or idea*. Some songs have pleasing melody lines that seem intrinsically attractive to a child; other songs have a catchy phrase or idea that motivates repetition of the song. Such songs include:

> Holiday and special occasion songs (Christmas, Valentine's Day, birthday, and so on)
> Hawaiian Rainbows (Groesbeck, 1968)
> Kumbaya (Gilbert, 1960) (This can be adapted to include names of children, such as: "Johnny's listening, Kumbaya", and so on)
> Lift Up Your Voice and Sing (Groesbeck, 1968)
> Skip to My Lou (Landeck, 1950)
> There's a Little Wheel a-Turnin' in My Heart (Landeck, 1950)

When children are changing from one activity to another it is pleasant occasionally to sing about what they are going to do next. Again, favorite songs can be adapted to fit the upcoming activity. One such *transition song* is "What Shall We Do When We All Go Out?" (Seeger, 1948).

Moving

Movement seems to be an integral part of every music skill. It is difficult to sing a song without accompanying it with movement. The very act of singing itself is a form of movement. It is hard to imagine playing an instrument without moving. The skill of creating usually involves some form of movement. And the demonstration of music-reading skill is basically an exercise in movement.

Movement has been called the "child's natural language." It depends on the messages the child receives through his senses and the way he interprets these messages. Music is just one of many areas in which the child's movement expresses his interpretation of the messages he receives from the senses.

But even though movement is "natural" to a child, he can learn to regulate his movements in patterns that help him do more with and understand more of his world. Most patterns of movement outside the simple locomotor skills of walking and running and the prehensory skills of holding an item and letting it go must be learned. Music is one area in which a child can use the movement skills he has learned. Children learn by *doing or moving.* If a child can move to recorded music or a voice or an instrument, he often can better understand the meaning of concepts and ideas that are taught in the lessons he receives.

There are numerous ways that movement can be used in a music lesson. Music movement possibilities depend on the basic movement skills discussed in Chapter 13. *Dramatization* is a form of movement in music where the children act out the story of a song or recorded instrumental music. *Imitation* is the movement interpretation by the child of the movements of an animal or an object described in a song or a recorded piece of music. Singing games involve movement of the whole body suggested by the words of a song. *Hand movements* are also suggested by some songs, such as "Where is Thumbkin?" Finger and hand movements are involved only, while the body remains in one place. Some songs are suitable for either singing games or hand movements.

Dance is frequently associated with music, although music is not necessary for dance. Shannon (1967) suggests that "dance is a . . . deliberate kind of movement" wherein the basic movement skills are used as tools to communicate concepts or ideas or feelings. It is possible to teach prescribed dance motions and steps to prekindergarten children, but it is probably more effective to allow the children to improvise their own steps to a given piece of music. For example, you can play a record and ask the children, "How does this music make you want to move? Show me with your body." Dance is a learning activity that can be used to demonstrate understanding of concepts, ideas, and feelings in each of the other areas of the curriculum as well as music.

Playing Instruments

Often when adults think of musical instruments they think of an expensive item that requires great technical skill. However, advanced technical skill is not necessary in order for a child successfully to use many kinds of musical instruments. Control of body movements and discrimination are necessary to play musical instruments, and both can be learned in the prekindergarten classroom.

It should be mentioned at this point that the musical instruments used in the prekindergarten classroom, though not as expensive as those used in a standard orchestra, need to be used with great care and discrimination. Children who are allowed to play out their aggressive feelings at random on musical instruments or who carelessly take an instrument from an odd assortment of instruments on a shelf for a few quick strokes can only become desensitized to the sounds they create; therefore, they will be unable to discover the distinctive tone qualities and possible sources of music enrichment in these same instruments.

Each instrument is unique in the tone it produces, its shape, the materials from which it is created, and its means for enriching one's skill and understanding of music. Musical instruments can be made available in the music-learning center one or two at a time under careful supervision by a teacher. It is best to make instruments available in the learning center only after the children have learned about how to use them during planned lessons in the music curriculum.

One effective way of teaching children about a musical instrument and how to play it is to begin by simply showing the instrument to the children and asking them to tell what they think it is. Then ask them if they think it makes a sound and if so, what kind of a sound. At this point children will want to try making the sounds the way they think the instrument should be played. If the instrument requires something else in order for a sound to be made (such as the felted stick for the drum or the metal striker for the triangle), let the children decide what it should be before showing it to them. After the children have learned the name of the instrument and the most appropriate way or ways to play it, they are ready for some practice with the instrument. You could then sing a song, indicating appropriate places where the instrument could be played, or create some simple exercises so that the instrument is played on one signal and is silent on another. Children can listen to a musical piece on the piano or on a record and play the instrument in an appropriate spot. Musical instruments are means to a musical end in most cases, rather than musical ends in themselves. They form appropriate accompaniment for songs or various movements or provide desired sound effects. Therefore, after the children have had the opportunity to explore the uses of an instrument, they can then experience its use as a means to an end, such as accompaniment to a song.

There are three basic types of instruments suitable for use by prekindergarten children: nonpitched percussion, pitched percussion, and stringed instruments. The name of each of these categories describes the unique sound quality of the instruments in that category. Each instrument is illustrated in Figure 14–1.

The term *percussion* refers to the striking together of two objects to produce sound. Percussion instruments are probably the most common type of instrument in prekindergartens because they are so easy to play and are relatively inexpensive. *Nonpitched percussion* instruments do not have a particular set frequency of tone. They are used where a certain tone frequency is unnecessary. Rhythm sticks, wood blocks, drums of different sizes, tambourines, jingle bells, triangles, hand and finger cymbals—all of these are

Nonpitched Percussion

Pitched Percussion

Stringed Instrument

Figure 14–1. Musical instruments in the prekindergarten.

nonpitched percussion instruments. Aronoff (1969) reports some of the discoveries children have made about a few of the nonpitched percussion instruments.

(1) A *triangle,* for example, can make only one sound, which is something like a "bright bell." The sound can last a long time, while the ringing gets softer and softer. An interesting way to play the triangle is to put the striker inside the triangle and hit the three sides by drawing little circles as fast as possible. The triangle and the striker are made of metal. The triangle must be held by a string or cord so that it can swing free and make the bell sound; when you hold the triangle with your hand, it doesn't make a very pleasant sound.

(2) The *tambourine,* on the other hand, is two instruments in one—a drum and jingles around the edges. You can't make a melody on it but it's fun to use for dancing. You can play the jingles without the drum just by shaking the tambourine. You can shake it high and low and make all kinds of shapes with your arms in space. You can play the drum part of the tambourine with your knee, knuckles, or elbow. Whenever you play the drum part, the jingles play, too.

(3) Another instrument, the *drum,* sounds lots of different ways, depending on how you play it. You can play it with a felted stick, with knuckles, or with fingers. When you play it with your fingers, you can play with the soft tips or with the fingernails gently scratching. They can scratch in a design, in a straight line, on the metal rim, or on the wood on the side of the drum. The drum can be soft, loud, or any place in between. It sounds best when you bounce away from it. The drum is made of wood sides and tightly drawn, very thin skin that is dried. You can play it while you carry it around or while you sit or while you stand still.

(4) *Rhythm sticks* are instruments that make dry clicks only the moment you play them; they don't ring and they don't sing. Also, they don't go higher and they don't go lower; you just tap one with the other. They're fine to help you keep the beat as you sing or march. If you want to make a scraping sound, rub one across the notches of the other. You can make a galloping rhythm by sitting on the floor and tapping the sticks together for the "short" sound and the floor with the other stick for the "long" sound.

Pitched percussion instruments are those that can make a variety of tones. Examples are the piano and song bells. Song bells usually come separate rather than hooked together. Each bell has a solid wood base with a metal strip suspended at the top of the base that is pitched to a particular frequency. The bells come in sets from one octave to three octaves, including the accidentals. Aronoff (1969) describes characteristics of the pitched percussion instruments as discovered by the prekindergarten children.

(1)   The *piano* has lots of keys, and each key has a different sound. The sounds go from very low to very high, and there are many different sounds in between; each sound can be loud or soft or in between. When you play the keys, they stop at once if you take your finger off the key. If you play a key with your foot on the damper pedal, the sound lasts a long time. Even if you keep your finger on a key, the sound fades away slowly. The piano can sound smooth and it can sound jumpy. You can use different fingers to play, and you can use all ten fingers to play. When you play sounds gently on the piano with more than one finger, you can decide if it's the kind of sound you want. You can make the sounds go high and low and anywhere you want them to go. And the sounds can go in steps or in wider spaces. There is just no end to the ways you can put chords and clusters together.

(2)   The *song bells,* on the other hand, can be used to make all kinds of melody shapes, but you can't slide with them. Each bell has a different sound. The sounds are soft and they fade gently away. The bells ring but they can't be jumpy. You can hit the metal with a mallet to make a sound, and you can stop the sound by touching the metal. Two or more people can play at the same time or one after another.

Stringed instruments are usually not as plentiful in the prekindergarten as percussion instruments because they usually require greater technical skill, are easily broken, and are more expensive. The most frequently used stringed instrument in the prekindergarten is the autoharp, because it is easy for the teacher to learn to play, is fairly sturdy, and is far less expensive than other stringed instruments. Anyone who can read and follow directions can play an autoharp. It requires the simple pressing of chorded bars. Two or three chords are usually sufficient for the accompaniment of any song in the prekindergarten. The strings are stroked with the fingers or with plastic or felt picks. Children can stroke the strings in appropriate rhythms while the teacher presses the bars for the correct chords. Under supervision in the music learning center, children can experiment by pressing the bars for chords while they stroke the strings.

Musical instruments in the prekindergarten classroom, together with the human voice (which is also an instrument), are especially good for demonstrating the elements of music discussed in the next section. It may be wise to select one or two instruments at a time and add to the prekindergarten collection as you gain skill and confidence in using them in the curriculum. It is better to pay a little more money and get a quality instrument rather than purchasing several instruments of low quality; instruments that produce poor-quality sounds are not instruments but noisemakers.

It is not necessary that each child in the group have an instrument whenever instruments are used for a lesson. Perhaps one instrument is all that is necessary, especially when you are introducing the instrument for the first time. In other cases, three or four different instruments may be used to accompany parts of a song or to demonstrate a concept. The children can take turns with the instruments. Remember, *all* children in the group should have the opportunity to play that instrument. The use of instruments in "rhythm bands" is not recommended in the classroom. Aronoff (1969) offers an opinion regarding rhythm bands:

> Classroom instruments, often called "rhythm instruments" and even "toy instruments," have traditionally been used to form a "rhythm band" or "toy orchestra." There seems little to recommend this kind of activity. Certainly little benefit can be gained from teaching set "orchestration" to young children, and having everyone "keep time with the music" with all the instruments sounding at once results in a cacophony which can only desensitize the children, to say nothing of the teacher [pp. 44–45].

Creating

When young children have had a variety of experiences with the skills of listening, singing, moving, and playing instruments and with some of the concepts of music, they begin to create their own musical expressions. The act of creating music is not simply a matter of random expression and exploration by the child; it is the ability to organize music skills and music concepts into new and novel combinations.

The musical creations of prekindergarten children should not be expected to be long or involved. Creating music, just like any other musical skill, develops in small steps. Creating can be as simple as taking the name of a child, clapping out the rhythm of the name, and selecting three notes on the piano or melody bells to use for a melody that fits the name. The important thing is the act of creating, not musical perfection or preservation of that which is created.

Creating with music can be accomplished in several ways. One way is to make up new words to a familiar song. Another way is to make up an introduction to a song. For example, a child can set the rhythmic and tempo pattern by strumming the autoharp or striking a song bell a few times before the children begin to sing a song. This same strumming or striking pattern also can be used at the end of a song as a coda. A third way of creating is making up body and hand movements to a song. A fourth way is making up a melody for words to a chant used by the children in their free-choice activity. Another way is creating both the words and the melody for a simple song.

Reading

You probably think that reading music means to look at the notes on a page of music manuscript and to translate those notes into a performance by the human voice or on a musical instrument. These are advanced demonstrations of music reading skills. However, there are beginning reading skills that can be learned by prekindergarten children.

One way that children in the first year of prekindergarten can demonstrate music reading skill is to move their hands up and down to fit the pattern of the melody of a song or instrumental piece. Their own hand movements help them to remember melody patterns. Another way children learn to read music is to follow the picture of a melody, or the melodic contour, as they sing a song. An example of a melodic contour is illustrated in Figure 14–2.

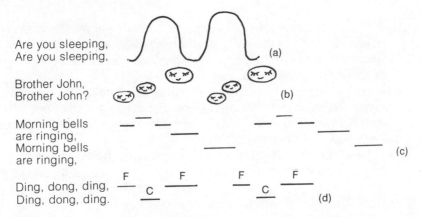

Are you sleeping,
Are you sleeping,   (a)

Brother John,
Brother John?   (b)

Morning bells
are ringing,
Morning bells
are ringing,   (c)

Ding, dong, ding,
Ding, dong, ding.   (d)

Figure 14–2. "Reading" music. Illustrations of contour and notation using the song, "Are You Sleeping?" (a) Melodic contour, (b) picture notation, (c) blank or line notation, (d) blank notation with letters added. Never put words under the contour or notation when using them in the prekindergarten.

In their second year of prekindergarten, children can learn to read blank notation or picture notation for rhythm only or for both rhythm and melody. Blank notation and picture notation are illustrated in Figure 14–2.

Skill Combinations

It is almost impossible to talk about one music skill without discussing another one because they are interdependent. Each of the music skills involves at least one other music skill. Here are a few more suggestions of ways to teach music skills to children that include singing plus at least one other skill:

1. Have the children find a way to move that expresses the feeling of a particular song sung at its normal speed. Then vary the speed of the song as you sing it, either slower or faster, and ask the children to show with their bodies how they would move differently than when the song is sung at its normal speed.

2. Play the rhythm of a favorite song on a drum. Let the children guess the name of the song by listening to the rhythm. After they guess the name of the song, let individual children play the rhythm of the song on the drum.

3. Have the children make up a melody for each child's name in the group. As each melody is sung, you can act as an echo repeating the name with the melody, and then you and the children can sing each new melody a third time.

4. Let each child in the group tell you something by singing it rather than saying it. Then everyone in the group can repeat the same melody.

5. Copy some novel words or phrases children have said during other activities. During music time have children create simple melodies and actions that go with the words you recorded.

The list of possibilities could go on and on. Let your own imagination guide you to new and interesting ways to help children practice and enjoy music skills.

THE ELEMENTS OF MUSIC

Music skills are developed through the use of the elements of music. These elements of music, as outlined on page 335, are rhythm, tempo, melody, tone quality (timbre), dynamics, harmony, and form. The elements of music, together with music skills, form the structure of music.

The names of the elements of music as written here are rather formal and academic. The important thing to remember is that repeated *firsthand experience* with each concept is the vital thing to a child, rather than the language label attached to that experience. In other words, it is not very important for a child to be able to say, "That is a loud note and the one before it was a soft one. That's called dynamics." However, we would want the child to be able to recognize the difference between soft and loud tones, to produce a soft or loud tone with his voice or another musical instrument when instructed, and to use the concepts "loud" and "soft" when creating new movement patterns or simple melodies on the melody bells. The academic names of these elements are abstract. But there are experiences you can give the prekindergarten children related to each of these music concepts that are concrete.

When a child is learning what a music concept or element of music is, he must also have experience with what it is *not* if he is to learn to discriminate appropriately. Bereiter and Engelmann (1966) provide persuasive evidence for this suggestion for teaching in their work with disadvantaged children, but it applies to all children regardless of their background when learning a new concept. If a child is learning the concepts of *high* and *low* (pitch) in music, he needs to learn what is *high* and what is *not high* before moving to the polar opposites of *low* and *not low.* The child first learns that *rough* sounds and *smooth* sounds (tone quality), *loud* sounds and *soft* sounds (dynamics) are not necessarily *high* or *low* sounds, and so forth.

The elements of music are interrelated. That is, one does not occur without at least one other. For example, melody always has some rhythm and tempo, timbre (or tone quality) is always related to dynamics, harmony to tempo, and so forth. No element of music stands alone. Nevertheless, when first teaching a music element to young children, you can focus on one element at a time. After a child has had a wide variety of experiences with each music element separately, he can begin to identify and use several elements of music in the same music experience.

Rhythm

Rhythm is an element or concept of music that refers to a regulated pattern formed by long or short notes. There are several sub-elements of this element. *Beat* is a regular and rhythmical unit of time, such as "each beat in a measure." *Accent* suggests a special stress given to a musical note within a phrase—for example, children can clap harder on some beats or notes than others. *Meter* indicates that written music is divided into measures or bars. The specific rhythm is determined by the number of beats and the time value assigned to each note in the measure. *Pattern* refers to the design of the rhythm, such as long-long-short, long-long-short or long-short-long, long-short-long, and so on. A *rest* in music is an interval of silence corresponding to one of the possible time values within the measure. *Prose rhythm* is the rhythm of natural speech or written prose or poetry.

Children can learn to be aware of rhythm by clapping the beat of a favorite song and then clapping the beat of another favorite song and comparing the differences. When children are first learning to clap a rhythm, only one song should be used. The song should have a simple rhythm pattern, such as "Skip to My Lou" (Landeck, 1950). If you play this rhythm on a drum at first, it will help the children learn to clap the rhythm. When first comparing the rhythm patterns of two favorite songs, select songs that have distinct contrasts in rhythm, such as "The Muffin Man" (Landeck, 1950) and "Kumbaya" (Gilbert, 1960). Children can also listen to the rhythm of a song and clap it and then find another way to move to the rhythm, such as galloping to "Looby Loo" (McLaughlin & Schliestett, 1967). When learning a new song, especially if it is a long one, children can immediately become involved if you help them clap hands or snap their fingers to the rhythm of the song. Whenever the rhythm of a song is a bit tricky, you might have the children clap the rhythm before they learn the song.

Tempo

When we talk about the relative speed of a musical composition or, in other words, how fast or slow it is to be sung or played, we're talking about tempo. For the musical artist, musical tempo is indicated by a descriptive word such as *moderato* or *adagio* or a metronomic direction such as "♩=60" (which means the rate should be 60 quarter notes to one minute). To the young child it simply means how fast or how slow the music is supposed to be and the variety of ways the music can be played faster or slower, such as "little by little" or "all at once."

The child who is learning the meaning of tempo is really learning the musical meaning of *fast* and *slow*. Therefore, he should have a variety of musical firsthand experiences that demonstrate *fast, not fast, slow,* and *not slow.* He can hear *fast* and *slow* through melody instruments, songs on a recording, recorded instrumental compositions, or nonpitched percussion instruments, to mention a few. He can sing fast songs and slow songs. He can play fast rhythms and slow rhythms on a drum. He can find ways to move his body fast and slow.

Melody

Melody is what most people think of usually when they think of music. It refers to a pleasing succession or arrangement of individual sounds or single notes. It has three sub-elements—pitch, direction, and shape. *Pitch,* in physics, is the sound frequency of any given musical tone. In simpler terms, it suggests how high or how low a note is. For children, the major musical concepts would be *high* and *low* and anything in between. *Direction* indicates the line a melody takes leading to a particular end or goal. The line can move *up* or it can move *down*, or it can stay level (*the same place*). But the line as it goes up or down or the same place can lead to only a certain goal. In other words, the melody "resolves" itself at the end. Try stopping any song at the end of the next to last line and see how it makes you feel, such as "There's a Little Wheel a-Turnin' in My Heart" (Landeck, 1950). The melody seems to be leading you someplace, and if you don't get there you feel uncomfortable. You might try this with children and ask them how it makes them feel and what they need to do to feel better about singing the song. *Shape* is the characteristic way a song goes up and down. As one child said, "You can tell a song by the way it goes up and down" (Aronoff, 1969).

When teaching the element of pitch to children, then, you are really teaching the concepts of *high* and *low,* and *up* and *down,* and *the same place* (level). By means of each of the musical skills they can learn to demonstrate their understanding of these concepts. One effective way to help children learn the meaning of melody as it goes up and down is to help them to use their hands in front of them as they sing to describe the level of each note in the song. When the melody goes way high, the hand goes "way high"; when the song is "very low," the hand goes to the floor. All the other notes in the melody have their relative place in between these two extremes of hand height. If you model this for the children, it will be easier for them to learn how to do it. This is a good experience for children when they have heard the melody of the song often enough to be very familiar with it.

Tone Quality (Timbre)

Tone quality or timbre is that characteristic of a sound that distinguishes it from other sounds of the same pitch and volume. In particular, it refers to the distinctive tone of a musical instrument, a voice, or a voiced speech sound. For example, the same note played on a piano, a song bell, and a violin is identical in pitch but has a different quality of sound in each instrument. This is one reason certain parts of the melody are played by some instruments rather than others in the orchestra, whereas the unique qualities of sound in each instrument can be very pleasing when played together in certain combinations.

Young children, when learning the concept of tone quality in music, can explore the sounds made by various objects in their environment as well as the sounds made by their own voices compared with the various types of musical instruments (nonpitched percussion, pitched percussion, stringed instruments). They can learn to identify an instrument by the sound it makes. They can explore the kinds of sounds they wish to accompany various kinds of songs or various kinds of feelings. The study of the music concept of tone quality is an extension of the topic *hearing* in the *our world* area of the prekindergarten curriculum (see Chapter 15).

Dynamics

The musical concept that deals with the variation in force or intensity in musical sound (that is, loud and soft and their variations) is called dynamics. Musical sound can get loud or soft gradually or, in the words of young children, "little by little." Or musical sound all of a sudden can become very loud or very soft. This is sometimes called *accent*. Thus children learn the concepts of *loud* and *soft* and their variations when learning the music concept of dynamics. They can explore these concepts again through the imaginative use of the various music skills. For example, they can listen to musical selections and identify the ones that are loud and the ones that are soft. They can sing songs softly and then sing the same song loudly and see what it makes them feel about the songs they sing this way. They can explore ways of playing various instruments loudly and then softly, such as a drum. (Note: playing an instrument loudly is not the same thing as playing it recklessly with abandon.) Children can create movements that express what they feel when something is loud or soft in volume.

Harmony

Harmony is the pleasing interaction or appropriate combination of several pitches at once. This forms what is known as a chord. Harmony is also the progression of chords and their relationship to one another. It probably is not a good idea to spend a great deal of time in the music curriculum on a study of harmony. As children get older, they will learn to sing in parts and this concept will take on greater meaning. However, the prekindergarten child could benefit from a few simple experiences related to harmony. For example, when you accompany a song with the autoharp while singing the song alone, ask the children to stop you when they hear you playing something that "doesn't sound right" or "doesn't fit" the music. If they can't guess it the first time around, do it again and exaggerate the "mistake." When they learn to recognize the chord that doesn't fit, ask them why it doesn't fit and what can be done to make it sound better. Then play some other chords that don't fit and the one that does, and let them decide which one sounds the best. You can also select a song that frequently uses one chord in its accompaniment, such as "Kumbaya" (frequent use of the tonic or I chord). Hand out to the children the mallets and the melody bells that comprise the notes in this chord and teach them to play the bells in the appropriate place in the song when you give them the signal. They need to learn both a "start" and a "stop" signal. You could play the other chords on the piano or guitar or autoharp.

Form

Songs have a beginning, a middle, and an end. They often have introductory passages and codas. Some songs have a verse (the words change each time this part of the melody is sung) and a refrain (the words stay the same each time this part of the melody is sung); these elements in varied arrangements form the basic pattern for a given song or musical composition. They provide unity and contrast in music. You can have the children listen to a song and identify the place where they hear a certain melody that you have hummed for them. Or you can sing a song and have the children determine which words are sung the same way each time (the verse). Every musical composition has a pattern. As you prepare lessons related to the music element of form, analyze the songs or music recordings you use for learning activities to determine the basic form or pattern of each. Learning activities related to form will depend on the particular pattern or form of a given musical composition.

PREPARING MUSIC LESSON PLANS

The chart in Table 14–1 has been helpful in preparing lesson plans in music. Once the decision is made as to whether the focus of a lesson is an element of music or a music skill, you can develop your learning activities using a combination of cells in the row or the column. For example, if you are planning a lesson on melody, you might wish to use each of the music skills in a learning activity related to that element (the Os on the chart down the "melody" column). If you want to teach a lesson on the music skill of playing instruments, you may wish to choose learning activities that include each of the elements of music (the Xs on the chart in the "playing instruments" row). You can select one skill or element, as the case may be, to develop a learning activity; or you may choose two, three, or all, depending on the objectives you wish to accomplish in the lesson.

Table 14–1. Elements of music and music skill planning chart.

| Music Skill | Rhythm | Tempo | Music Concept | | Dynamics | Harmony | Form |
			Melody	Tone quality			
Listening			O				
Singing			O				
Moving			O				
Playing instruments	X	X	O X	X	X	X	X
Creating			O				

But What If ... ?

Music is probably the one area in the curriculum more teachers feel uncomfortable about than any other area. Many feel that because they are not professional musicians they cannot teach music to young children. There are other related problems. Let's look at a few of the questions such people often ask.

I'm not a trained musician. How can I teach music to young children? It is not necessary for a teacher to have advanced training in music in order to teach it. If he enjoys music, he probably can learn to teach it. The elements of music and music skills that young children can learn are also ones that an adult without musical training can learn—but faster. Such a person should be willing to take a beginning music class for teachers of young children at a local college or university. There are many books and articles available to provide a wide background of information on music for young children. Above all, such a person should be willing to practice the skills of music that he will be teaching the children. When teaching music to young children, the nonmusician teacher should start with simple music behavior and lesson plans and gradually increase the complexity of lessons as his music teaching skills are rewarded and continue to develop. One can always observe sounds around himself, study, attend seminars and classes, talk to musicians, and practice.

But what if I don't play the piano?   A person who doesn't play the piano is probably better off teaching music to younger children than to older ones because skill on the piano is not necessary in the prekindergarten. As a matter of fact, skilled pianists have often found other music activities far more successful and satisfying with young children. The piano in most schoolrooms is used as an instrument to accompany singing or movement activities. This requires considerable technical skill. However, instruments such as the autoharp or song bells are extremely easy to learn to play for accompaniment purposes and are often far more satisfactory because they allow the teacher to be close to the children and in direct eye contact with them. It is difficult to play the piano and maintain eye contact with children, regardless of skill. Most, if not all, music skills and concepts can be adequately taught without a piano. But even a person who doesn't play the piano can help children explore the unique tone quality of a piano and the way a piano works.

Occasionally, as a novel experience for the children, a teacher who doesn't have a piano can have someone record the piano accompaniment on audio tape. The recorded accompaniment can then be used for the song desired.

What if I can't read music?   It is a distinct disadvantage when a prekindergarten teacher is unable to read music. However, if the teacher can read, he can learn to read music. Again, a beginning music class should be a high-priority item if such a skill is to be developed. There are introductory programmed texts available to aid the beginning student in music notation. Such an individual must be willing to study and practice. Exploring the uses of a piano, a guitar, a recorder, or a song flute helps considerably. It is surprising how quickly music-reading skill can be developed. The prekindergarten teacher at least should be able to understand examples given in a book or article and be able to pick out a melody on a musical instrument.

I've never tried to teach songs to children. I've only sung with adults. Should I try to teach young children to sing?   Such a person probably would not take long getting "the swing of things" with young children. Observation of young children is necessary before teaching them anything, if for no other reason than to learn what kinds of responses to expect from young children. Practicing the suggestions in this chapter could help such a person.

What if I can't carry a tune?   Not all music learning activities require the teacher's singing voice as a model. However, the basic assumption here is that some individuals sing in monotones. This just is not true. Longer practice of simple melodies will be required. In the meantime, the person who "can't carry a tune" can record someone singing and playing songs and use the recordings in class to teach songs to the children. At the same time, such an individual can sing along enthusiastically with the recording, both in private and with the children. He also can listen to the sounds of his own voice, imitate sounds in the environment such as fire engines and ticking clocks, and take a few lessons from a voice teacher.

How much space is needed for music and movement experiences with young children?   Children should be able to walk and run and gallop freely without bumping into one another. There should be enough space so that a child can move his arms in all directions without touching anyone. However, too much room can be quite disturbing to children. A large room does not have the built-in limits of smaller space; music sometimes cannot be heard and group cohesiveness can be lost. Some rules may be necessary, such as, "Move so that you don't touch anyone else" or "Move all in the same direction."

What can I do with children who can't carry a tune?   Again, no child really sings in a monotone; he can be taught to sing a melody line.

Sometimes teachers sing too high or too low for some children to follow. It might be advisable to play some singing games with each individual child requiring that he echo back what you sing to him in short phrases. Help the child imitate environmental sounds around him. Have him purposely speak in a monotone and then in his regular voice and note the differences. Above all, never make an issue out of the fact that a child doesn't seem to be able to carry a tune. Spend your time diagnosing and treating the problem.

When can I use records in the prekindergarten?   Unfortunately, records are used as almost the sole music experience for the children in some prekindergartens because their teachers feel inadequate to teach music. A record can be used for a lesson in music when it can help the children learn a music skill or music concept, but many children's records on the market are sheer entertainment and of little use as music learning activities. "Entertainment" is not necessarily a bad thing, but the constant din and blare of records in a prekindergarten can desensitize children to records' entertainment and/or musical qualities. A small selection of carefully selected records, some or all of which have been used during a music lesson, should always be available in the music learning area where children can listen at their leisure during free-choice periods.

SAMPLE LESSON PLAN

Area of curriculum: Music

Music focus: Playing instruments

Behavioral objectives: Each child will:

1. Choose one way the notched rhythm stick might make a sound and demonstrate his idea with the instrument. (Problem solving.)
2. Play the notched rhythm stick to simulate the sound of a duck in the appropriate places in "Six Little Ducks" (Winn, 1966) when it is his turn in the group. (Motor sequence, serial memory.)

To the teacher: For this lesson you will need at least one notched rhythm stick and a chopstick with which to play it. Smooth, round chopsticks are more suitable than unfinished, square ones and can be purchased in quantity at some import houses.

It is assumed that the children are well acquainted with "Six Little Ducks" but have never learned to play the notched rhythm sticks. The emphasis in this lesson is exploring a new musical instrument and the sounds that it makes.

Learning Activities:

Posttest   (behavioral objective from previous lesson). Each child will sing correctly from memory all the words to the song "Six Little Ducks" (Winn, 1966). (Serial memory.)

Show.   Place a notched rhythm stick in the center of the table (or floor, if you and the children are seated on a rug) without the chopstick.

Discuss, apply.   Ask, "What do you think that is? What does it look like? What do you think you could do with it? What kind of a sound do you think it makes?" When you get to the last question, the children may suggest making a sound by tapping the stick on the floor, rubbing their fingernails across the notches, or even blowing on it. Let children try their ideas. Encourage children as they respond. Then hold up a chopstick and ask the children if the chopstick could help them play the notched rhythm stick and if so, how it could be used. Let each child use the chopstick and the rhythm stick together to make a sound of his choice. Most of the children may tap the notched stick with the chopstick. Help them to discover, if necessary, that the notched rhythm stick is played by drawing the chopstick across the notches.

Show, discuss, apply.   Tell the children that the notched rhythm stick can be played to sound like a duck. Demonstrate by drawing the chopstick across the notches in two quick strokes to sound like a "quack, quack." Then sing "Six Little Ducks" with the children and have them tell you where the words *quack, quack, quack,* are sung. Suggest that they could play the notched rhythm stick when these words are sung in the song. Hand out two other notched rhythm sticks with accompanying chopsticks if you wish, and let each child have at least one turn playing the notched stick in the appropriate place in the song. Give verbal encouragement and prompts as necessary.

Posttest.   Test both of these objectives one week later.

Music topical outline.

6.1.   Music skills
    6.1.1.   Listening
    6.1.2.   Singing
    6.1.3.   Moving
    6.1.4.   Playing instruments
        6.1.4.1.   Nonpitched percussion: rhythm sticks, wood blocks, drums of different sizes, tambourines, jingle bells, triangles, cymbals
        6.1.4.2.   Pitched percussion: song bells, piano
        6.1.4.3.   Stringed instruments: autoharp
    6.1.5.   Creating
    6.1.6.   Reading
6.2.   Elements of music
    6.2.1.   Rhythm
        6.2.1.1.   Beat
        6.2.1.2.   Accent
        6.2.1.3.   Meter
        6.2.1.4.   Patterns
        6.2.1.5.   Rests
        6.2.1.6.   Prose rhythm
    6.2.2.   Tempo
        6.2.2.1.   Changing rate
    6.2.3.   Melody
        6.2.3.1.   Pitch (high and low)
        6.2.3.2.   Direction (up, down, level)
        6.2.3.3.   Shape
    6.2.4.   Tone quality (timbre)
        6.2.4.1.   Voice
        6.2.4.2.   Nonpitched percussion
        6.2.4.3.   Raw sounds
        6.2.4.4.   Pitched percussion
        6.2.4.5.   Stringed instruments
        6.2.4.6.   Wind instruments
    6.2.5.   Dynamics (loud and soft)
        6.2.5.1.   Changing
        6.2.5.2.   Accent
    6.2.6.   Harmony
    6.2.7.   Form

REFERENCES

Aronoff, F. W. *Music and young children.* New York: Holt, Rinehart and Winston, 1969.

Bailey, C. *Sing a song with Charity Bailey.* New York: Plymouth Music, 1955.

Beattie, J. W. (Ed.) *The American singer: No. 1.* New York: American Book, 1954.

Bereiter, C., & Engelmann, S. *Teaching disadvantaged children in the preschool.* Englewood Cliffs, N. J.: Prentice-Hall, 1966.

Gilbert, R. (Ed.) *The Weaver's song book.* New York: Harper & Row, 1960.

Groesbeck, L. S. (Ed.) *Songs for children.* Provo, Utah: Brigham Young University Press, 1968.

Landeck, B. *Songs to grow on.* New York: William Sloane Associates, 1950.

Landeck, B. *More songs to grow on.* New York: William Sloane Associates, 1954.

Lloyd, N. *The new golden song book.* New York: Golden Press, 1966.

McLaughlin, R., & Schliestett, P. *The joy of music: Early childhood.* Evanston, Ill.: Summy-Birchard, 1967.

Seeger, R. C. *American folk songs for children.* New York: Doubleday, 1948.

Shannon, L. Types of teaching in the dancing field. Chico, Calif.: Author, 1967.

Winn, M. (Ed.) *The fireside book of children's songs.* New York: Simon and Schuster, 1966.

Chapter 15

Our World

Who makes the sky blue? Who makes the clouds move? Why does water run? Does it hurt the ground when you dig in it? Who makes the fish die? These questions and thousands like them are asked by prekindergarten children everywhere. Young children often give animate characteristics to inanimate objects or phenomena, characterized by beginning a question with *who* instead of *what.* But their questions indicate a keen awareness of many of the biological and physical events about them.

Children, as well as adults, can easily develop mystical and superstitious ideas about the world they live in because of their relative lack of experience and information. They make sense out of what they observe by piecing together their past experiences, which can lead to inaccurate information when the child has little if any opportunity to talk about what he experiences and to have experiences in appropriate sequences. The prekindergarten can offer a wide variety of firsthand experiences related to the biological and physical phenomena in the child's world and opportunity for the children to talk about and clarify and develop these experiences.

The prekindergarten child obviously is not expected to know all there is to know about the biological and physical sciences before he leaves the prekindergarten. Experiences with the sciences begin at birth and continue throughout one's lifetime. As the child grows in his ability to use language, he learns to understand more and more the experiences he has with his world.

You don't need to be a professional scientist to give children good experiences with science concepts and ideas. You do need firsthand experiences of your own with science that you understand through doing and talking about your experience. You can provide firsthand experiences for children related to their everyday world and provide accurate information. You can help them find answers to their own questions.

As you teach the children, you have special opportunities to help them develop skills that are basic to any scientific endeavor. First, you can help the children develop their powers of observation. The subtopics in the *our world* curriculum lend themselves exceptionally well to firsthand experiences for children; they can develop their powers of perception and observation aided by the questions you ask. Second, children can build on their observation experiences to predict what might happen under given conditions; this is an effective problem-solving strategy. Third, children can learn to classify what they perceive and discuss (concept learning). Fourth, prekindergarten children can learn to make simple measurements of the phenomena they study in this area of the curriculum. For example, they can keep track of how much food each pet in the prekindergarten eats each day, how far down the glass the water comes after it has been boiled a few minutes, how many different kinds of food each child eats in a day, and so forth. Finally, children can learn to draw conclusions based on the evidence of their observations and measurements.

Ideas and concepts in the biological and physical sciences appropriate for prekindergarten children can be developed from the topical outline on pages 348–352.

THE WORLD OF LIVING THINGS

For prekindergarten children, the world of living things includes those topics related to the biological sciences: animals, insects, birds, fish, people, plants, food, and trees.

Animals. In general, the animals a child learns about should be those with which he can have direct contact. Animals in one geographical area may differ considerably from those in another.

Pets include dogs, cats, guinea pigs, hamsters, white mice, and any other domestic animal that children consider a pet. Wild animals such as monkeys and baby lions are sometimes kept as pets but frequently die in captivity unless they have the special care and treatment provided in a zoo. Therefore lessons about pets should revolve around domestic animals only. Farm animals include cows, horses, sheep, goats, pigs, and other animals normally found on a farm. Turkeys and chickens can be discussed as birds (fowl) rather than as animals. Deer, bears, moose, squirrels, chipmunks, beavers, porcupines, gophers, coyotes, field mice, and others are forest and field animals. Zoo animals include elephants, monkeys, tigers, lions, camels, giraffes, kangaroos, polar bears, zebras, and others. Prehistoric animals include the dinosaurs and other kinds of animals that lived in prehistoric times.

When possible, the child should have more than just the opportunity to see the real animal. He will learn more accurate information about the animal if he can touch it, smell it, hear the sounds it makes, and even taste the foods it produces, such as milk and cheese. This gives the child a greater variety of experiences from which to draw when he tells about his feelings and interprets his experiences with an animal.

Children live in homes, eat food, and have baby brothers or sisters. They can learn that animals, too, have special kinds of homes, eat special kinds of foods, and have babies. They can learn appropriate labels for various animal homes, foods, and babies. They can also learn the reasons why animals live in certain kinds of homes and eat certain foods.

Each animal has a unique movement pattern. Children can learn what these movement patterns are and why each animal moves the way it does. Children enjoy imitating various animal movements.

Some animals help man by producing certain kinds of food. Sheep produce wool. In some geographical areas, horses are still used to pull a plow.

Insects. Most children are fascinated by the varieties of insects they see in their world. Some children, through the example of adults and older children, have learned to fear some insects. But generally an insect is an object of great curiosity to a child. Prekindergarten children can learn to identify each insect they might encounter and to distinguish between those that are pests (flies and mosquitoes) and those that are useful (some bees make honey and the preying mantis eats insect pests). Children can learn about insect homes, food, and even how insects grow, such as caterpillars growing into beautiful butterflies.

Birds.   There are varieties of birds in virtually every geographical area. Those most common in your geographical area can be used as the focus of lessons about birds. Children can learn how to identify each kind of common bird. They can learn how birds grow from eggs, what each bird egg looks like, and how long it takes the bird to hatch. They can examine the nests of birds and find out how they are made. They can learn how and what birds eat. Some children will probably ask why birds can fly. Children can examine the bones of birds and note that they are hollow, which makes it possible for birds to fly with the aid of wing movements. Some birds are useful to man because they produce food such as eggs or feathers for pillows or decoration, or because they eat insects that destroy food crops.

Fish.   Wherever there is a lake, a stream, or an ocean, there are usually fish of various kinds. You can find out what fish are found in the area you live in, how they grow, what they eat, how they move, and what their babies are like. You can also find out if they live in a stream, in a lake, or in the ocean. Children occasionally wonder if fish sleep. You can gather this information and prepare lessons related to the fish the children you teach can actually see, smell, touch, and even taste as food. Some fish such as goldfish are pets, whereas other fish such as trout or lobster are primarily of interest because of their meat.

People.   Suggestions for lessons related to people are found in Chapters 10 and 11.

Plants.   All children have some experiences with growing things such as vegetables, fruits, flowers, shrubs, and even weeds. Children can learn to name the plants they see and to classify them as food, flowers, shrubs, or weeds. They can care for plants and watch them grow, learning to identify the parts of the plant as it grows, such as the root, the stem, the leaf, the bud, the flower, and the fruit. Some plants are used for food such as beans and tomatoes, some for clothing such as cotton, and some for decoration such as flowers.

Food. Food for man has been divided into four main classifications: meat, fish, and poultry; fruits and vegetables; breads and cereals; dairy products and eggs. Children can see and taste a variety of foods in each of these categories and learn to name and classify each food. Children enjoy identifying the source of each food, such as milk from cows, beans from a bean plant, cherries from a cherry tree, bread from wheat, and eggs from chickens. They can also learn which foods are eaten raw or cooked or in juice form, and why some foods are eaten in one form but not another. The preparation of foods is discussed in Chapter 11.

Trees. Varieties of trees grow in almost every geographical area. Children can learn to identify the most common ones by their shape and form and by the configuration of their leaves. Trees have parts such as roots, trunk, branches, leaves, and bark. They grow similar to the way a plant grows, but they are generally taller and stronger and take longer to grow. Incidentally, the leaves from several trees can be used as an interesting variety of collage in the graphic arts.

THE PHYSICAL WORLD

The physical world refers to the inanimate things in the child's world. Weather, the seasons, the heavens, our senses, water, rocks and soil, and miscellaneous topics such as magnets and air and mechanics—all are part of the physical world. The emphasis in lessons for prekindergarten children should be on phenomena that children normally experience in their world of here and now.

Weather.   There are many different kinds of weather that children experience: sunshine or fair weather, rain, wind, clouds, snow, frost, hail, lightning and thunder. Lessons generally should revolve around only those kinds of weather experienced by the children you teach. Snow has little meaning to a child who has never seen it. Related to weather can be lessons about temperature changes in different kinds of weather, what people do in various kinds of weather, and what they wear in different kinds of weather.

Seasons.   Some geographical areas experience all four seasons each year, and others have just two or three seasons, such as warm-dry and cool-wet. Children can learn about the seasons they experience in their own locality. Different seasons have unique characteristics; people do things in some seasons that they don't do in others.

The heavens.   Children are aware of the sun, the moon, and the stars. They can learn about the passage of time as they relate the sun to daytime and the things people do during the day and the moon and stars to nighttime and things people do at night. Some children are afraid of the dark. Often these fears can be allayed by discussions of what makes the night, how living things have a chance to sleep at night, and how peaceful nighttime can be. Complicated theories and ideas about heavenly bodies are best learned in later years.

Our senses.   The child gets his information about the world he lives in through his senses of hearing, seeing, touching, tasting, and smelling. Children therefore should be given a variety of specific experiences related to each of the senses (see pages 7-9). This topic area of the curriculum probably should be the most extensive of all the topic areas in the physical world. Children can learn to identify various sensory phenomena, to relate these phenomena to one another, and to solve problems using their senses.

Water.   Water is so common that we often take it for granted. It can do several things—evaporate, cause steam, freeze to a solid state, make things grow. People use water for many things, including bathing and washing, cleaning clothes and other objects, drinking, preparing foods, and participating in recreational activities. Children can also learn where water comes from (for example, rivers, streams, pipes, and faucets).

Rocks and soil.   Rocks and soil exist virtually everywhere. Children often wonder where rocks come from and what makes "dirt." Simple experiences can be provided to help children identify different kinds of common rocks and their sources, to determine what man can do with rocks, to determine what soil is and how it is used, and to identify the differences and similarities between sand and soil. If the children are in an area where moon rocks are on display, they can visit the exhibition and compare the moon rocks with those they see in their own geographical area.

Miscellaneous topics related to the physical world.   Children experience many other kinds of physical science phenomena that can be demonstrated and discussed and practiced in the prekindergarten. Some examples of such phenomena are temperature, appliances in the home, light, shadow and dark, friction, balance, magnets, magnification, wheels, air, parts of things (for example, the legs, seat, and back of a chair), rockets and spaceships, mechanics, electricity, force, energy, thrust, and vehicles.

STUDYING ECOLOGY IN THE PREKINDERGARTEN

Ecology is defined as the relationship between organisms and their environments. The *our world* area of the curriculum is ideal for the study of this relationship. Such a study can wed the biological and physical sciences.

Subtopics in the typical ecology curriculum would include fish, minerals, population, climate, thermal disturbances (man-made and natural), pesticides, water, animals, trees, and air pollution related to airplanes, autos, industry, and burning wastes. Each of these topics can be broken down into categories, rules (or ideas), and problem-solving situations useful for lessons the children can understand. For example, when studying the topic *trees*, children can learn the following uses of trees: shade, climbing, swinging, lumber to build houses, paper, fuel, and homes for birds and insects. Problems arise when too many trees are cut in a given area (that is, soil erosion results), when too much paper becomes waste, when burning wood fouls the air, when animals and insects lose their homes. Children can learn to help solve these problems by doing things like recycling paper, using less paper, and using scrap paper whenever possible. Emphasis always should be on ecological phenomena the child himself can observe firsthand.

It is probable that prekindergarten children who study ecology today will best develop the skills and attitudes necessary to save our environment tomorrow.

LEARNING ACTIVITY SOURCES

The *our world* content area of the curriculum can be the broadest and most extensive in the prekindergarten curriculum. The scope of the subject in terms of learning activities is far too broad for adequate coverage in this book. You probably will want to look at a few sources specifically devoted to the study of science with young children. Texts prepared for elementary teachers often provide the best references for science learning activities. Three of these sources are Greenlee (1955), Hone, Joseph, and Victor (1971), and Lewis and Potter (1970). Be sure to adapt ideas gleaned from such sources to the learning level of the children you teach.

SAMPLE LESSON PLAN

Area of curriculum: Our world

Our world focus: Types of food

Behavioral objective: Each child will correctly select from real food items not used before in instruction those that represent the food category *breads and cereals*. (Concept learning.)

To the teacher: You will need the following items for this lesson:

A tray for demonstration

A small tray for each child in the group

Six or seven real foods representing the *breads and cereals* category
  (some of these will be duplicated for use in the apply step)

Three or four foods in food categories other than *breads and cereals*
  (some of these will be duplicated for use in the apply step)

The children can be seated on chairs around a table or on the carpet in a semicircle where they can see, touch, and possibly taste the real foods.

Learning Activities:

Posttest   (behavioral objective from previous lesson). Each child will correctly select from real food items not used before in instruction those that represent the food category *fruits and vegetables*. (Concept learning.)

Pretest.   Prepare a tray of items you will not use in the following lesson plan. Test the children on the new objective for this lesson.

Show, discuss.   (1) Put three real foods on a tray in front of the children, two of which are breads and cereals. These food items should be varied, such as a slice of whole wheat bread, a banana, a bowl of prepared dry cereal. As you pick up the *bread and cereal* items say, "This belongs to a type of food we call breads and cereals, so this is a bread and cereal food. Say it with me. This is a bread and cereal food." As you pick up the item that is not a bread and cereal product say, "This is *not* a bread and cereal food. Say it with me. This is *not* a bread and cereal food." Allow the children to hold the items while they look at them for a few seconds. Allow those who wish to taste the foods. (2) Put three more food items on the tray, two of which are bread and cereal foods such as a hard roll and a sample of uncooked oatmeal. As you pick up each bread and cereal item say, "This is a bread and cereal food. Say it with me.

This is a bread and cereal food." As you pick up the item that is not a bread and cereal food say, "This is *not* a bread and cereal food. Say it with me. This is *not* a bread and cereal food." Allow the children to hold the objects while they look at them for a few seconds. Allow those who wish to taste the foods. (3) Put all six food items on a tray, mixed at random so the bread and cereal foods are not separated from the other foods. Put the tray in front of each child in turn and say, "Show me something that is a bread and cereal food" or "Show me something that is *not* a bread and cereal food." Be sure that each child in the group has the opportunity to respond to *both* requests. If a child points to or picks up an incorrect item, say, "No, that is (or is *not*) a bread and cereal food. *This* [picking up a correct item] is *not* (or is) a bread and cereal food [that is, you ask him the original question again]." Continue asking both questions until each child can respond correctly each time he is asked.

Show, apply.   Put in front of each child a small tray containing four food items, two or three of which are bread and cereal foods. These items should *not* be items used in the previous instructional process. Ask each child to take out of his tray each item that is a bread and cereal food. If any child takes out incorrect items, go through the correction process with that child.

Posttest.   Repeat the apply step the following day and again a week later, using food items not previously used in instruction.

Our world topical outline.

7.1.   The world of living things
      7.1.1.   Animals
            7.1.1.1.   Pets
                  7.1.1.1.1.   Identification of pets
                  7.1.1.1.2.   Where pets live
                  7.1.1.1.3.   What pets eat
                  7.1.1.1.4.   How pets move
                  7.1.1.1.5.   Pet babies
                  7.1.1.1.6.   Care of pets

7.1.1.2. Farm animals
    7.1.1.2.1. Identification of farm animals
    7.1.1.2.2. Where farm animals live
    7.1.1.2.3. What farm animals eat
    7.1.1.2.4. How farm animals move
    7.1.1.2.5. Farm animal babies
7.1.1.3. Forest and field animals
    7.1.1.3.1. Identification of forest and field animals
    7.1.1.3.2. Where forest and field animals live
    7.1.1.3.3. What forest and field animals eat
    7.1.1.3.4. How forest and field animals move
    7.1.1.3.5. Forest and field animal babies
7.1.1.4. Zoo animals
    7.1.1.4.1. Identification of zoo animals
    7.1.1.4.2. Where zoo animals live
    7.1.1.4.3. What zoo animals eat
    7.1.1.4.4. How zoo animals move
    7.1.1.4.5. Zoo animal babies
7.1.1.5. Prehistoric animals
7.1.1.6. How animals help people
7.1.2. Insects
    7.1.2.1. Identifying various kinds of insects
        7.1.2.1.1. Those that help man
        7.1.2.1.2. Pests
    7.1.2.2. How insects grow
    7.1.2.3. Insect homes
    7.1.2.4. Insect food
7.1.3. Birds
    7.1.3.1. Identifying varieties of birds
    7.1.3.2. How birds grow
    7.1.3.3. Bird homes
    7.1.3.4. Food for birds
    7.1.3.5. How birds help man
7.1.4. Fish
    7.1.4.1. Identifying varieties of fish
    7.1.4.2. How fish grow
    7.1.4.3. Fish homes
    7.1.4.4. Food for fish
    7.1.4.5. How fish move
    7.1.4.6. Fish babies

7.1.5.   People (see Health and Safety curriculum and Living
         in a World of People curriculum)
7.1.6.   Plants
         7.1.6.1.   Identifying varieties of plants
         7.1.6.2.   How plants grow
         7.1.6.3.   Parts of a plant or flower
         7.1.6.4.   How plants are used
         7.1.6.5.   Care of plants
7.1.7.   Food
         7.1.7.1.   Identifying varieties of food
                    7.1.7.1.1.   Meat, fish, and poultry
                    7.1.7.1.2.   Fruits and vegetables
                    7.1.7.1.3.   Breads and cereals
                    7.1.7.1.4.   Dairy products and eggs
         7.1.7.2.   Sources of food
         7.1.7.3.   Foods in various forms
         7.1.7.4.   Preparing foods (see Living in a World of
                    People curriculum)
7.1.8.   Trees
         7.1.8.1.   Identifying various kinds of trees
         7.1.8.2.   How trees grow
         7.1.8.3.   Parts of a tree
7.2.   The physical world
7.2.1.   Weather
         7.2.1.1.   Varieties of weather
                    7.2.1.1.1.   Sunshine
                    7.2.1.1.2.   Rain
                    7.2.1.1.3.   Wind
                    7.2.1.1.4.   Clouds
                    7.2.1.1.5.   Snow
                    7.2.1.1.6.   Frost
                    7.2.1.1.7.   Hail
                    7.2.1.1.8.   Lightning and thunder
         7.2.1.2.   Temperature changes in different kinds of
                    weather
         7.2.1.3.   What people do in different kinds of
                    weather
         7.2.1.4.   What people wear in different kinds of
                    weather
7.2.2.   Seasons
         7.2.2.1.   Variety of seasons
                    7.2.2.1.1.   Spring
                    7.2.2.1.2.   Summer
                    7.2.2.1.3.   Autumn (fall)
                    7.2.2.1.4.   Winter

7.2.3. The heavens
    7.2.3.1. Sun
    7.2.3.2. Moon
    7.2.3.3. Stars
7.2.4. Our senses*
    7.2.4.1. Hearing
        7.2.4.1.1. Rhythm
        7.2.4.1.2. Pitch
        7.2.4.1.3. Shape of sound
        7.2.4.1.4. Tone quality
        7.2.4.1.5. Volume (Dynamics)
    7.2.4.2. Seeing
        7.2.4.2.1. Color (see Graphic Arts curriculum)
        7.2.4.2.2. Spatial relations
        7.2.4.2.3. Shape (see also Graphic Arts curriculum)
        7.2.4.2.4. Motion
        7.2.4.2.5. Light
        7.2.4.2.6. Shade—shadow
    7.2.4.3. Touching
        7.2.4.3.1 Texture
        7.2.4.3.2. Temperature
        7.2.4.3.3. Shape (see Graphic Arts curriculum)
        7.2.4.3.4. Size
        7.2.4.3.5. Pressure
        7.2.4.3.6. Position
        7.2.4.3.7. State of motion
        7.2.4.3.8. Weight
    7.2.4.4. Tasting
        7.2.4.4.1. Saltiness
        7.2.4.4.2. Sourness
        7.2.4.4.3. Bitterness
        7.2.4.4.4. Sweetness
    7.2.4.5. Smelling
        7.2.4.5.1. Ethereal
        7.2.4.5.2. Fragrant
        7.2.4.5.3. Burned
        7.2.4.5.4. Putrid
        7.2.4.5.5. Resinous
        7.2.4.5.6. Spicy

---

*Based on a taxonomy of the senses in *The Classification of Educational Objectives: Psychomotor Domain* by Elizabeth Jane Simpson. U. S. Office of Education Contract No. OE-5-85-104, 1966.

7.2.5. Water
      7.2.5.1. What water can do
            7.2.5.1.1. Evaporate
            7.2.5.1.2. Steam
            7.2.5.1.3. Freeze
            7.2.5.1.4. Help things grow
      7.2.5.2. What man can do with water
            7.2.5.2.1. Bathing, washing
            7.2.5.2.2. Cleaning clothes and objects
            7.2.5.2.3. Drinking
            7.2.5.2.4. Use in food preparation
            7.2.5.2.5. Recreation
      7.2.5.3. Sources of water
7.2.6. Rocks and soil
      7.2.6.1. Identifying varieties of rocks
      7.2.6.2. Sources of rocks
      7.2.6.3. What man can do with rocks
      7.2.6.4. What soil is
      7.2.6.5. How soil is used
      7.2.6.6. Sand and soil: similarities and differences
      7.2.6.7. Moon rocks
7.2.7. Miscellaneous topics related to the physical world
      7.2.7.1. Temperature
      7.2.7.2. Appliances in the home
      7.2.7.3. Light, shadow, and dark
      7.2.7.4. Friction
      7.2.7.5. Balance
      7.2.7.6. Magnets
      7.2.7.7. Making things look bigger
      7.2.7.8. Wheels
      7.2.7.9. Air
      7.2.7.10. Parts of things
      7.2.7.11. Rockets and spaceships
      7.2.7.12. Mechanics (levers, pulleys, machines)
      7.2.7.13. Electricity
      7.2.7.14. Force, energy, thrust
      7.2.7.15. Vehicles

REFERENCES

Greenlee, J. *Teaching science to children.* Dubuque, Iowa: Wm. C. Brown, 1955.

Hone, E. B., Joseph, A., & Victor, E. *A sourcebook for elementary science.* (2nd ed.) N. Y.: Harcourt Brace Jovanovich, 1971.

Lewis, J. E., & Potter, I. C. *The teaching of science in the elementary school.* (2nd ed.) Englewood Cliffs, N. J.: Prentice-Hall, 1970.

Chapter 16

Reading

Interest in providing reading instruction in the prekindergarten has been growing rapidly since the early part of the 1960s. To teach or not to teach reading, however, is and probably will remain for many years a highly controversial issue. There is a vast amount of myth as well as research related to beginning reading. You can read Chall (1967) for a review of the research and the status of beginning reading in this country. Della-Piana and Endo (in press) review research findings and research methods related to reading. This chapter is a brief discussion of the meaning of reading, the concept of reading readiness, and some information you might wish to have about beginning reading if you decide to include reading as part of the prekindergarten curriculum.

THE MEANING OF READING

Reading is basically "decoding the written language into the spoken language which the child already knows" (Pick, 1970). The child who can look at the written symbols *h-a-t,* and say to himself silently or orally "hat" is demonstrating ability to decode, or read, written language.

Learning to read involves four basic skills. First, the child must be able to discriminate one letter from another. This is basically a visual process. Second, the child must be able to discriminate one sound from another, primarily an auditory process. Third, the child must be able to blend sounds. Blending the letter sounds of *m-a-n* into "man" is sound-blending. Fourth, the child must be able to understand the meaning of a word in context. If the child can understand the meaning of *left* in "left turn" as well as in "he left the light on," he is demonstrating understanding of the meaning of a word in context.

Reading thus becomes a matter of learning the letters of the alphabet, decoding the letters into sounds, and processing longer and more complex units of the written language (Pick, 1970).

Proponents of some reading programs suggest that reading is nothing more than word recognition, or knowing what the words "say" (Chall, 1967). This principle suggests that a child can read when he has learned to "crack the code" and name or recognize a letter or a word or a series of words. Proponents of other reading programs suggest that reading goes beyond word recognition to include word meaning (Chall, 1967). Jacobs (1971) suggests that the

> . . . skills of word recognition and abilities of comprehension and rate of reading are functions of the reading act which are so taught that the child recognizes them not as the ends of reading but rather as the instrumentalities that make reading possible.

READING READINESS

Prekindergarten has been looked on traditionally as a good place to teach the child to "get ready" to read. The child under 5 has been viewed as physically and experientially unprepared to face the tasks required in the process of learning to read.

Few writers in early childhood education have investigated reading readiness in terms of *what* the child is ready for. For example, there is a difference between recognizing the letters *d-o-g* as *dog* and knowing what *dog* means. When the sequence of behavior in the reading act has been determined and the child's mastery of a given behavior is evaluated, then *what* reading behavior the child is ready for can be determined intelligently. Readiness is something that is taught. For example, if you wish to teach a child to recognize and name the letter O, you don't use a wooden circle or some other object; you use the letter itself.

O. K. Moore of "talking typewriter" fame is quoted in Chall (1967) as suggesting that the most important reading readiness factors are the ability to sit, to speak, and to listen to a natural language. Another reading program proponent is quoted in Chall (1967) regarding reading readiness:

> Reading readiness is vastly overemphasized. I would think that reading readiness is just like talking readiness. We don't investigate too closely whether a child is ready to talk or not. . . . Blaming such factors as "difficulty at home, " "shyness," or "personal problems" as reasons for not being "ready" is ridiculous. In fact, if the shy or troubled child is taught, it ameliorates his problems [p. 57].

A factor often overlooked in the reading readiness controversy is the degree of preparation by the teacher. Most prekindergarten teachers have had little or no training in reading instruction. Effective reading instruction is a skill requiring expert training and supervision during practice. Many a prekindergarten child's lack of "reading readiness" probably is a matter of teacher "unreadiness."

WHEN A PREKINDERGARTEN CHILD BEGINS TO READ

As early as 1937 it was recognized that children could learn to read before the age of 6 (Gates, 1937). Evidence indicated even then that the child's mental age was not as crucial as other factors such as the materials used, the method of teaching, the skill of the teacher, the size of the class, the amount of preparatory work, the type of evaluation, and other factors.

If the child can read before age 5, a major question becomes, "What method of instruction is best?" Method refers to the sequencing, focusing, and pacing of learning activities (Chall, 1967). The great debate in learning to read is whether the code-emphasis method (letter and word recognition) is better than the meaning-emphasis method in reading. Research indicates that code emphasis is more effective when children are beginning to read than meaning emphasis (Chall, 1967). However, there is apparently little evidence to indicate that one code-emphasis program is better than another. It is important to remember that "knowledge of both letter names and letter sounds are indispensable for further acquisition and development of hierarchical reading skills [such as comprehension]" (Della-Piana & Endo, in press).

Chall (1967) concludes that the ability to give names to letters prior to learning to read helps the child, regardless of which method is used. It also is important that the child be able to produce the sound value for any given letter.

If you decide to include reading in your prekindergarten curriculum, it probably is best to select one that uses a code (letter and word recognition) emphasis, with the early stages of the program including letters that are easily distinguished from one another and words that are used in the child's everyday experiences. As Della-Piana and Endo (in press) suggest, "it may be unlikely that we will 'find' one best method of instruction but it is not unlikely that we will *develop* best methods for specific outcomes, populations, personnel, and time-cost factors."

Even though children *can* learn to read during ages 3 and 4, you may be wondering if they *should* learn to read. After all, it is quite possible that a child could learn to "crack the code" but also learn to hate reading at the same time. Reading has value only as a means to an end. It can open up a whole new world of experience to the child. If reading is related to something important to the child, then it probably has value and the child *should* learn to read. Reading can broaden and deepen the child's understanding of his world. If "cracking the code" is the ultimate goal of reading in the prekindergarten, then reading probably should not be part of the curriculum. According to Jacobs (1971), "If reading in Johnny confirms and extends his ways of knowing about his world and those who live therein, he can at least potentially increase his humaneness."

Chall (1967) reports evidence that children of lower average intelligence and socioeconomic status do better in early code-emphasis reading programs than do middle-class children. She hastens to add, however, that we need longitudinal evidence when children in both categories are tested beyond the fourth grade. It is possible that gains are made much faster when a child is first learning a skill than when he has had a good deal of experience with that same skill. Middle-class children probably have books and other kinds of reading exposure in their homes to a far greater degree than disadvantaged children. Therefore, they probably start their formal reading experiences at a higher level of proficiency than most children of below average intelligence and social class. This simply means you need to know what the child already knows before you begin to teach him how to read. Many children enter prekindergarten with the ability to name many or all of the letters in the alphabet as well as many common words. If you attempt to teach the child what he already knows, he will soon lose interest in the learning tasks. Assessing preinstructional behavior is as important in the reading curriculum as it is in any other content area in the prekindergarten. Many of the claims regarding "pressuring" or "forcing" the prekindergarten child to read probably mean that instruction started where the child wasn't!

REFERENCES

Chall, J. S. *Learning to read: The great debate.* New York: McGraw-Hill, 1967.

Della-Piana, G. M., & Endo, G. T. Reading research. In R. M. W. Travers (Ed.), *AERA Handbook of research on teaching.* Chicago: Rand McNally, in press.

Gates, A. I. The necessary mental age for beginning reading. *The Elementary School Journal,* 1937, **37**(7).

Jacobs, L. B. Humanism in teaching reading. *Phi Delta Kappan,* April 1971.

Pick, A. D. Some basic perceptual processes in reading. *Young Children, 1970,* **25**(3), 162–181.

Index